TAMIL TEACHER

Volume I

with my novel scientific way of ***making 'your own'*** *Tamil sentences.*
This book walks you holding your finger

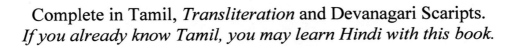

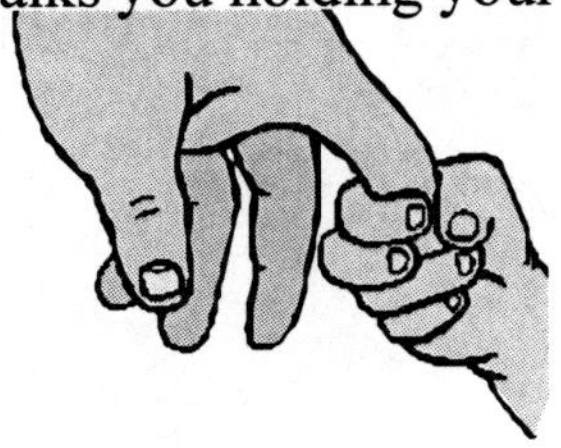

Complete in Tamil, *Transliteration* and Devanagari Scaripts.
If you already know Tamil, you may learn Hindi with this book.

PRIMARY to INTERMEDIATE

Prof. Ratnakar Narale
பறொ. ரத்னாகரன் நராலே

Ratnakar
PUSTAK BHARATI
BOOKS-INDIA

Author :

Dr. Ratnakar Narale

B.Sc. (Nagpur Univ.), M.Sc. (Pune Univ.), Ph.D. (IIT), Ph.D. (Kalidas Sanskrit Univ. Nagpur);
Prof. Hindi. Ryerson University, Toronto
web : www.books-india.com * email : books.india.books@gmail.com

Book Title :

Tamil Teacher : Teach or Learn to 'Make Your Own Sentences' and then Speak Tamil.

Primary to Intermediate, *With my novel scientific method.*

Tamil Teacher is a step-by-step progressive approach with cumulative learning from the basic alphabet to making your own Tamil sentences comfortably. It walks you carefully holding your finger. It is fully English transliterated for your help. It is also coupled with Devanagari script for those who know Hindi or Sanskrit. It has nice diagrams, colourful Chart of Alphabet, valuable Tables, Answers to all Exercises and Examples, Transliterated Students Dictionary of vocabulary, important Notes at the beginning of each chapter and at each step, and much more. Uniquely, in this book you will learn the interrelation between Tamil and Sanskrit.

Fonts used in the Book :

Ratnakar-T and Unicode for Tamil typing

Ratnakar-H for Hindī typing

Ratnakar-E for *Transliteration* Typing

Published by :
PUSTAK BHARATI (Books India)
Division of PC Plus Ltd.,

For :
Sanskrit Hindi Research Institute, Toronto

Copyright ©2014

ISBN 978-1-897416-58-7

ISBN 978-1-897416-58-7
90000
9 781897 416587

© All rights reserved. No part of this book may be copied, reproduced or utilised in any manner or by any means, computerised, e-mail, scanning, photocopying or by recording in any information storage and retrieval system, without the permission in writing from the author.

Dedicated to

My Caring Wife
Sunita Narale
and my Loving Grandchildren
Samay, Sahas, Saanjh, Saaya Narale

INDEX

LIST OF TABLES

MODEL FORMAT FOR THE **FIRST** QUARTERLY TEST

QUESTION 1 : Read and Write the Following Tamil words five times.

1. **பாரம்** ---

2. **வணக்கம்** ---

3. **கடல்** ---

4. **மரம்** ---

5. **பழம்** ---

QUESTION 2 : Say it in Tamil.

1. I am a student. -----------------------------------
2. My name is xxxxxx. --------------------------
3. We drink milk . ---------------------------------
4. They are going. ------------------------------
5. You are speaking Tamil. -----------------------
6. He is writing. ---------------------------------

QUESTION 3 : Say and write it in Tamil.

1. She was here. ---
2. I was there. ------------------------------------
3. Anita is eating a mango. ---
4. They run 10 km. --
5. You are a teacher. ------------------------------

QUESTION 4 : Write the names of the verbs (action words) in Tamil :

1. cry ---------	2. go ---------	3. eat --------	4. come --------	5. say --------	6. sing ---------
7. do --------	8. become ------	9. give ------	10. take -------	11. walk ------	12. see --------
13. learn ---------	14. drink ---------	15. read -------	16. stand --------	17. run ---------	18. begin ------

QUESTION 5 : Say and write it in Tamil.

1. She is fighting. -------------------------------------
2. He falls. --
3. She is writing. -------------------------------------
4. I am writing. --
5. I am going to India. -------------------------------
6. He speaks Punjabi. ----------------------------------
7. She takes flowers. ---------------------------------
8. These are books. -----------------------------------
9. I drink milk. ---------------------------------------
10. Is that a parrot? -----------------------------------
11. Is that a goat? ------------------------------------
12. Hello! --
13. Is your mothertongue Tamil ---

14. Say the following numbers in Tamil : 5, 3, 100, 10, 4, 2, 7, 20, 9

MODEL FORMAT FOR THE <u>SECOND</u> QUARTERLY TEST

QUESTION 1 : Write all vowels of Tamil Alphabet in proper order.

QUESTION 2 : Write the Tamil names of following things :

1. boy ---------	2. girl ---------	3. dog --------	4. cat --------	5. letter ---------	6. tea ---------
7. ear ---------	8. nose --------	9. hand ----------	10. leg ----------	11. egg ---------	12. tail ---------
13. mango ---------	14. apple --------	15. banana ------	16. plate ---------	17. car ---------	18. knife ---------
19. fan -----------	20. book --------	21. ball ---------	22. chair ---------	23. key ---------	24. window -----

QUESTION 3 : Say and write in Tamil :

1. I drank milk. --
2. He walked 2 km. --
3. She was reading a Hindi book. --
4. She will take flowers. --
5. She will go. ---

QUESTION 4 : Answer and write in Tamil :

1. What is your name? ---
2. Where do you live. --
3. How are you? --

QUESTION 5 : Say and write in Tamil :

1. I sleep at 10.00 O' Clock. ---
2. You (all) will give money. ---
3. I will eat fruits. --

QUESTION 6 : Say and write in Tamil :

1. Rādhā goes to school. --
2. Sītā will come to New York. ---
3. Rājan reads a Tamil book. --

QUESTION 7 : Write Tamil consonants in Alphabetical order.

MODEL FORMAT FOR THE <u>THIRD</u> QUARTERLY TEST

QUESTION 1 : Write the Tamil suffixes used for saying following expressions :

1. to --------- 2. by ---------------- 3. from ---------- 4. for -----------------5. in --------------------

6. on -------- 7. near ------------- 8. together with ------------------------ 9. of ---------------------

QUESTION 2 : Say and write in Tamil :

1. The dog will eat the bone --

2. The bricks will fall ---

3. I am ok! ---

4. What is the news? ---

5. Don't worry! --

6. Who is she? --

7. Where is the dog? ---

QUESTION 3 : Find the Intransitive and Transitive actions and say them in Tamil :

1. to sing --------------- 2. to fall ------------------- 3. to walk ------------------- 4. to buy ------------

5. to see ----------------- 6. to hear -------------------7. to write ----------------- 8. to stand -----------

QUESTION 4 : Say and write in Tamil :

1. Yesterday monring. --

2. You are welcome. --

3. Where are you going? --

4. I am going to Chennai. --

QUESTION 5 : Say and Answer in Tamil :

1. What's your native language? ---

2. How are you? --

3. Do you want coffee? ---

4. Do you know Tamil? --

5. What is your name? ---

6. Who is she? --

7. Who is he? ---

MODEL FORMAT FOR THE <u>**FOURTH**</u> QUARTERLY TEST

QUESTION 1 : Say and write in Tamil :

1. Please come in. --
2. Please excuse me. --
3. Open the door! ---
4. Please be quite. --
5. Hurry up! ---

QUESTION 2 : Say and write in Tamil :

1. to her --------------	2. to them ------------------	3. for her ------------------	4. to us -----------
5. near him --------------	6. from you ----------------	7. by train -----------------	8. from you -------
9. for us -------------	10. by them ----------------	11. in him -----------------	12. of our ---------

QUESTION 3 : Say, answer and write in Tamil :

1. What is her name? ---
2. Who is he? ---
3. What is his mother tongue? ---
4. Is your mothertongue English? ---
5.

QUESTION 4 : Say and and write in Tamil :

1. Please have a seat. ---
2. Please listen. ---
3. Please wait. ---
4. Please come again. ---
5. Say yes! --
6. Is your mothertongue Sanskrit? --
7. Please close the window. ---
8. A letter to <u>my</u> brother --
9. The bird on the tree. ---
10. My house. ---

INTRODUCTION

What you are about to discover in this book is a wholly novel way of learning and teaching Tamil, which you have never seen before, even if you already know or teach Tamil. Believe me, even if you JUST READ every word of this book, patiently and thoughtfully, you will understand how to make your own Tamil sentences and speak Tamil with confidence.

The significant factor in the approach and structure of this book is the input over number of years from the students regarding their needs and difficulties in learning Tamil. Thus, while putting this book together, first consideration is given to the fact that learners may not know the Tamil (Devanāgarī) script if they came from the countries outside India or from the provinces of India where Tamil not the first language. For such first time Tamil learners, the complete package includes a 20-step Programmed Text Book, 20-step Course Syllabus, 20-step Homework Book with 20-stepTeachers guide and Four Quarterly Tests . With this lightly priced full package, the Teachers can monitor the progress of their students in a programmed manner; the Learners can feel their daily improvement; and the parents can witness the proof of the progress of their children. Many people living in Guyana, the West Indies, Suriname, Fiji, Canada, USA, UK, Africa and Europe; also children of Indian parents living outside India, so also many students in India, learning the English Medium Schools and in the non-Tamil speaking Indian provinces, want to learn Tamil through English Medium. For them, this is perfect level-I Tamil learning book.

What is unique of this book is my innovative but proven scientific method of teaching Tamil, even to absolutely new learners. Here, purposefully, the consonants are discussed first and then the vowels. Within the consonants, the characters are grouped into sets based on their shapes. With this new way, even absolutely new learners learn to read Tamil within a very short time of only few hours. Unique charts are key tools in this book. One of them you will find on the back cover of this book, in the form of the 'Chart of Tamil Alphabet.' In our Institute it is a large 3' x 4' size poster. Students love it.

Many excellent books are written to learn Tamil through Tamil medium or through English Medium, but in the usual way of providing you pre-made Tamil sentences. It means they must assume that the self-learners already know Tamil well enough to follow the book. Here the learner's purpose has to be to 'improve' the skill, rather than 'to learn' the language from level zero. How suitable is a book written in the very language that a learner is trying to learn? For example, is it a good idea to learn Chinese through a book written in Chinese? The learning book must be written in a language the learner already knows, and it must teach how to MAKE your own sentences, and not through pre-made Tamil sentences. The teachers and learners who teach or self-learn Tamil, through a book written in Tamil must appreciate this basic difference, if they are serious in achieving full benefit for their efforts.

The Tamil teachers and learners who use books written in Tamil medium and pre-made, will at first surely hesitate to try this new method, but they should rest assured that once they discover the astonishing effectiveness of this book, they will be glad to have given it a try.

For 'teaching' Tamil from level zero, in this book it is first assumed that the reader does not know Tamil at all. Thus, right from Lesson one till the end, you will notice the meticulous care assuring that the material discussed on every page deals ONLY with the information covered in previous pages, a common sense but very rarely practiced. In addition, after every step, the material covered up to that point is cumulatively reviewed under a novel entry called, '**what we have learned so far**.' This **cumulative learning** is one of the beautiful aspects of this book.

While learning Tamil, you must understand **how to make your own sentences**, rather than memorize pre-made 'pet-sentences.' By remembering the pet-sentences you and people may think you have learned Tamil in a week, but then you will have to wait until you get an opportunity to use the pre-made sentences that you remember. However, by knowing the simple technique given in this book, **for making your own sentences to express your original thoughts**, all you have to remember is the technique, and then the sky is the limit.

In this book you will discover unique Tables, Charts and Notes that I have discovered, after long research and contemplation, to reveal the inner structure of the Tamil language, like no other book does. You will find them useful, interesting and educational.

Another uncommon but valuable feature in this book is "Answers and word meanings" (**in English transliteration as well as in Tamil**) for all Questions asked in the Exercises and Examples, this makes it a true self-tutor, **'without any help form anyone whatsoever.'** Without this idea, the self learners would have been left in the dark and helpless, wondering at each question, '**Did I Get it Right**?' and '**Did I Say it Correctly**?' I have many Guyanese, West Indian, Canadian and South Indian students who want to learn to 'speak' in Tamil, without any particular preference to writing it, other than writing their name etc. Even for them, who want to learn Tamil **without a teacher** and **wholly through transliteration**, this book is right one.

If you like this book, please use my **Tamil level II** book for further learning. You will greatly benefit.

LESSON 1

THE TAMIL ALPHABET

Tamil Vowels :

அ	ஆ	இ	ஈ	உ	ஊ	எ	ஏ	ஐ	ஒ	ஓ	ஔ	ஃ
अ	आ	इ	ई	उ	ऊ	ए	ऍ	ऐ	ओ	ओऽ	औ	अख्
a	ā	i	ī	u	ū	e	ē	ai	o	ō	au	akh

In this row of 12 vowels, vowel number 2, 4, 6, 8 and 11 are extended sounds of the short vowel number 1, 3, 5, 7 and 10.

Tamil Full Consonants :

க	ங	ச	ஞ	ட	ண
क, ग	ङ	च, स	ञ	ट, ड	ण
ka, ga	ṅga	cha, sa	ñya	ṭa, ḍa	ṇa
த	ந	ப	ம	ய	ர
त, द	न	प, ब	म	य	र
ta, da	na	pa, ba	ma	ya	ra
ல	வ	ழ	ள	ற	ன
ल	व	ऴ	ळ	ऱ्	न
la	va. wa	lá	ḷa	ra	na
ஷ	ஸ	ஹ	க்ஷ	ஜ	ஸ்ரீ
श, ष	स	ह	क्ष	ज	श्री
śa, ṣa	sa	ha	kṣha	ja	shrī

Tamil Half Consonants

Tamil Consonants without their inherant vowel ‘a’

க்	ங்	ச்	ஞ்	ட்	ண்
क्, ग्	ङ्	च्, स्	ञ्	ट्, ड्	ण्
k, g	ṅg	ch, s	ñy	ṭ, ḍ	ṇ

த்	ந்	ப்	ம்	ய்	ர்
त्, द्	न्	प्, ब्	म्	य्	र्
t, d	n	p, b	m	y	r

ல்	வ்	ழ்	ள்	ற்	ன்
ल्	व्	ऴ्	ळ्	ऱ्	ऩ्
l	v. w	l´	ḷ	ṟ	n

ஷ்	ஸ்	ஹ
श्, ष्	स्	ह्
ś, ṣ	s	h

Tamil and Devanagari Sanskrit Alphabet Charts

Side by Side Comparison

TABLE 1 : **Tamil - Sanskrit inherent interrelationship**

Tamil Vs *Devanagari* Sanskrit **VOWELS**							
Tamil	अ அ *a*	आ ஆ *ā*	इ இ *i*	ई ஈ *ī*	उ உ *u*	ऊ ஊ *ū*	
Devnagari	अ	आ	इ	ई	उ	ऊ	
Tamil	ए எ *e*	एॅ ஏ *ē*	ऐ ஐ *ai*	ओ ஒ *o*	ओऽ ஓ *ō*	औ ஔ *au*	अख् ஃ *akh* *
Devnagari	ए	एॅ	ऐ	ओ	ओऽ	औ	अह् : *

Tamil Vs Devanagari Sanskrit **CONSONANTS**						
Tamil	क् க் *k*	ङ् ங் *ṅg*	च् ச் *ch*	ञ् ஞ் *ñy*	ट् ட் *ṭ*	ण् ண் *ṇ*
Devnagari	क् ख् ग् घ्	ङ्	च् छ् ज् झ्	ञ्	ट् ठ् ड् ढ्	ण्
Tamil	त् த் *t*	न् ந் *n*	प् ப் *p*	म् ம் *m*	य् ய் *y*	र् ர் *r*
Devnagari	त् थ् द् ध्	न्	प् फ् ब् भ्	म्	य्	र्
Tamil	ल् ல் *l*	व् வ் *v*	ळ् ள் *ḷ*	ऴ् ழ் *l′*	ऱ् ற் *r*	ऩ् ன் *n*
Devnagari	ल्	व्	ळ् **			
Tamil	श्, ष् ஷ் *sh*	स् ஸ் *s*	ह् ஹ் *h*	क्ष् க்ஷ் *kṣh*	ज् ஜ் *j*	**These five are adopted** *Granthaksharam* **characters**
Devnagari	श्, ष्	स्	ह्	क्ष्	ज्	

* अख् ஃ *akh* (अह् :) is Semi Consonant, Semi Vowle.

NOTES : (i) Quite contrary to the common belief that Tamil language is totally independent and unrelated to Sanskrit, the above vowel consonant tables (as well as the following lessons and rules on Sandhi, Samasa etc. in Tamil grammar) clearly exhibit that the relationship between these two ancient languages is beyond just a coincidence. These two languages may have been developed separately, but their millenniums of common inheritance on the Indian subcontinent clearly reveals their common imprint. One language may or may not have come from or influenced the other, but there is a common thread for sure.

** (ii) Some Hindi speaking people may think that letter ळ is not a Devanagri or Sanskrit character. Even though it did not reach Hindi, the Sanskrit has it. Letter ळ appears in the very first verse of the Rigveda (अग्निमिळे पुरोहित). You can also hear their sounds in Tamil, Telugu, Kannad, Malyalam, Marathi and Gujrati languages. Same is true for the letters एॅ and ऑ. In Hindi, vowels ऐ and ओ are used in their place. See the language charts in the Appendix.

LESSON 2

SPEAKING THE TAMIL CHARACTERS

1. The Vowels :

Alphabet		Hindī	Sounds like, as in		
அ	(a)	(अ)	a	in	particular
ஆ	(ā)	(आ)	a	in	pāpā
இ	(i)	(इ)	I	in	pin
ஈ	(ī)	(ई)	ee	in	peel
உ	(u)	(उ)	u	in	pull, put
ஊ	(ū)	(ऊ)	oo	in	pool
எ	(e)	(ए)	e	in	pen
ஏ	(ē)	(ऍ)	ay	in	pay
ஐ	(ai)	(ऐ)	i, ai	in	Spine, Saigaon
ஒ	(o)	(ओ)	o	in	polute
ஓ	(ō)	(ओऽ)	o, au	in	pore
ஔ	(au)	(औ)	ow	in	powder

2. The Consonants :

Alphabet		Hindī	Sounds like, as in		
க	(ka)	(क)	k	in	pink
ங	(ṅga)	(ङ)	ṅg	in	spring
ச	(cha)	(च)	ch	in	chum
ஞ	(ñya)	(ञ)	n	in	Puñjāb
ட	(ṭa, ḍa)	(ट, ड)	t, d	in	tape, pet, paddy, pant
ண	(ṇa)	(ण)	English does not have it		
த	(ta, da)	(त, द)	th	in	they
ந	(na)	(न)	m	in	nap
ப	(pa, ba)	(प, ब)	p, b	in	pub
ம	(ma)	(म)	m	in	map
ய	(ya)	(य)	y	in	yup
ர	(ra)	(र)	r	in	rap
ல	(la)	(ल)	l	in	lap
வ	(va)	(व)	v. w	in	Volkswagon
ழ	(lá)	(ऴ)	English does not have it		
ள	(ḷa)	(ळ)	English does not have it		
ற	(ṛa)	(र)	r	in	park
ன	(na)	(न)	n	in	pan
ஷ	(ś́h, ṣh)	(श, ष)	sh	in	push
ஸ	(sa)	(स)	s	in	sap
ஹ	(ha)	(ह)	n	in	hip
க்ஷ	(kṣha)	(क्ष)	ksh	in	rikshaw
ஜ	(ja)	(ज)	j	in	jump

Like Sanskrit, the Tamil characters

க, ச, ட, த, ப क, च, ट, त, प

are considered Hard Consonants

LEARN TO PRONOUNCE TAMIL CHARACTERS

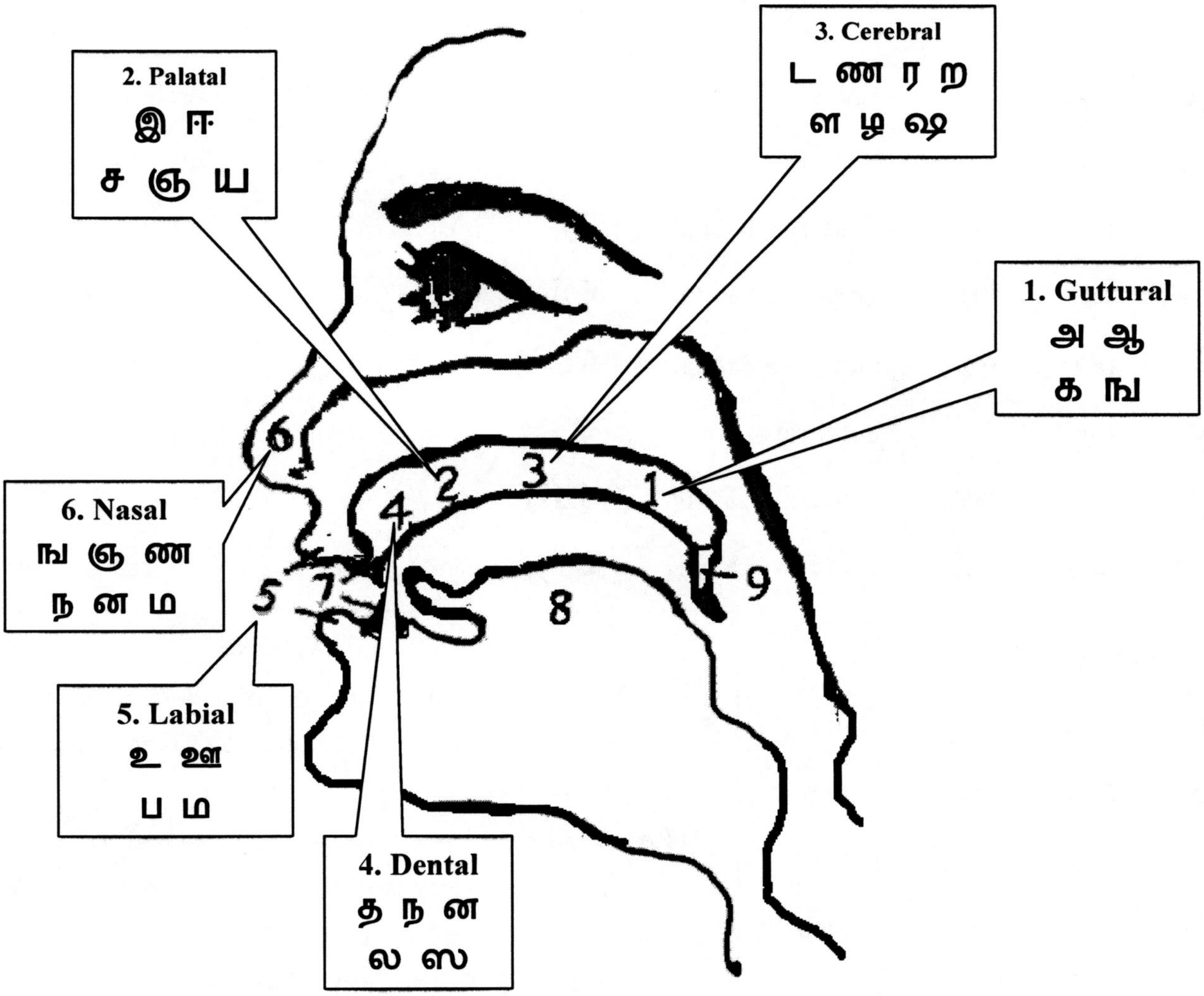

(1)	**Guttural**	कण्ठ्य *kaṇṭhya*	=	with throat
(2)	**Palatal**	तालव्य *tālavya*	=	with palate
(3)	**Cerebral**	मूर्धन्य *mūrdhanya*	=	with cerebrum
(4)	**Dental**	दन्त्य *dantya*	=	with teeth
(5)	**Labial**	ओष्ठ्य *oṣṭhya*	=	with lips
(6)	**Nasal**	अनुनासिक *anunāsik*	=	with nose

 # 7 = Teeth, # 8 = Tongue, # 9 = Uvula

(1) THE VOWELS :

அ	(a)	(अ)	Guttural
ஆ	(ā)	(आ)	Guttural
இ	(i)	(इ)	Palatal
ஈ	(ī)	(ई)	Palatal
உ	(u)	(उ)	Labial
ஊ	(ū)	(ऊ)	Labial
எ	(e)	(ए)	Guttural+Palatal
ஏ	(ē)	(एॅ)	Guttural+Palatal
ஐ	(ai)	(ऐ)	Guttural+Palatal
ஒ	(o)	(ओ)	Guttural+Labial
ஓ	(ō)	(ऑ)	Guttural+Labial
ஔ	(au)	(औ)	Guttural+Labial

(3) THE CONSONANTS :

க	(k) hard	(क)	Guttural
ங	(ṅg)	(ङ)	Guttural
ச	(ch) hard	(च)	Palatal
ஞ	(ñy)	(ञ)	Palatal
ட	(ṭ, ḍ) hard	(ट, ड)	Cerebral
ண	(ṇ)	(ण)	Cerebral
த	(t, d) hard	(त, द)	Dental
ந	(n)	(न)	Dental
ப	(p, b) hard	(प, ब)	Labial
ம	(m)	(म)	Labial
ய	(y)	(य)	Palatal
ர	(r) soft	(र)	Cerebral
ல	(l)	(ल)	Dental
வ	(v)	(व)	Dental + Labial
ழ	(ĺ)	(ऴ)	Cerebral
ள	(ḷ)	(ळ)	Cerebral
ற	(r) hard	(र)	Cerebral
ன	(n)	(न)	Dental
ஷ	(śh, ṣh)	(श, ष)	Cerebral
ஸ	(s)	(स)	Dental
ஹ	(h)	(ह)	Guttural
க்ஷ	(kṣh)	(क्ष)	Guttural+Cerebral

PRONUNCIATIONS

(1) **GUTTURALS :** The characters pronounced by touching the hind part of the tongue to the THROAT (Gutter).

(2) **PALATALS :** The characters pronounced by touching the middle part of the tongue to the middle roof of the mouth i.e. the PALATE.

(3) **CEREBRALS (Retroflex)** : The characters pronounced by momentarily touching tip of the tongue against roof of the mouth (the CEREBRUM) and then dropping the tongue down suddenly..

(4) **DENTALS :** The characters pronounced by touching tip of the tongue against the base of the TEETH.

(5) **LABIALS :** The characters pronounced by touching the LIPS together.

The Tamil Compound Letters

i. Remember that the **<u>dots</u>** placed above the Tamil Characters <u>are NOT the Anusvara Nasal Dots</u>. A dot above any Tamil letter means the letter below that dot is MUTE, half or without the inherent vowel a (अ). A Tamil letter with a dot over it is equivalent of the Sanskrit or Hindi half letter or a letter with the *Halant* slash under it e.g. **ம், த், க்** = म्, त्, क् etc. Thus, **ம் + அ = ம** (म् + अ = म) etc.

ii. A consonant can not be pronounced without any vowel to it. Thus like Sanskrit or Hindi, vowel **அ** *a* अ is considered inherent in each full consonant. Without it, the consonant is considered mute or half.

iii. Unlike Sanskrit or Hindi, the Tamil letters of a compound characters are written one after another. They are not written with half letter attached to full letter. e.g. **க்க, ப்ப, ப்ல** = क्क, प्प, प्ल, etc.

Thus, the Sanskrit (and Hindi) compound letters will be written in Tamil as shown below :

क्त, क्र, त्त, ट्ट, त्र, द्र, द्ब, द्य, द्द, द्ध, द्म, श्र, क्ष, ज्ञ ॐ

க்த, க்ர, த்த, ட்ட, த்ர, த்ர, த்ப, த்ய, த்த, த்த, த்ம, ஷ்ர, க்ஷ, ச்ஞ ஓம்

The Devanagari *Anusvara* and *Visarga* in Tamil

1. The Anusvara Nasal Dot :

In Tamil writing there are no *Anusvāra* Nasal dot like the Hindi writing has. But, like Sanskrit, for writing nasal pronunciations in the words, the 'Kindred' or Class Nasal Consonants are used. The following chart of Devanagari Class Consonants helps understanding how the Nasals work in Tamil as well as in Sanskrit, because both are exactly same (for detailed discussion on this aspect, please refer to my *"Learn Sanskrit through English Medium"* Lesson 3.2).

TABLE 2 : The Devanagari Class Consonants and Nasals in relation to the Tamil Nasals :

	Devanagari Class	Sanskrit Class Characters that may come after the Kindered Nasal Characters shown in the last colomn.	Equivalent Tamil Character that may come after the Kindered Nasal Characters shown in the last colomn.	**Kindered Nasal Characters** Sanskrit & Tamil (Soft Characters)
1	*k* Class क वर्गः	क् (ख् ग् घ्) *k (kh g gh)*	**க்** k Class	ङ् *ng* **ங்**
2	*ch* Class च वर्गः	च् (छ् ज् झ्) *c (ch j jh)*	**ச்** ch Class	ञ् *ñy* **ஞ்**
3	*ṭ* Class ट वर्गः	ट् (ठ् ड् ढ्) *ṭ (ṭh ḍ ḍh)*	**ட்** t Class (retroflex)	ण् *ṇ* **ண்**
4	*t* Class त वर्गः	त् (थ् द् ध्) *t (th d dh)*	**த்** th Class	न् *n* **ந்**
5	*p* Class प वर्गः	प् (फ् ब् भ्) *p (ph b bh)*	**ப்** p Class	म् *m* **ம்**
6	Non-class Characters	य् र् ल् व् श्-ष् स् ह् ळ् *y r l v* *ś́h-ṣh s h ḷ*	**ய் ற் ல் வ்** *y r l v* **ஷ் ஸ் ஹ் ள்** *ś́h-ṣh s h ḷ*	अं m̃ **ன்**

This Table is developed by Sanskrit Hindi Research Institute for *"Learn Tamil Through English/Hindi"* by Ratnakar Narale.

The above tables shows that the Tamil characters of Alphabet are in exactly same order as the Sanskrit Alphabet. The words with nasal sounds will be written in Tamil and Sanskrit as shown in the following Table :

TABLE 3 : The Devanagari - Tamil Nasals :

		Devanagari Class	Tamil words	Sanskrit	Hindi	English
1	க	*k* Class क वर्गः	**சங்கு** (चङ्कु, सङ्कु)	शङ्ख, शङ्ख	शंख	Conch
2	ச	*ch* Class च वर्ग	**பஞ்சமம்** (पञ्चमम्)	पञ्चमम्	पंचम	Fifth
3	ட	*ṭ* Class ट वर्गः	**காண்டாமிருகம்** (काण्डामिरुगम्)	गण्डकमृगम्, गण्डः	गेंडा	Rhino
4	த	*t* Class त वर्गः	**கூந்தல்** (कून्तल्)	कुन्तल	कुंतल	Hair
5	ப	*p* Class प वर्गः	**கம்பளம்** (कम्बळम्)	कम्बलम्	कंबल	Blanket
6		Non-class	**சிங்கம்** (सिंगम्) **ஸம்ஸாரம்** (संसारम्)	सिंह संसार	सिंह, सिंघ संसार	Lion World

This Table is developed by Sanskrit Hindi Research Institute for *"Learn Tamil Through English/Hindi"* by Ratnakar Narale.

2. The Visarga Dots ஆய்தம் (आयतम्)**:**

i. In Tamil, in order to write some Tamil words with visarga sound or for the Sanskrit words with Visarga **(:)** , the (∴ *akh*) sign is used. This ∴ sign is called **ஆய்தம் āytham** or **முப்புள்ளி muppuḷḷi.**

ii. Although in Sanskrit words the visarga could come after any vowel, in Tamil words it usually comes after a short vowel and before a hard consonant. e.g. எஃகு *eḥku* (Steel); **அஃகம்** = **தானியம்** (धान्यम्) grains; **அஃது** अःदु (That). நமஃ *namaḥ* नमः (Salute).

TABLE 4 : CHARACTER PRONUNCIATION GUIDE

	Hard Character.	Nasal	Semi	Short Vowels	Long Vowels	Dipthongs
Gutturals	க ∴	ங		அ	ஆ	எ ஏ
Palatals	ச ற	ஞ ன	ய	இ	ஈ	ஐ
Cerebrals	ட	ண	ழ ள			
Dentals	த	ந	ர ல			
Labials	ப	ம	வ	உ	ஊ	ஒ ஓ ஔ

This Table is developed by Sanskrit Hindi Research Institute for *"Learn Tamil Through English/Hindi"* by Ratnakar Narale.

BEFORE YOU BEGIN, PLEASE KNOW THIS

1. The Tamil alphabet is derived from the ancient Indian inscriptional *Brahmi* script and was known as *Brahmi-Tamil* script.

2. Like Sanskrit (unlike Hindi and English), the Tamil vowel letter shapes (**அ, ஆ, இ,** ஈ...ஔ) can come only at the beginning of a word. They never come in the middle or at the end of a word. In the middle or end they are used only in their sign (मात्रा) forms attached to the right, left, up or below a consonant.

3. In Tamil there are 12 vowels and 18 Consonants. Like Sanskrit or Hindi (unlike English), in Tamil there are no Capital letters.

4. Tamil short vowels are pronounced more abruptly than the corresponding Hindi or English sounds.

5. When there are short and long vowels within a word, the long ones are pronounced more distinctly.

6. While learning the 18 consonants by heart, the first 10 consonants are repeated in five pairs of two consonants each, then the rest eight consonants are said singly or in pairs of two.

7. The long Tamil vowels like (एँ, ऑ) have a drawing pronunciation (like Punjabi ए, ई in ओए! भाई!). They can not be exactly rendered in Hindi or English.

8. Please remember that English equivalent pronunciations of Tamil characters are rarely exact. If you can read Sanskrit/Hindi, you can write, read and express them quite exactly.

9. Each letter of the alphabet can be named by adding (suffixing) **கரம்** करम् *karam* to short letters, **காரம்** कारम् *kaaram* to long letters and prefixing **இ** इ *i* to the mute Tamil letters. e.g. **அ** अ *a* = अकर *a-kar*; **ஆ** आ *aa* = आकार, **க** क् *k* = इक् *ik* etc.

10. Tamil is spoken by over 80 million people in the world. Tamil is spoken by people in almost every country in the world.

NOW YOU ARE READY TO LEARN : READING AND WRITING THE TAMIL SCRIPT.

LESSON 3

READING AND WRITING TAMIL CONSONANTS

3.1 The First Two Tamil Consonants :

க	ங
ka	***nga***
क (... ख, ग, घ)	**ङ**

1. <u>The First Tamil Consonant</u> : க (*ka* क) :

i. Tamil க *ka* क is written in the strokes of 1, 2 and 3, 4, 5 as shown with the numbered arrows below.

ii. The Tamil consonant க stands for Devanagari consonant क, ख, ग, or घ, depending on the how the word is pronounced.

iii. **The sound of க is like English letter *k*** (as in *Kit*) or Hindi क (as in कमल), when :

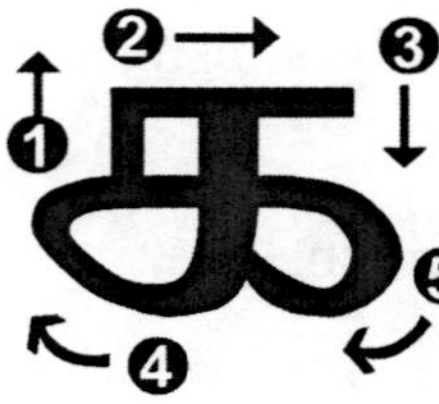

(a) a Tamil word starts with letter க,

(b) when the க is in the (middle of the) word is mute (i.e. half க் क् *k*)

(c) when it is doubled (க்க क्क *kk*),

(d) க is at the end of a syllable,

(e) or when க comes after letter ட் *ṭ* द् ;

(f) or when க comes after ண (n ऩ्);

(g) when க comes after letter ற் *ṟ* ऱ्

(h) when க is between two vowels.

e.g. கடல் *kaḍal* कडल = Ocean; சக்கரம் *chakkaram* चक्करम् = Wheel (Sanskrit चक्रम् *chakram;* Hindi चक्र *chakra);* வைகாசி *vaikasi* वैकासि = April-May (Sanskrit वैशाख, Hindi बैसाख); கட்கம் *kaḍkam* कट्गम् = Sword (Sanskrit खड्गम् *khaḍgam;* Hindi खड्ग *khaḍga);* பற்கள் पऱ्कळ, पर्कळ् *parkal* (teeth); வணக்கம் वणक्कम् *vaṇakkam* = Hi (Sanskrit/Hindi नमस्ते).

iv. **The sound of க is like English letter *g*** (as in *gut*) or Hindi letter ग (as in गरम), **when க comes after the nasal consonants ங் (ng ङ) , ண (ṇ ण) or after letter ர் (r र्)** , e.g. சங்கம் सङ्गम् *saṅgam* = Group (Sanskrit सङ्गः Hindi संग, संघ); அவர்கள் अवर्गळ् *avargaḷ* (they).

v. When letter க क *ka* comes in the middle of a word between two consonants, that letter க *ka* क may sound like letter ह *h* or घ *gh.* e.g. நகம் नहम्, नघम् *naham, nagham* (Nail), மகன் मगन् *magan* (*mahan, maghan* महन्, मघन् *)* (Son).

viii. The க *ka* क at the end of a word, if follows vowel आ *ā,* it sounds like ह *h.* e.g. உனக்காக (For you) उनक्काक = उनक्काह *unakkāk = unakkāh.*

ix. In a word of several syllables, the க क *ka* of the last syllable sounds like ह *h.* e.g. அவர்கள் अवर्गळ् *avargaḷ* (They).

x. When a Sanskrit or Hindi word is written in Tamil, the sound of the letter க will be क, ख ग or घ, (*k, kh, g, gh*) depending on its sound in that language. e.g. नखम् = நகம், घड़ी = கடி, etc.

NOTE : In Hindī (in English too), if a word ends in a simple consonant, this ending consonant is said with less stress. eg◦ *kaba* (कब) is actually said as if it was *kab* कब् *baka* (बक) as *'bak* बक् *'* and so on. But, In Tamil (as in Sanskrit) the last letter is pronounced full, unless it actually is a half letter, e.g. கட்கம் *kaḍkam* कट्गम् = Sword (Sanskrit खड्गम् *khaḍgam)*

2. The Second Tamil Consonant : ங (*nga* ङ)

i. Tamil ங *nga* ङ is written in the strokes of 1, 2 and 3, 4, 5, 6 as shown with numbered arrows below.

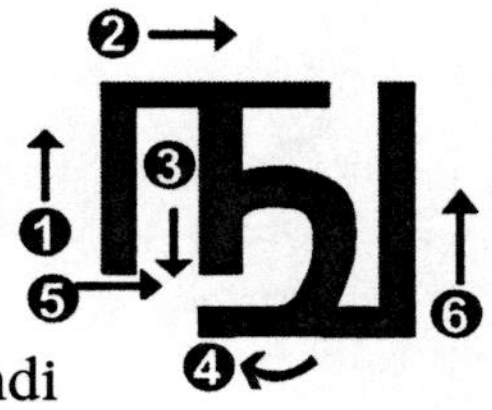

ii. The Tamil letter ங is not in English language. In Hindi it is rarely used if at all, but in Sanskrit and Tamil it is used frequently. It is usually used as mute consonant ங் followed by its kindred letter க *k* क, and the pair ங்க gives the composite sound of *nga* ङ्ग or ङ्ग e.g. சங்கம் सङ्गम् *saṅgam* = Group (Sanskrit सङ्गः Hindi संग; English : Dung)

iii. Also, like Sanskrit, no Tamil word begins with consonant ங் or ங. That is, this letter never comes as an initial letter of a Tamil or Sanskrit word.

iv. When a word ending in letter ம் *m* म् is followed by a word beginning with letter க k क, the letter ம் *m* म् is changed to letter ங் *ng* ङ् (like the *parasvarna sandhi* of Sanskrit grammar). e.g. பழம்

palám पळ्म् Fruit + **கள்** *kal* कळ् a suffix of pluralization = **பழங்கள்** *palángaļ* पळ्ंगळ् Fruits.

However, in some cases the **ம்** m म् changes to **க்** *k* क् e.g. **நகம்** *naham* नहम् Nail +**கண்** *kan* कण् Eye = **நகக்கண்** *nahakkan* नहक्कण् Nail and Eye (संस्कृत द्वंद्व समास)

v. When a word ending in letter **ம்** *m* म् is followed by the honorary suffix **ங்க** *ngg* ङ्ग, the **ம்** m म् is dropped, like the Sanskrit *parasvarna sandhi*..e.g. **வணக்கம்** *vanakkam* वणक्कम् (Hi नमस्ते) + **ங்க** (Sir जी*)* = **வணக்கங்க** *vaṇakkang* वणक्कङ्ग (Hello Sir, नमस्ते जी)

vi. When an adjective ending in letter **ம்** m म् is followed by its noun, the end letter **ம்** m म् of the adjective is dropped

3.2 The Third and Fourth Tamil Consonants :

ச	ஞ
cha	***ñya***
च (... छ, ज, झ)	**ञ**

3. <u>The Third Tamil Consonant</u> : **ச** (*ch* च) :

i. Tamil **ச** *cha* च is written in the strokes of 1, 2 and 3, 4, 5 as shown with the numbered arrows.

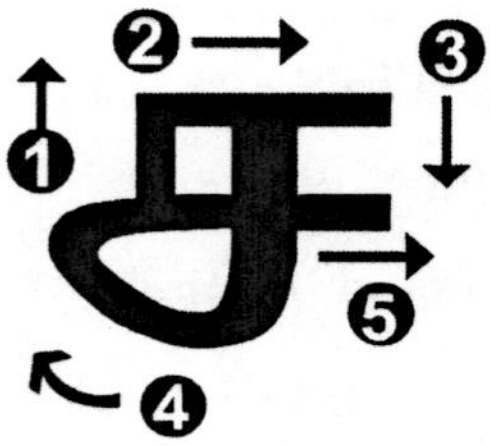

ii. The Tamil consonant **ச** stands for Devanagari consonant च, छ, ज, or झ, depending up on the how the word is pronounced.

iii. When a Tamil word starts with letter **ச**, or when the **ச** in the word is mute (i.e. half **ச்** च् *ch*) or when it is doubled (**ச்ச** च्च *chcha*), the sound of **ச** is like the Hindi letter च (as in चम्मच), and Sanskrit letter च *ch,* as in the Sanskrit verb चर्च् *√charch* (to violate, to rebuke). English language does not have letter *ch*, but only the sound of *ch* is there as in English word *Church.*

iv. In the Tamil words adopted from Sanskrit, the sound of **ச** may be like ज j. e.g. **சனம்** = **ஜனம்** जनम् *janam* (People), Sanskrit and Hindi जन *jana* (People).

v. Like the Sanskrit rule of Third Consonant, when letter ச *cha* च comes after letter ஞ் (ञ् *ny*), the letter ச takes sound of Hindi letter ज English j. e.g. பஞ்சு पञ्जु *pañju* (Cotton).

vi. When ச *cha* च is mute or doubled, it sounds like छ *chh*. e.g. இச்சை इच्छै *icchai* (Desire), Sanskrit and Hindi इच्छा *ichhā*.

vii. When ச *cha* च comes after letter ட் ट् t or ற் र् r, it maintains its च *ch* sound. e.g. திராட்சை दिराट्चै *diratchai* (Grapes); Sanskrit, Hindi द्राक्ष *drāksha.*

viii. When ச *cha* च comes after letter ப் प *p*, it sounds like स *s*. e.g. பசு पसु *pasu* (Cow), Sanskrit पशु *pashu* (Animal).

ix. When letter ச *cha* च comes after letter ஞ், the letter ச *cha* च is pronounced as ज *j* and letter ஞ் is pronounced somewhat like न् *n.* e.g. பஞ்சாபி (written पञ्चापि) spoken पंजाबी *pañjābī.*

x. When ச comes as initial letter, or if it comes in the word as a full simple consonant, it sounds like स *s*. e.g. சரம் सरम् *saram* (Movement) Sanskrit सर *sar* (move); ரசம் रसम् *rasam* (Juice) Sanskrit रसम् *rasam* (juice).

xi. When a word ending in ம் म् *m* is followed by a word starting with letter ச च *ch*, the ம் म् *m* is <u>usually</u> changed to ஞ் ञ् *ny*; in some cases it is changed to ச் च् *ch.* e.g. பழம் + செய்யப்பட்ட = பழஞ்செய்யப்பட்ட पळञ्चैप्पट्ट *pal̥añchaippaṭṭa* (an Old Sandal); மரம் + சட்டம் = மரச்சட்டம் मरच्चट्टम् *marachchaṭṭam* (a Wood-frame).

xii. In Sanskrit words, the ச *cha* च can sound like letter स *s or* श *sh.* e.g. சந்நியாசி संन्यासी *sanyasi* (Hermit). தேசம் देसम्, देशम् *desam, desham* (Country)

PLEASE DO NOT JUMP TO NEXT LESSON WITHOUT DOING THIS ONE PROPERLY.

4. The Fourth Tamil Consonant : ஞ (*ny* ञ) :

i. Tamil ஞ *ny* च is written in the strokes of 1, 2 and 3, 4, 5 as shown with the numbered arrows.

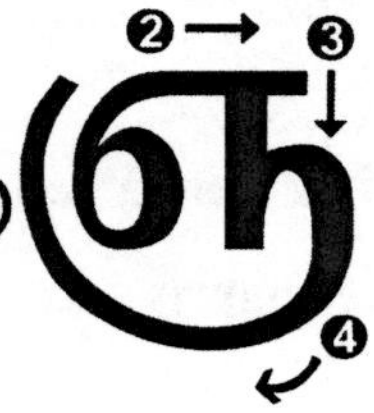

ii. The Tamil letter ஞ (*ny* ञ) is not in English language and its pronunciation can not be correctly expressed in English, but it approximately sounds like *ny*. In Hindi it is rarely used. In Sanskrit and Tamil it is used frequently. It is usually used as a mute consonant ஞ் *ny* ञ्

iii. For joining with vowels, letter ஞ *ny* ञ takes only vowels அ, ஆ, எ, ஏ and ஒ अ, आ, ए, ऍ, and ओ (*a, ā, e, ĕ* and *o*).

iv. When letter ச *cha* च comes after letter ஞ், the letter ச *cha* च is pronounced as ज *j* and letter ஞ் is pronounced somewhat like न् *n.* e.g. பஞ்சாபி (पञ्चापि) पंजाबी *pañjābī.*

v. When a word ending in ம் म् *m* is followed by a word starting with letter ச च *ch*, the ம் म् *m* is <u>usually</u> changed to ஞ் ञ् *ny*; in some cases it is changed to ச் च् *ch.* e.g. பழம் + செய்யப்பட்ட = பழஞ்செய்யப்பட்ட पळ्ञ्चैप्पट्ट *paḷañchaippaṭṭa* (an Old Sandal); மரம் + சட்டம் = மரச்சட்டம் मरच्चट्टम् *marachchaṭṭam* (a Wood-frame).

3.3 The Fifth and Sixth Tamil Consonants :

ட	ண
ṭa	*ṇa*
ट (...ठ, ड, ढ)	ण

5. <u>The Fifth Tamil Consonant</u> : ட (*ṭ* ट) :

i. Tamil ட *ṭ* ट is written in a stroke of 1, 2 as shown.

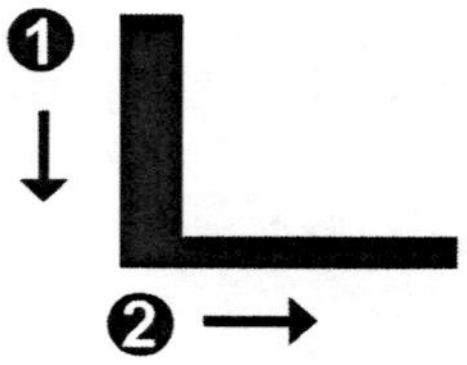

ii. The Tamil consonant ட stands for Devanagari consonant ट, ठ, ड, or ढ, depending up on how the word is pronounced.

iii. Tamil ட has a very hard metallic cerebral sound which is not in English. It comes in Sanskrit word टिट्टिभी *tittibhee* (a Sandpiper) and Hindi word टमटम *tamtam* (a One horse carriage, Tonga).

iv. The Tamil ட *t* ट (ट, ड, ढ) gives the preceding vowel a wider sound than it's normal sound. e.g.

ஈடு ईडु *eedu* (Suffer); ஏடு एँडु *ĕdu* (a Leaf); ஓடு ऑडु *ŏdu* (Run, hasten)

v. The original Tamil words do not begin with letter ட, but the adopted words begin with double ட்ட (ट्ट *tt*). e.g. ட்டாணா ट्ठाना *tthānā* (Police station) Hindi थाना *thana*. Sanskrit स्थान *sthana*.

6. <u>The Sixth Tamil Consonant</u> : **ண** (*ṇ* ण) :

i. Tamil **ண** *ṇ* ण is written in the strokes of 1, 2, 3 and 4 as shown with the numbered arrows below.

ii. To pronounce this retroflex letter **ண** *ṇ* ण, curl the tongue back towards the throat and touch it at middle part of the cerebrum plate and then suddenly drop it to say the sharp **ண** *ṇ* ण .

iii. The Tamil **ண** has a hard metallic cerebral sound which is not in English. It is in Sanskrit and Hindi word बाण *bāṇa* (an Arrow).

iv. When a word ending in **ண** *ṇ* ण् is followed by a word beginning with **க்**, **ச்**, or **ப்** क्, च् or प् *k, ch* or *p* , the final **ண** *ṇ* ण becomes ட் द् *t*. e.g. மண் + மூர்த்தம் = மட்மூர்த்தம் मण् + मूर्त्तम् = मट्मूर्त्तम् *maṇ* (Earthen) + *moorttham* (Idole, मूर्ति) = *maṭ-mūrtam* (Clay-idole)

v. In Tamil, Sanskrit and Hindi **ண** *ṇ* ण never comes as initial letter of a word.

EXERCISE : Read the following Tamil letters and words

க ங ச ஞ ட ண

கண் (Eye), சட்(Haa!), டக்டக் (Tapping souns), டங்க (Twang sound)

3.4 The Seventh and Eighth Tamil Consonants :

த	**ந**
ta	***na***
त (...थ, द, ध)	**न**

7. <u>The Seventh Tamil Consonant</u> : த (*t* त) :

i. Tamil dental த *t* त is written in the strokes of 1, 2 ans 3, 4, 5 as shown.

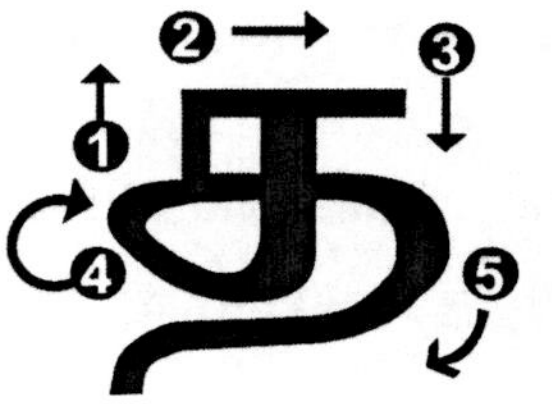

ii. This pure dental consonant த stands for Devanagari dental consonants त, थ, द, ध, depending on how the word is pronounced. The most common Tamil sound of த is more close to थ *th* than त *t* or द *d.*

Specially between two vowels the த *sound mote like th* थ than त t. e.g. ஸீதா सीता *seetha*; Sanskrit, Hindi सीता *Seethā* கதை कथै *kathai* (Story) = Sanskrit कथा *kathā.*

English *th* has two sounds as in *<u>th</u>*under and *<u>th</u>*en, but both of these *th* sounds are different than the Tamil த *th*. This sound is not in English.

iii. The letter த is stand alone, initial letter, mute or doubled, it has a sound of त, थ *t, th*; but when it is in the middle or at the end of a word, it sounds like द, ध *d, dh*. In Sanskrit originated words, it is pronounced accordingly. e.g. தானம் दानम् *dānam* (Charity); தேவி देवि *devī* (Goddess देवी).

iv. The Tamil ட *t* ट (ट, ड, ढ) gives the preceding vowel a wider sound than it's normal sound. e.g. ஈடு ईडु *eedu* (Equal); ஏடு एॅडु *ĕdu* (a Leaf); ஓடு ऑडु *odu* (Run, hasten)

v. When letter த *t* त comes after letter ந் *n* न्, it sounds like द d. e.g. இந்த इन्द *ind* (this), வந்தனம் वन्दनम् *vandanam* (Salute संस्कृत वन्दनम्).

8. <u>The Eighth Tamil Consonant</u> : ந (*n* न) :

i. Tamil ந *n* न is written in the strokes of 1, 2 and 3, 4 as shown with the numbered arrows.

ii. To pronounce this न *n* sound, touch the tip of your tongue to the tip of upper teeth and say it softly.

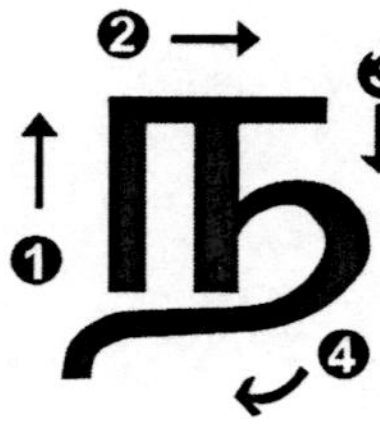

iii. There are two न *n* letters in Tamil (The other न *n*, is the consonant number 18, given ahead). This ந न *n* NEVER comes at the end of a word. This ந न *n* comes only as INITIAL letter or in the middle of the word.

If the न *n* comes before letter த त, द *t, d*, then this ந is used. e.g. பதினைந்து पदिनैन्दु *padinaindu* (Fifteen); பந்து पन्दु *pandu* (Ball, Sanskrit कन्दुक), பஞ்சதஷம் *pañchadasham* शंचदशम् (Sanskrit पंचदश *pañchadasha*, Hindi पन्द्रह *pandraha*).

NOTE that there is not much essential difference between this ந and the other Tamil ண न n, other than that for the first ந the tongue touch is heavier with the teeth than ண न n. <u>In written Tamil, these two letters are often interchanged</u>.

EXERCISE : Read and Write the following Tamil letters

க ங ச ஞ ட ண த ந

3.5 The Ninth and Tenth Tamil Consonants :

ப	ம
pa	***ma***
प (...फ, ब, भ)	**म**

9. <u>The Ninth Tamil Consonant</u> : ப (*p* प) :

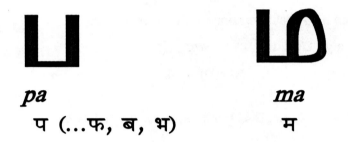

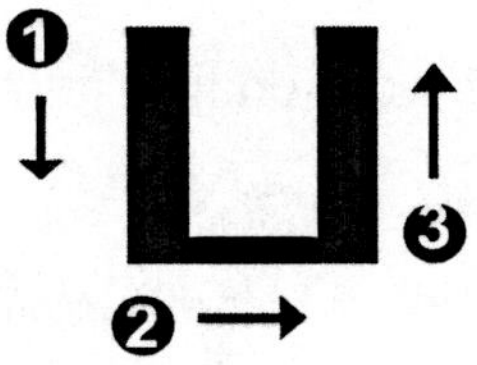

i. Tamil ப *p* प is written in a stroke of 1, 2, 3 as shown .

ii. The consonant ப stands for Devanagari consonant प, फ, ब, or भ, depending on how the word is pronounced.

iii. When letter ப comes as stand-alone, initial, mute or doubled, it sounds like प *p* as in பணம் पणम् *paṇam* (Coin); Sanskrit पण् *paṇ* (to buy), English word *pan* (Pot).

iv. When letter ப comes as after letter ட ट *t* or ற र *r*, it sounds like प *p* as in பாடம் पाठम् *pāṭham* (Lesson); Sanskrit, Hindi पाठ *pāṭh* (Lesson),

v. When letter ப is doubled, it also sounds like प *p* as in கப்பல் कप्पल् *kappal* (Ship).

vi. Other than above three situations, when letter ப comes in the middle or at the end of a word, it sounds ந்ike ब or भ *b* or *bh*. e.g. கம்பர் कम्बर *kambar* (A Tamil Poet);

vii. In adopted words it sounds like ब *b*. e.g. புத்தி बुद्धि *buddhi* (Intelligence); பந்து बन्धु *bandhu;* பஞ்சாபி पंजाबी *pañjābī*

viii. Between two vowels Tamil ப *p* प has *ph* फ like sound. e.g. தபம் तफम् *tapham* (Austerity) Sanskrit तपम् *tapam* (Austerity)

ix. In Sanskrit words written in Tamil, the letter ப *p* प may sound as प, फ, ब, भ *p, ph, b, bh.* e.g. भयम् *bhayam* (Fear), बन्धु *bandhu* அண்ணன், தம்பி (Relative, Brother).

10. The Tenth Tamil Consonant : ம (*m* म) :

i. Tamil letter ம *m* म is written in a stroke of 1, 2, 3 as shown with the numbered arrows below.

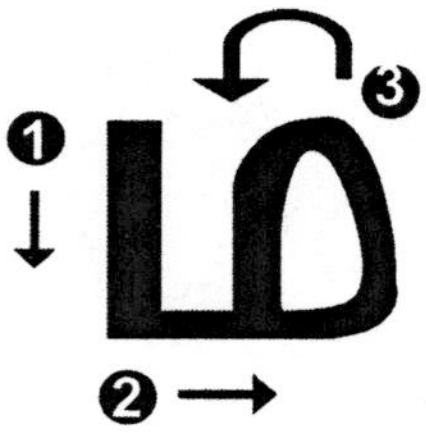

ii. The mute consonant ம் is used as a nasal component of the preceding consonant, vowel or syllable. e.g. பணம் पणम् *paṇam* (Coin)
பணம் पणम् *paṇam* = प + णम् *pa* + *ṇam;* NOT प + ण + म् *pa* + *ṇa* + *m*

iii. While saying ம் म् *m*, the lips are kept closed, but while saying ம म *ma*, the lips are opened.

iv. When a word ending in ம் म् *m* is followed by a word beginning with letter க क *k*, the ம் म् *m* changes to ங் ङ् *ng*. e.g. பக்கம் + கள = பக்கங்கள் - பக்கம் *pakkam* पक्कम् (Side) + கள *kaḷ* (plural) = பக்கங்கள் *pakkaṅkaḷ* पक्कङ्कळ् (Sides)

v. When a word ending in ம் म् *m* is followed by a word beginning with letter ச च *ch*, the ம் म् *m* changes to ஞ் ञ् *ny*. like Sanskrit sandhi. e.g. மரம் *maram* मरम् (tree) + சாகை (chāgai, sāgai सागै = संस्कृत शाख) = மரஞ்சாகை *marañchāgai* मरंसागै or *marankiḷai* மரக்கிளை मरंक्किळै).

vi. When a word ending in ம் म् *m* is followed by a word beginning with letter த त, द *t, d* the ம் म् *m* changes to ந் न् *n*. e.g. (i) மனம் *manam* मनम् (mind) + திறந்து *thirandu* तिरंदु (open) = மனந்திறந்து *mananthirandu* मनन्तिरंदु (open mind); (ii) மரம் *maram* मरम् (tree) + தழை (daḷai दळै; संकृत दल, मराठी दळ) = மரந்தழை *marañdaḷai* मरंदळै).

vii. When a word ending in ம் म् *m* is followed by a word beginning with letter ம் म *m*, the ம் म् *m* is dropped. e.g. வணக்கம் *vanakkam* वणक्कम् (Hi नमस्ते) + முருகன் (Murugan मुरुगन्) = வணக்கம்முருகன் *vaṇakkammurugan* वणक्कम्मुरुगन् (Hello Mr. Murugan नमस्ते मुरुगन् जी)

EXERCISE : Read and Write the following Tamil letters and words

க ங ச ஞ ட ண த ந ப ம

சங்கம் (Gathering संघ), **சசம்** (Hare सं. शशक), **சட்டம்** (Picture frame), **படம்** (Picture), **மண்** (the Earth), **நகம்** (Nail नख), **கன்னம்** (Cheek), **பட்டம்** (Kite पतंग), **பணம்** (Money पण)

3.6 The Eleventh and Twelfth Tamil Consonants :

ய	ர
ya	***ra***
य	**र**

11. <u>The Eleventh Tamil Consonant</u> : ய (*y* य) :

i. Tamil ய *y* य is written in the strokes of 1, 2 and 3, 4 as shown with the numbered arrows below.

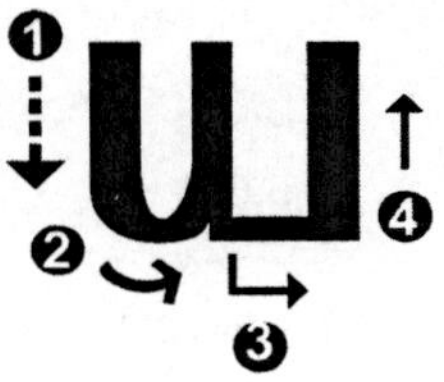

ii. The sound of this letter is closer to English letter *y* or Sanskrit-Hindi य.
e.g. நாய் नाय् *nāy* (Dog)

iii. Similar to Hindi, the ய य *y* sound is some times interchanged with ए *ai* sound. e.g. Tamil நரசய்யா नरासय्या, नरसैया *Narasayya, Narasaiya;* Hindi गये, गए.

iii. In a word where ய *y* य comes after ஆ எ ஏ ஓ आ, ए, ऍ, ओऽ *ā, e, ĕ ŏ,* the ய sounds like इ *i.* e.g. ஓய்வுக்காலம் ओइवुक्कालम् *oivukkālam* (Life at retirement)

iv. Double ய்ய has pure य *y* sound. e.g. அய்யா, அய்யர் अय्या, अय्यर *iyyā, iyyar* (Sir)

v. Final ய் has ई *ī* sound. e.g. தாய் दाई *dāī* (Mother)

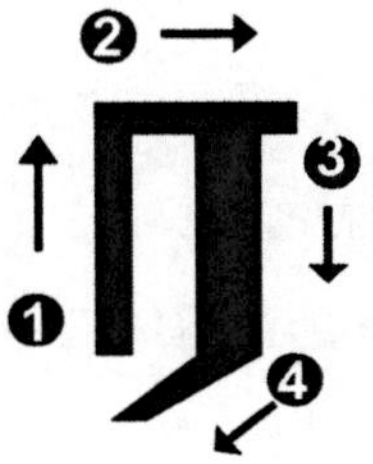

12. <u>The Twelfth Tamil Consonant</u> : ர (*r* र) :

i. Tamil ர *r* र is written in the strokes of 1, 2 and 3, 4 as shown with the numbered arrows below.

ii. There are two र *r* letters in Tamil. (The other र *r*, is consonant number 17, given ahead). This ர *r* र never comes in compound letters. The other ற *r* र comes in compound letters. This ர *r* र is never doubled. The other ற *r* र may be doubled or even tripled in a row. e.g. கற்றளி (Stone temple); காற்று (Wind); கற்றறிமோழை (an Educated fool).

iii. This ர *r* र is plain र r as in மரம் मरम् *maram* (Tree). The other ற *r* र has rough or slurred sound like Sanskrit/Hindi double *rr* र्. e.g. ஸர்ப்பம் सर्प्पम् *sarppam* (Snake), Sanskrit सर्प *sarp* (Snake).

iv. The two ர and ற *r* र are not interchangeable. The meaning will change. e.g. மரம் मरम् *maram* (Tree) மறம் मर्म *maram* (Valour). As also in Sanskrit करण (Instrumental Case) and कर्ण (Ear).

v. This ர *r* र is usually written as ா̇ (same as vowel sign ா आ *ā)*, except in the places when it could be confused with vowel sign आ *ā*. In that case a dot is placed over it ா̇ to say it is ர *r* र. e.g. மரம் or மா̇ ம (not ம ா̇ம்)

vi. No pure original Tamil word starts with ர *r* र. The Tamil words that now do begin with ர *r* र, the ர in them is compounded with vowel உ, ஐ, ஒ or ஓ उ, ऐ, ओ or ऑ (u, ai, o or ŏ), or vowel இ इ *i* is prefixed to it. This initial இ may not actually be written, pronounced or may be pronounced very lightly. e.g. இரண்டு इरण्डु or रण्डु *iraṇḍu* or *raṇḍu* (Two).

vii. Letter ர *r* र (not ற *r* र्) comes before letters க் க ச் ச த் த ப் ப क्, क, च्, च, त् त, प् प *k, ka, ch, cha, t, ta, p, pa.*

viii. Note letter ர *r* र is written in ா shape for writing ர் ரி ரீ ரு ரூ (र्, रि, री, रु, रू *r, ri, rī, ru, rū*) and in ர shape to write ர ரா ரெ ரே ரொ ரௌ (र, रा, रे, रॅ, रो, रॉ *r, rā, re, rĕ, ro, rŏ*)

EXERCISE : Read and Write the following Tamil letters and words

க ங ச ஞ ட ண த ந ப ம ய ர

மரம் (Tree), கப்படம் (Clothes कपड़े), சபம், ஜபம் (Mutter, Chant, जप), சயம், ஜயம் (Victory जय), சர்க்கம் (Chapter), சரம் (Movable चर), மணம் (Smell), அரங்கம் (Theater रंगभूमि), யமகம் (Rhyme अनुप्रास), தடாகம் (Lake तडाग), தயக்கம் (Hesitation), நகம் (Nail)

3.7 The Thirteenth and Fourteenth Tamil Consonants :

ல	**வ**
la	***va, wa***
ल	**व**

13. <u>The Thirteenth Tamil Consonant</u> : ல (*l* ल) :

i. Tamil ல *l* ल is written in a stroke of 1, 2, 3 as shown with the numbered arrows below.

ii. No pure original Tamil word starts with ல *l* ल . The Tamil words that now do begin with ல *l* ल , the ல in them is compounded with vowel உ, ஐ, ஒ or ஓ उ, ऐ, ओ or ऑ (u, ai, o or ŏ), or the vowel இ इ *i* is prefixed to it. This initial இ may not actually be written or pronounced or may be pronounced very lightly. e.g. இலக்கம் इलक्कम् or लक्कम् *ilakkam* or *lakkam* (One Lack, One Hundred Thousand); Sanskrit लक्षम् *laksham*; Hindi लाख *lakh.*

iii. When a word ending in ல் ल् *l* is followed by a word beginning with க், ச், or ப் क्, च् or प् *k, ch* or *p* , the final ல் ल् *l* becomes ற் र् *r.* e.g. பல் पल् *pal* + போடி पोडी *podi* = பற்போடி पल् + पोडि = पर् (teeth) + पोडी *podi* (powder) = *parpodi* पर्पोडी (Tooth-powder)

14. <u>The Fourteenth Tamil Consonant</u> : வ (*v, w* व) :

i. Tamil வ *v* व is written in a stroke of 1, 2, 3, 4 as shown with the numbered arrows below.

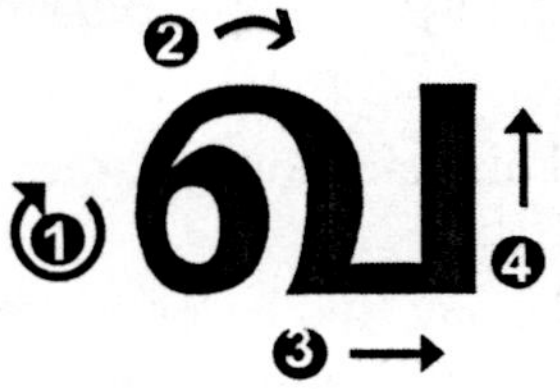

ii. Similar to Sanskrit and Hindi, the Tamil has only one வ *v* व sound, as against the two English v and w letters. e.g. வட்டம் वट्टम् *vaṭṭam* (a Circle), Sanskrit वृत्तम *vṛttam* (a Circle), Hindi वृत्त *vṛtta* (a Circle); பர்வதம் पर्वदम् *parvadam* (Mountain) Sanskrit पर्वत *parvat* (Mountain) Hindi पर्वत, पर्बत *parvat, parwat, parbat* (Mountain); நவம் नवम् *navam* (New) Sanskrit नवम् *navam* (New) Hindi नव, नया *nava, nayā* (New); வசந்தம் वसन्दम् *vasandam* (the Spring season) Sanskrit वसन्तम् *vasantam* (the Spring season) Hindi वसंत, बसंत *vasant, wasant, basant* (the Spring season), ... etc.

EXERCISE : Read and Write the following Tamil characters and words

க ங ச ஞ ட ண த ந ப ம ய ர ல வ

பல் (Tooth), **வயல்** (Farm, field), **கப்பல்** (Ship, boat), **கடல்** (Ocean), **வண்ணம்** (Colour), **மட்டம்** (Flatness, Evenness), **யவம்** (Paddy जव, जौं), **ரசம்** (Juice रस), **ரத்தம்** (Blood रक्त), **வங்கம்** (Bengal वङ्ग), **வட்டம்** (Circle वृत्त), **வடம்** (Rope), **வர்க்கம்** (a Group, class वर्ग), **வரம்** (Boon वर), **வர்ணம்** (a Group, class; Colour वर्ण), **லட்சம்** (One hundred thousand लक्ष, लाख), **லயம்** (Melody लय), **லவணம்** (Salt लवण).

3.8 The Fifteenth and Sixteenth Tamil Consonants :

ழ	ள
ĺa	*ḷa*
ऴ	ळ

15. <u>The Fifteenth Tamil Consonant</u> : **ழ** (*í* ऴ) :

i. Tamil **ழ** *ĺ* ऴ is written in the strokes of 1, 2, 3 and 4, as shown with the numbered arrows below.

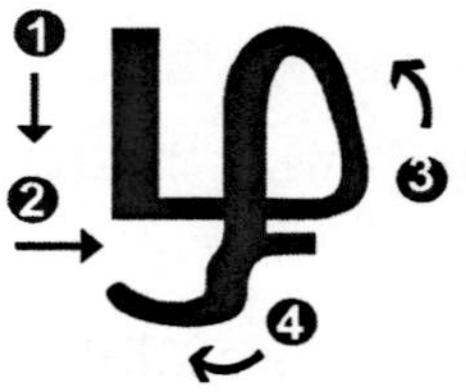

ii. This *ĺ* ऴ is NOT a half *l* ळ, but written as Devanagari *ĺ* ऴ just to differentiate it from the other similar Tamil letter **ள** *ḷ* ळ (letter #6).

iii. Letter **ழ** *ĺ* ऴ never comes as initial letter of a word.

e.g. **பழம்** पऴम् *paĺam* (Fruit) Sanskrit फलम् *phalam* (Fruit), Hindi फल *phal* (Fruit).

iii. This letter or the sound is not found in English and Hindi languages.

iv. To say this letter, either do not move the tongue or bend it to the throat as far as you can but do not touch it to the palate, and then say the Devanagari character ळ or Hindi ड़ or English *rl*.

16. <u>The Sixteenth Tamil Consonant</u> : **ள** (*ḷ* ळ) :

i. Tamil **ள** *ḷ* ळ is written in the strokes of 1, 2 and 3, as shown with the numbered arrows below.

iii. Like Sanskrit, no Tamil word starts with letter **ள** *ḷ* ळ.

e.g. **மஞ்சள்** मञ्जळ् *mañjaḷ* (*Yellow colour*). Note that, as said above, this ள *ḷ* ळ् is different than the other ழ *l̒* ऴ् , even if they are written same in Devanagari.

iii. This letter or the sound is not found in English and Hindi languages.

iv. To say this letter, either do not move the tongue or bend it to the throat as far as you can but do not touch it to the palate, and then say the Devanagari character ळ or Hindi ड़ or English *rl.*

v. When a word ending in ள் ळ् *ḷ* is followed by a word beginning with க், ச், or ப் क्, च् or प् *k, ch* or *p* , the final ள் ळ् *ḷ* becomes ட் ट् ṭ. e.g. பொருள் + கள் = பொருட்கள் पोरुळ् + कळ् = पोरुट्कळ् *poruḷ* (Matter) + *kaḷ* (Suffix of pliral) = *poruṭkaḷ* (Many बहुत)

EXERCISE : Read and Write the following Tamil letters and words

க ங ச ஞ ட ண த ந ப ம ய ர

ல வ ழ ள

மகள் (Daughter), **கச்சம்** (Dress), **கச்சல்** (Bitter Taste), **கட்டம்** (Hardship कष्ट, Square space), **சரதம்** (Truth), **சல்லடம்** (Shorts), முள்ளம்பன்றி (Porcupine), **தட** (Large), **விஷம்** (visam or vidam = Poison विष).

3.9 The Seventeenth and Eighteenth Tamil Consonants :

ற	ன
r	*n*
ऱ्	ऩ्

17. The Seventeenth Tamil Consonant : ற (*r* ऱ्) :

i. Tamil ற / ऱ् is written in a stroke of 1, 2, 3 as shown.

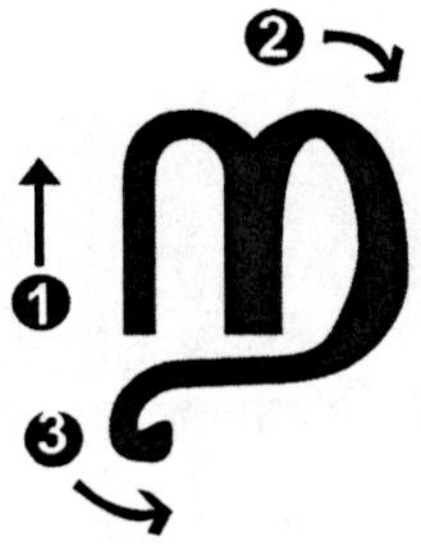

ii. The *r* ऱ् is NOT a half *r* ऱ्, but written as Devanagari *r* ऱ् only to identify it from the Tamil letter ர *r* र. See Table 5.

iii. Letter ற / ऱ् never comes as initial letter of a word.

e.g. அறம் अरम् *aram* (Dharma), Sanskrit धर्म *dharma,* Hindi धरम *dharam.* **r** ऱ्

iv. As said before, there are two र *r* letters in Tamil. (The other र *r*, is consonant number 11, given before). This ற *l* ऱ् comes in compound letters. The other ர *r* र. does not come in compound letters. The other ர *r* र is never doubled. This ற *r* र may be doubled or even tripled in a row. e.g. கற்றளி (Stone temple); காற்று (Wind); கற்றறிமோழை (an Educated fool).

v. This ற *r* र has rough or slurred sound like Sanskrit/Hindi double *rr* र्. e.g. ஸர்ப்பம் सर्प्पम् *sarppam* (Snake), Sanskrit सर्प *sarp* (Snake), Hindi सर्प *sarp* (Snake),

vi. The two ர and ற *r* र are not interchangeable. The meaning will change. e.g. மரம் मरम् *maram* (Tree) மறம் मर्म *marm* (Violence). Same as in Sanskrit करण (Instrumental Case) and कर्ण (Ear).

vii. When ற *l* ऱ् is doubled, they sound like *ṭr* ट्र. e.g. காற்று *kaṭru* काट्रु (Wind)

viii. When ற *l* ऱ् is mute, it may take ट *ṭ* or र r sound. See Table 6.

ix. When this ன *n* न् comes before ற் र *r* , it's sound changes to ण *ṇ* and then the ன்ற் नऱ् *nr* is pronounced as ण्ड्र *ṇḍr.* e.g. கன்று कण्ड्रु *kaṇḍru* (Calf). See Table 16.

x. When a word ending with letter ல் *l* ल् is joined with or followed by a word beginning with letter க, ச or ப क, च or प *k, ch* or *p,* the ல் ल् *l* is changed to ற *l* ऱ्. e.g. கடல் கப்பல் = கடற்கப்பல் कडल् कप्पल = कडऱ्कप्पल कडर्कप्पल *kadal kappal - kadarkappal* (Ocean liner). See Table 16.

xi. When letter ல் ल् *l* is followed by letter த त *t*, both these letters are changed in to ற்ற र् *rr*. e.g. கூந்தல் தலை = கூந்தற்றலை कून्दल् + तलै *kūndal + talai* = कून्दर्लै *kūndarralai* (Hairy head). See Table 16.

xii. ற *r* ऱ् never comes before letters க் க ச் ச த் த ப் ப क्, क, च्, च, त् त, प् प *k, ka, ch, cha, t, ta, p, pa.*

18. <u>The Eighteenth Tamil Consonant</u> : ன (*n* न्) :

i. Tamil ன *n* न is written in the strokes of 1, 2, 3 and 4, as shown with the numbered arrows below.

ii. Letter ன *n* न् never comes as initial letter of a word. It always comes as a middle or the end letter of a word. e.g. நண்பன் नण्बन् *naṇban* (a Friend)

கன்னம் कन्नम् *kannam* (cheeks) *Sanskrit* कर्ण *karṇa,* Hindi कान *kān.*

iii. When this ன் *n* न् comes before ற் र *r* , it's sound changes to ण *ṇ* and then the ன்ற் न्र् *nr* is pronounced as ण्ड्र *ṇḍr.* e.g. கன்று कण्ड्रु *kaṇḍru* (Calf). See Table 16.

EXERCISE : Read and Write the following

க ங ச ஞ ட ண த ந ப ம ய ர
ல வ ழ ள ற ன

மஞ்சள் (Yellow colour), நண்பன் (Friend), கன்னம் (cheeks), மகன் (Son), தச்சன் (Carpenter तक्षक), சிப்பி (Shell सीप), பவ்வம் (Knot), பயம் (Fear भय), நலம் (Goodness), நல்ல (Good).

.

VOWEL- CONSONANT RULE : When a word ending in a vowel is followed by a word beginning with consonant क्, च्, त्, or प्, *k, ck, t,* or *p* that consonant is doubled.

.

TABLE 5 : SUMMARY OF CONSONANT MODIFICATIONS (संधि)

	க்	ச்	த்	ந்	ம்	ப்
ண்	ட்க்	ட்ச்	ண்ட்	ண்ண்		ப்ப்
ம்	ங்க்	ஞ்ச்	ந்த	ந்	ம்	
ல்	ற்க்	ற்ச்	ற்ற், ன்ற்	ன்ன்	ன்ம்	ற்ப்
ள்	ட்க்	ட்ச்	ட்ட் , ண்ட்	ண்ண	ண்ம், ண்ண்	ட்ப்
ன்	ற்க்	ற்ச்	ன்ற், ற்ற்	ன்ன்		ற்ப்
Vowel	க்க	ச்ச	த்த			ப்ப

This Table is developed by Sanskrit Hindi Research Institute for *"Learn Tamil Through English/Hindi"* by Ratnakar Narale.

CONSONANT PRONUNCIATION

TABLE 6 : SUMMARY OF CONSONANT PRONUNCIATION

				AFTER THIS									
This ↓	Initial letter	Mute	Double	ங்	ஞ	ட்	ண்	ர்	ற்	Between two vowels	Between two Consonants.	Last letter	Other places
க	क *k*	क *k*	क *k*	ग *g*		क *k*	ग *g*	ग *g*	क *k*	क *k*	ह *h*	क *k*	ग *g*
ச			च *ch*		ज *j*	च *ch*			च *ch*				स *s* श *sh*
ட		ट *ṭ*	ट *ṭ*										ड *ḍ*
த	त *t* थ *th*	त *t* थ *th*	त *t* थ *th*										द *d*
ப	प *p*	प *p*	प *p*										ब *b*
ற	द् *ṯ*	द् *ṯ*	द् *ṯ*						ट्र *tr*				र् *ṟ*

This Table is developed by Sanskrit Hindi Research Institute for *"Learn Tamil Through English/Hindi"* by Ratnakar Narale.

READING AND WRITING TAMIL GRANTHAKSHARs

ஜ ஸ ஷ ஹ க்ஷ

ja	*sa*	*sha*	*ha*	*ksha*
ज	स	श, ष	ह	क्ष

1. <u>The First Tamil Granthakshar</u> : ஜ (*ja* ज)

i. Tamil ஜ *j* ज is written in a single stroke of 1, 2, 3, 4 as shown :

ii. The Tamil letter used in place of ஜ is ச and pronounced as ज j or स s.
e.g. சனம் जनम् *janama* (People) Sanskrit जन *jana* (People);
பசு पसु *pasu* (Cow), Sanskrit पशु *pashu* (Animal, Cow).

2. <u>The Second Tamil Granthakshar</u> : ஸ (*sa* स)

i. Tamil ஸ *sa* स is written in a single stroke of 1, 2, 3 as shown :

ii. Tamil ஸ *sa* स is always used as a mute character and joins another consonant or a vowel. e.g. புத்தகம் (புஸ்தகம்) पुत्तहम् *puttaham* (Book), Sanskrit पुस्तकम् *pustakam*, Hindi पुस्तक *pustak* (Book).

<u>NOTE</u> : The த त *t* that joins with स *s* has a sound of थ *th*. e.g. ஸ்தரீ स्त्री स्त्री *stree* (Woman).

3. <u>The Third Tamil Granthakshar</u> : ஷ (*sha* श, ष)

i. The Tamil ஷ *sha* श, ष is written in the strokes of 1, 2, 3 and 4

ii. Tamil letter used in place of ஷ is ட and pronounced as ट t.
e.g. கஷ்டம் कष्टम् *kashṭam* = கட்டம் कट्टम् *kaṭṭam* (Trouble)

4. <u>The Fourth Tamil Granthakshar</u> : ஹ (*ha* ह)

i. Tamil ஹ *ha* ह is written in the a single stroke of 1, 2, 3, 4, 5 as shown :

ii. Tamil ஹ *ha* ह is used only for the words that came from Sanskrit.
For Tamil words letter **க** is used for ह *h*. e.g. **நகம்** नहम् *naham* (Nail),

5. <u>The Fifth Tamil Granthakshar</u> : **க்ஷ** (*ksha* क्ष)

i. Tamil **க்ஷ** *ksha* क्ष is written in the strokes of 1, 2; 3, 4, 5 and 6 as shown :

ii. Tamil **க்ஷ** *ksha* क्ष is used only for the words that came from Sanskrit.
For Tamil words letters **ட்ச** are used for क्ष *ksh.* e.g. **மோக்ஷம்** मोक्षम् *moksham* = **மோட்சம்** मोट्सम् *moṭsam* (Liberation).

EXERCISE : Read and Write the following

க ங ச ஞ ட ண த ந ப ம ய ர

ல வ ழ ள ற ன ஜ ஸ ஷ ஹ க்ஷ

ஸர்ப்பம் (Snake सर्प), ஜகத் (the World जगत्), ஜடம் (Insensitive person जट), ஜபம் (Repeated chant जप), ஜயம் (Victory जय), ஜலம் (Water जल), ஜனம் (People जन), ஸமம் (Equality सम), ஸமரஸம் (Harmony समरस), ஸர்வம் (All सर्व), ஹரன் (Shiva हर), ஹலம் (Plough हल).

LESSON 4

READING AND WRITING TAMIL VOWELS

4.1 The First Two Tamil Vowels :

அ	ஆ
a	***ā, aa***
अ	**आ**

THE VOWEL SIGN :

◌ா

ā, aa

आ

1. <u>The First Tamil Vowel</u> : அ (*a* अ) :

i. Tamil அ *a* अ is written in the strokes of 1, 2, 3 and 4 as shown with the numbered arrows below.

ii. Notice the striking similarity between Tamil அ and Sanskrit अ

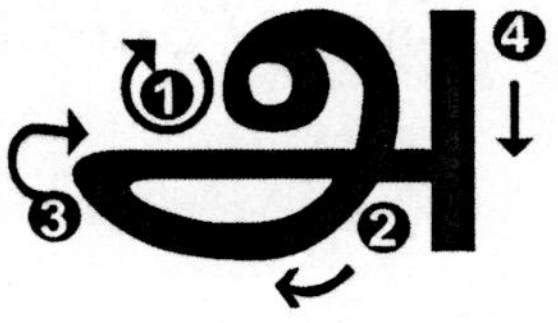

iii. The Tamil pronouns that begin with letter அ *a* अ denote the quality of furtherness. e.g. அவன் अवन् *avan* = m. That (man); இவன் इवन् *ivan* = m. This (man).

iv. When vowel அ *a* अ is prefixed to a Tamil noun, the initial letter of that noun gets doubled, and then it imparts furtherness to that noun. e.g. நகரம் नगरम् *nagaram* (City), அந்நகரம் अन्नगरम् *annagaram* (That city); Sanskrit नगरम् *nagaram* (City), Hindi Sanskrit नगर *nagar* (City)

v. Similar to Sanskrit and Hindi, the letter அ *a* अ does not have a "Vowel Sign" assigned to it. This is because the vowel அ *a* अ is inherent in each Tamil, Sanskrit and Hindi consonant. Without this inherent அ *a* अ, the consonant is mute or half and is written with a dot over it for a Tamil letter; and with a *halant* (हलन्त) slash, or in it's half shape for a Sanskrit and Hindi consonant. e.g. Tamil க் Sanskrit-Hindi क् or क ; English *k.*

2. <u>The Second Tamil Vowel</u> : ஆ (*ā* आ) :

i. Tamil ஆ *ā* आ is written in the strokes of 1, 2, 3 and 4, 5 as shown..

ii. The Vowel Sign for letter ஆ *ā* आ is ◌ா (like Greek letter *pi*), placed on the right side of a consonant. க் + ஆ = கா क् + आ = का $k + \bar{a} = k\bar{a}$

iii Vowel Sign *ā* आ ◌ா is used for all consonants other than ண, ற, ன ण्, र् न् *ṇ, ṛ n* e.g. கா, ஙா, சா, ஞா, டா, தா, நா, பா, மா, யா, ரா, லா, வா, ழா, ளா का, ङा, चा, ञा, टा, ता, ना, पा, मा, या, रा, ला, वा, ऴा, ळा *kā,ṅgā,chā, ñā, ṭā, tā,, nā, pā, mā, yā, rā,,lā,vā,ḻā,, ḷā.*

EXERCISE : Read and Write the following Tamil letters and words :

கா ஙா சா ஞா டா ணா தா நா பா மா யா ரா
லா வா ழா ளா றா னா ஜா ஸா ஷா ஹா க்ஷா

பால் (Milk), நாய் (Dog), காற்று (Air वायु), வானம் (Sky), ராஜா (King राजा), ஸர்ப்பம் (Cobra सर्प), ஹாரம் (Garland हार), மாம்பழம் (Mango), யானை (Elephant), காகம் (Crow काक), அப்பா (Father)அம்மா (Mother), தாத்தா (Grandfather दादा), மாமா (Uncle मामा).

4.2 The Third and Fourth Tamil Vowels :

இ	ஈ
i	*ī, ee*
इ	ई

THE VOWEL SIGNS :

i	*ī, ee*
इ	ई

3. <u>The Third Tamil Vowel</u> : இ (*i* इ) :

i. Tamil இ *i* इ is written in the strokes of 1, 2, 3, 4 as shown.

ii. The sound of letter இ *i* इ is normally prefixed to the words that begin with ர or ல र, ल *r, l*, therefore, in original Tamil Dictionaries, words beginning with ர and ல र, ल *r, l*, are listed under letter இ *i* इ.

e.g. ராமன் = இராமன் रामन् = इरामन् *rājan* = *irāman* (Rāma);

லக்குமண் = இலக்குமணன் लक्कुमण् = इलक्कुमणन् *Lakkumaṇa* = *ilakkumaṇanan* (Lakshman)

iii. When letter இ *i* इ is followed by a retroflex consonant (ट, ठ. ड, ढ *ṭ, ṭh, ḍ, ḍh*), the இ *i* इ is pronounced longer like ई *ī.*

iv. The words (pronouns and nouns) beginning with letter அ *a* अ that denote fartherness, will denote nearness when the initial அ *a* अ is replaced with இ *i* इ.

e.g. அவள் अवळ् *aval* = f. That (girl); இவள் इवळ् *ival* = f. This (girl); நகரம் नगरम् *nagaram* (City), அந்நகரம் अन्नगरम् *annagaram* (That city), இந்நகரம் इन्नगरम् *innagaram* (This city)

v. Vowel Sign for letter இ *i* इ ி is (similar to Sanskrit/Hindi vowel sign ि) attached to the right side of consonant. e.g. விஷம் विषम् *visham* (Poison), Sanskrit विषम् *visham,* Hindi विष *vish* (Poison)

EXERCISE : Read and Write the following Tamil characters and words

கி ஙி சி ஞி டி ணி தி நி பி மி யி ரி
லி வி ழி ளி றி னி ஜி ஸி ஷி ஹி க்ஷி

இரத்தம் (Blood रक्त), விஷம் (Poison विष), நரி (Fox), மணி (Bell), சிங்கம் (Lion सिंह), திராக்ஷை (Grapes द्राक्ष), ஆசிரியன் (Teacher), நாற்காலி (Chair), பன்றி (Pig), ஈ (Fly, Bee), மயில் (Peacock मयूर), தரணி (the Earth धरणी), பாட்டி (Grandmother), சித்தி (Aunt, mother's younger sister).

4. <u>The Fourth Tamil Vowel</u> : ஈ (*i* इ) :

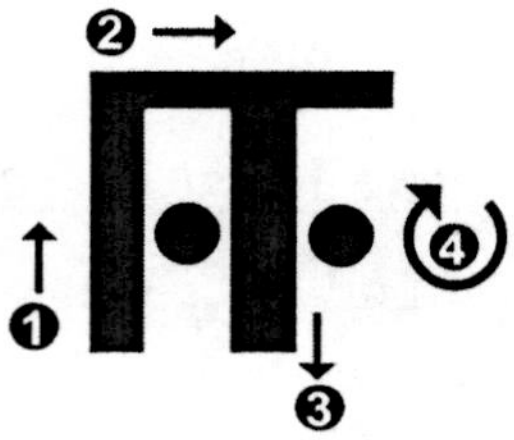

i. Tamil ஈ *ī* ई is written in the strokes of 1, 2 and 3 and 4 as shown.

ii. Sign for vowel ஈ *ī* ई is ீ placed above the consonant. e.g. நீ नी *nee* (You)

iii. The letter ஈ *ī* ई is also a unilettered-word. e.g. ஈ *ī* ई means a Fly, Bee.

iii. When short letter இ *i* इ and long letter ஈ *ī* ई are not interchangeable, the meaning of the word will change. e.g. கிரி किरि *kiri* = Hill; கீரி कीरि *keeri* = Mongoose (नेवला)

EXERCISE : Read and Write the following

கீ ஙீ சீ ஞீ டீ ணீ தீ நீ பீ மீ யீ ரீ
லீ வீ ழீ ளீ றீ னீ ஜீ ஸீ ஷீ ஹீ க்ஷீ

மீன் (Fish मीन), நீலம் (Blue नील), கண்ணீர் (Tears), சீழ் (Pus), வீக்கம் (Swelling).

4.3 The Fifth and Sixth Tamil Vowels :

உ ஊ

i इ

ī, ee ई

THE VOWEL SIGNS :

u उ

ū, oo ऊ

5. <u>The Fifth Tamil Vowel</u> : உ (*u* उ) :

i. Tamil உ *u* उ is written in a single stroke of 1, 2, 3 as shown.

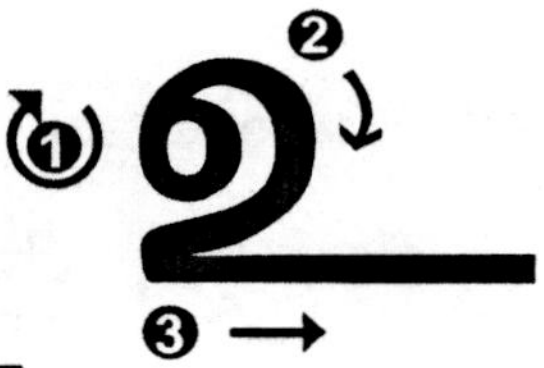

ii. The sign for the vowel உ *u* उ has three (four) variations.

1. A curved arch below the consonant (almost like Sanskrit/Hindi), from right to left. e.g. கு, டு, மு, ரு, ழு, ளு (कु, डु, मु, रु, ळु, ळु *ku, tu, mu, ru, lu, lu*)
2. A short downward vertical line attached at the south-east corner of the consonant. e.g. சு ஙு, பு, யு, வு (चु ङु, पु, यु, वु *chu, ngu, pu, yu, vu*)
3. A curved loop drawn under the consonant and ending it in a vertical line on the right side of the consonant. e.g. ஞு, ணு, து, நு, லு, று, னு (ञु, णु, तु, नु, लु, रु, नु *ñyu,ṇu, tu, nu, lu, ru, nu*)

4. The vowel sign of vowel உ *u* उ for the Granthakshars ஜ ஸ ஷ ஹ க்ஷ ज, स, श(ष), स, ह, क्ष *(j, s, sh, h, ksh)* is ௵ attached to the top right corner of these five consonants. See below.

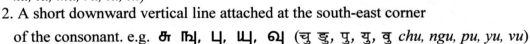

EXERCISE : Read and Write the following

கு ஙு சு ஞு டு ணு து நு பு மு யு ரு

லு வு ழு ளு று னு ஜு ஸு ஷு ஹு க்ஷு

பசு (Cow पशु), பஞ்சு (Cotton), கிணறு (a Well), நண்டு (Scorpion), பந்து (Ball गेंद), விளக்கு (Lamp), புஸ்தகம் (Book पुस्तक), புஷ்பம் (Flower पुष्प), குதிரை (Horse), குரங்கு (Monkey), புலி (Tiger), முயல் (Rabbit), எறும்பு (Ant), பாம்பு (Snake), குளவி (Honeybee), புறா (Pigeon), குயில் (Blackbird कोयल), கருடன் (Eagle गरुड).

6. <u>The Sixth Tamil Vowel</u> : ஊ (*ū* ऊ) :

i. Tamil ஊ *ū* ऊ is written in the strokes of 1, 2, 3 and 4. and 5 shown with the numbered arrows.

ii. The sign for the vowel உ *u* उ has two variations.

1. A curved arch below the consonant from right to left ending in a small rounded loop knot. e.g. கூ, ஙூ, சூ, டூ,ரூ, ழூ, ளூ (कू, ङू, चू, टू, रू, ळू, ळू *kū, ṅgū, chū, tū, rū, lū, lū*)

2. A curved loop drawn under the consonant and ending it in *pi* sign on the right side of the consonant. e.g. ஞூ, ணூ, தூ, நூ, லூ, றூ, னூ (ञू, णू, तू, नू, लू, रू, नू *ñyū,ṇū, tū, nū, lū, rū, nū*)

iv. The vowel sign of vowel ஊ *ū* ऊ for the Granthakshars ஜ ஸ ஷ ஹ க்ஷ ज, स, श(ष), स, ह, क्ष *(j, s, sh, h, ksh)* is ூ attached to the top right corner of these five consonants. See below.

EXERCISE : Read and Write the following

கூ ஙூ சூ ஞூ டூ ணூ தூ நூ பூ மூ யூ ரூ

லூ வூ ழூ ளூ றூ னூ ஜூ ஸூ ஷூ ஹூ க்ஷூ

கூடு (Nest नीड), பூட்டு (Lock), மூன்று (Three), நூறு (One Hundred), மூடி (Lid).

4.4 The Seventh and Eighth Tamil Vowels :

எ	ஏ
e	*ĕ*
ए	ऍ

THE VOWEL SIGNS :

ெ◌	ை◌
	ை ஐ
e	*ĕ*
ए	ऍ

7. **<u>The Seventh Tamil Vowel</u>** : எ (*e* ए) :

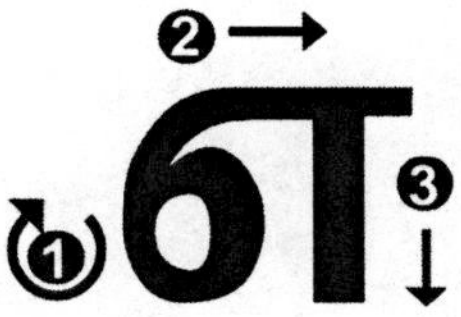

i. Tamil எ *e* ए is written in the strokes of 1, 2 and 3 as shown.

ii. The vowel எ *e* ए is pronounced like English *ay* as in Ray when it comes before retroflex consonants (ट, ठ. ड, ढ, *ṭ, ṭh, ḍ, ḍh*).

iii எ *e* ए is pronounced like English *e* as in Red when it comes before other consonants.

iv. The Tamil pronouns that begin with vowel எ *e* ए denote Interrogation.
e.g. **என்ன** एन्न *enna* = What? **ஏன்** एन *en* = Why? **எந்த** एन्द *enda* = Which?

v. When letter எ *e* ए is prefixed to a Tamil noun, the initial letter of that noun gets doubled, and then the noun denotes interrogation. e.g. **நகரம்** नगरम् *nagaram* (City), **எந்நகரம்** एन्नगरम् *ennagaram* (Which city?)

vi. The Vowel Sign for letter எ *e* ए is ெ◌ attached on the left side of the consonant (somewhat like the vowel sign for Sanskrit-Hindi small इ ि). e.g. **பெண்** पेण् *peṇ* (Girl)

EXERCISE : Read and Write the following

கெ ஙெ செ ஞெ டெ ணெ தெ நெ பெ மெ
யெ ரெ லெ வெ ழெ ளெ றெ னெ ஜெ ஸெ
ஷெ ஹெ க்ஷெ

எலி (Mouse), எறும்பு (Ant), பெயர் (Name), பெண் (Girl), நெற்றி (Forehead), நெருப்பு (Fire), வெற்றி (Victory), சீடன் (Follower, pupil),. மயில் (Peacock), உடல் (Body), உப்பு (Salt), உலகம் (the World), ஈரம் (Wet), ஆணி (Nail), பெட்டி (Box).

8. <u>The Eighth Tamil Vowel</u> : ஏ (*ĕ* ऎ) :

i. Tamil ஏ *ĕ* ऎ is written in the strokes of 1, 2 and 3, 4 as shown with the numbered arrows below.

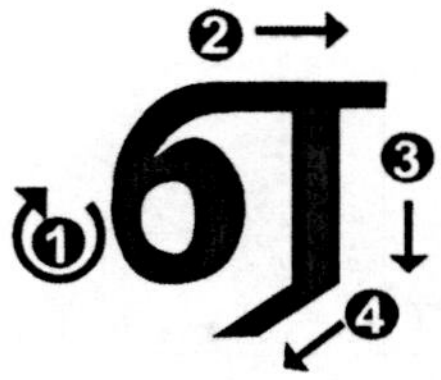

ii. The vowel ஏ *ĕ* ऎ is pronounced like English *a* as in Rat when it comes before retroflex consonants (ट, ठ. ड, ढ, *ṭ, ṭh, ḍ, ḍh*).

iii. Vowel ஏ *ĕ* ऎ is pronounced like English *eye* when it comes as initial letter of a word, or when it comes in a word of mono-syllable. e.g. **ஏகம்** ऎकम् *ekam* (unique); Sanskrit एकम् *ekam* (unique); **தேர்** थेर् *ther* (a Chariot, a divine Chariot, a Chariot or vehicle for God, a Chariot driven by Gods)

vi. The Vowel Sign for letter ஏ *ĕ* ऎ is ே◌ attached on the left side of the consonant.

e.g. **தேசம்** देसम् *desaṃ* (Country); Sanskrit-Hindi देश *desh* (Country)

EXERCISE : Read and Write the following

கே ஙே சே ஞே டே ணே தே நே பே மே யே ரே

லே வே ழே ளே றே னே ஜே ஸே ஷே ஹே க்ஷே

ஏணி (Ladder), ஏழு (Seven), கை (Arm, hand), வேர் (Root), தேனீ (Hornet).

4.5 The Ninth Tamil Vowel :

ஐ

ai
ऐ

THE VOWEL SIGN :

ை◌

ai
ऐ

9. <u>The Ninth Tamil Vowel</u> : ஐ (*e* ए) :

i. Tamil ஐ *ai* ऐ is written in a single stroke of 1, 2, 3, 4 as shown with the numbered arrows below.

ii. The vowel ஐ *ai* ऐ does not have a sound in English language, but sounds approximately like *i* as in Rite. It sounds like Hindi *ai* ए as in *ai Malik* ऐ मालिक!

iv. The Vowel Sign for letter ஐ *ai* ऐ is ை◌ attached on the left side of the consonant. e.g. **சித்திரை** चित्तिरै *chittiraị* (April); **அம்மை** अम्मै *ammaị* (Goddess, Amma, Amba); Sanskrit-Hindi अम्बा *ambā* (Devi, Ambā).

<u>Note</u> that, in above example (அம்மை अम्मै *ammaị*) the vowel sign ை◌ *ai* ऐ is placed between ம் and ம म् and म (*m* amd *ma*), therefore, it is more like अम्मै than अम्मै.or अंमै. <u>This hint holds good for the other vowel signs as well</u>.

EXERCISE : Read and Write the following Tamil letters and words

கை ஙை சை ஞை டை ணை தை நை

பை மை யை ரை

லை வை ழை ளை றை னை ஜை

ஸை ஷை ஹை க்ஷை

சட்டை (Coat, Jacket), **தவளை** (Frog), **அறை** (Room), **வாழை** (Banana), **பூனை** (Cat), **கோழி** (Hen)

4.6 The Tenth and Eleventh Tamil Vowels :

ஒ	ஓ
o	*ŏ*
ओ	ऑ

VOWEL SIGNS :

ெ ◌ ா	ே ◌ ா
o	*ŏ*
ओ	ऑ

10. The Tenth Tamil Vowel : ஒ (*o* ओ) :

i. Tamil ஒ *o* ओ is written in a single stroke of 1, 2, 3, 4 as shown.

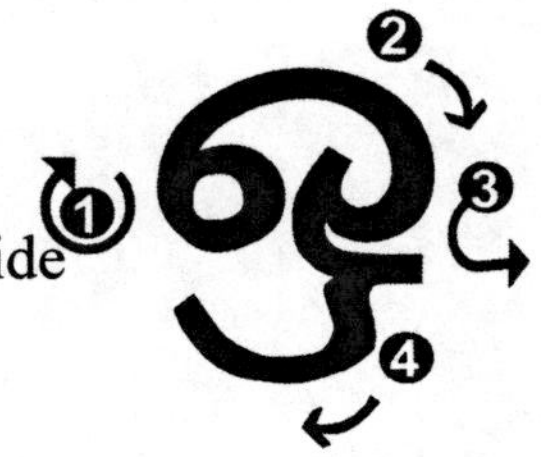

ii. The vowel sign for vowel ஒ *o* ओ is ெ◌ா, with ெ◌ placed on the left side of the consonant and ◌ா placed on the right side. e.g. கொய்யா कोय्या *koyyā* (Guava)

EXERCISE : Read and Write the following

கொ ஙொ சொ ஞொ டொ ணொ தொ

நொ பொ மொ யொ ரொ

லொ வொ ழொ ளொ றொ னொ ஜொ

ஸொ ஷொ ஹொ க்ஷொ

கொசு (Mosquito), கொய்யாப்பழம் (Guava), கொய்யாமரம் (Guava tree), பொடி (Powder), நொண்டி (Handicapped), தொழிலாளி (Worker, laborer), தொப்பி (Cap टोपी).

11. The Tenth Tamil Vowel : ஓ (*ŏ* ऑ) :

i. Tamil ஓ *ŏ* ऑ is written in the strokes of 1, 2 and 3, 4, 5 as shown with the numbered arrows.

ii. While the vowel ஒ *o* ओ is pronounced like *o* as in Row, vowel ஓ *ŏ* ऑ is pronounced like English *aw* as in Raw. Hindi does not have this ஓ *ŏ* ऑ pronunciation, instead just the ஒ *o* ओ sound is used in Hindi.

ii. The vowel sign for vowel ஒ *o* ओ ஓ *ŏ* ऑ is ே◌ா, with ே◌ placed on the left side of the consonant and ◌ா placed on the right side. e.g. தோள் तोळ् *toḷ* (Shoulder)

EXERCISE : Read and Write the following

கோ ஙோ சோ ஞோ டோ ணோ தோ நோ
போ மோ யோ ரோ
லோ வோ ழோ ளோ றோ னோ ஜோ ஸோ
ஷோ ஹோ க்ஷோ

மோதிரம் (Ring मुंदरी), **தோள்** (Shoulder), **ரோகம்** (Disease रोग), **கொட்டாவி** (Yawn).

4.7 The Twelfth Tamil Vowel :

ஔ

au

औ

VOWEL SIGN :

ெ◌ள

au

औ

10. <u>The Tenth Tamil Vowel</u> : **ஔ** (*au* औ) :

i. Tamil **ஔ** *au* औ is written in the strokes of 1, 2, 3 and 4, 5, 6 and 7 as shown with the numbered arrows below.

ii. The vowel sign for vowel **ஔ** *au* औ is **ெ◌ள**, with ெ◌ placed on the left side of the consonant and ள placed on right side.

e.g. **வௌவால்** वौवाल् *vauval* (the Bat mammal)

iii. The sound of vowel **ஔ** *au* औ is nearly like *ou* in English word Powder; or like *au* in Sanskrit-Hindi word औषधि *aushadhi* (Medicine)

EXERCISE : Read and Write the following

கௌ ஙௌ சௌ ஞௌ டௌ ணௌ
தௌ நௌ பௌ மௌ யௌ ரௌ
லௌ வௌ ழௌ ளௌ றௌ னௌ
ஜௌ ஸௌ ஷௌ ஹௌ க்ஷௌ

ஔடதம் (Medicine औषध), **ஔதாரியம்** (Generosity औदार्य), **ஔவி** (Jaelousy),
சௌந்தரியம் (Beauty सौंदर्य), **சிங்காரம்** (Beauty शृंगार),
தௌகித்தரி (Daughter's daughter दोहित्री), **பௌத்தரி** (Son's daughter पौत्री).

PLEASE DO NOT GO TO NEXT LESSON WITHOUT DOING PREVIOUS LESSONS PROPERLY.

THE TAMIL AAYDAM (VISARGA विसर्ग)

ஃ

ḥ
अः

i. The use of *visarga* (विसर्गः) is quite frequent in Sanskrit, much less in Tamil, rare in Hindi and does not exist in English. In Sanskrit, it usually comes at the end, but sometimes in the middle.

In Sanskrit it is pronounces as *ḥ* ह्, in Tamil it is *h, ch* or *kh* ह, च or ख. e.g. Sanskrit दुःखम् *duḥkham* (Pain); Tamil **அஃது** or **அது** अखदु, अच्दु, अहदु or अदु *akhdu,achdu, ahdu* or *adu* (This), **பஃது** or **பத்து** *paḥdu* पःदु *or* पद्दु (Ten), **பஃறி** पःरि *pḥari* (Ship) *etc.*

Aaytham is mostly used in poetry that too when required to comply with the metre.

SUMMARY OF VOWELS & THEIR SIGNS

TABLE 7 : Vowels and their Signs

VOWEL	VOWEL SIGN(s)	EXAMPLE(s)
அ		மரம் (Plant, tree)
ஆ	◌ா	மாதா (Mother माता), அண்ணா (Father, Elder brother)
இ	◌ி	மிக்க (Great)
ஈ, ஈ	◌ீ	மீதி (*nux vomica* मेथी)
உ	ு ு ு ு	முகம் (Face मुखम्), புவனம் (पवनम् Wind, Sky), துக்கம் (Pain दुःखम्), சுடு (Hot)
ஊ	ூ ூ ூ ூ	மூச்சு (Breath) பூமி (Earth) தூக்கம் (Sleep) கூரை (Roof)
எ	ெ◌	மெய் (Truth)
ஏ	ே◌	மேகம் (Cloud, Sanskrit मेघ)
ஐ	ை ை	மை (Ink), பூனை (Cat)
ஒ	ெ◌ா	மொக்கு, மொட்டு (Flower bud)
ஓ	ே◌ா	மோகம் (Delusion, Sanskrit मोघम्)
ஔ	ெ◌ள	மௌனம் (Silence, Sanskrit मौनम्)
This Table is developed by Sanskrit Hindi Research Institute for *"Learn Tamil Through English/Hindi"* by Ratnakar Narale.		

CHART OF ALPHABET WITH VOWEL SIGNS

a	*ā*	*i*	*ī*	*u*	*ū*	*e*	*ĕ*	*ai*	*o*	*ŏ*	*au*
अ	आ	इ	ई	उ	ऊ	ए	ऍ	ऐ	ओ	ऑ	औ
அ	ஆ	இ	ஈ	உ	ஊ	எ	ஏ	ஐ	ஒ	ஓ	ஔ
	◌ா	◌ி	◌ீ	◌ு	◌ூ	ெ◌	ே◌	ை◌	ெ◌ா	ே◌ா	ெ◌ள
क	का	कि	की	कु	कू	के	कॅ	कै	को	कॉ	कौ
க	கா	கி	கீ	கு	கூ	கெ	கே	கை	கொ	கோ	கௌ
ங	ஙா	ஙி	ஙீ	ஙு	ஙூ	ஙெ	ஙே	ஙை	ஙௌ	ஙோ	ஙௌ
ச	சா	சி	சீ	சு	சூ	செ	சே	சை	சொ	சோ	சௌ
ஞ	ஞா	ஞி	ஞீ	ஞு	ஞூ	ஞெ	ஞே	ஞை	ஞொ	ஞோ	ஞௌ
ட	டா	டி	டீ	டு	டூ	டெ	டே	டை	டொ	னோ	னௌ
ண	ணா	ணி	ணீ	ணு	ணூ	ணெ	ணே	ணை	ணொ	ணோ	ணௌ
த	தா	னி	னீ	னு	னூ	னெ	னே	னை	னொ	னோ	னௌ
ப	பா	பி	பீ	பு	பூ	பெ	பே	பை	பொ	போ	பௌ
ம	மா	மி	மீ	மு	மூ	மெ	மே	மை	மொ	மோ	மௌ
ய	யா	யி	யீ	யு	யூ	யெ	யே	யை	யொ	யோ	யௌ
ர	ரா	ரி	ரீ	ரு	ரூ	ரெ	ரே	ரை	ரொ	ரோ	ரௌ
ல	லா	லி	ல	லு	லூ	லெ	லே	லை	லொ	லோ	லௌ
வ	வா	வி	வீ	வு	வூ	வெ	வே	வை	வொ	வோ	வௌ
ள	ளா	ளி	ளீ	ளு	ளூ	ளெ	ளே	ளை	ளொ	ளோ	ளௌ
ற	றா	றி	றீ	று	றூ	றெ	றே	றை	றொ	றோ	றௌ
ன	னா	னி	னீ	னு	னூ	னெ	னே	னை	னொ	னோ	னௌ

books-india.com

BEFORE YOU PROCEED FURTHER, PLEASE KNOW THIS

1. Like Sanskrit and Hindi, the **அ, இ, உ** अ, इ, उ are Basic or Simple Vowels. The rest nine vowels **ஆ, ஈ, ஊ, எ, ஏ, ஐ, ஒ, ஓ, ஔ** आ, ई, ऊ, ए, ऍ, ऐ, ओ, ऑ, औ are Compound Vowels, composed of the Basic three vowels. e.g. ஆ = அ + அ; ஈ = இ + இ; ஊ = உ + உ; எ = அ + இ; ஏ = அ + ஈ; ஐ = அ + அ + இ; ஒ = அ + உ; ஓ = அ + ஊ; ஔ = அ + அ + உ. आ = अ + अ; ई = इ + इ; ऊ = उ + उ; ए = अ + इ; ऍ = अ + ई; ऐ = अ + अ + इ; ओ = अ + उ; ऑ = अ + ऊ; औ = अ + अ + उ.

2. Like Sanskrit, and unlike Hindi and English, the last consonant (with vowel अ a), is pronounced with full stress (long). e.g. Tamil : **பக** (पक, बक depart); Sanskrit : बक (*baka* Stork); Hindi : बक (*bak* pronounced as बक् Stork); English : Buck (बक् *buk* Dollar).

3. While learning the 18 consonants by heart, the first 10 consonants are repeated in five pairs of two consonants each, then the rest eight consonants are said singly or in pairs of two.

4. When there are short and long vowels within a word, the long ones are pronounced more distinctly.

5. Within the above mentioned five pairs, each initial consonant is followed by its corresponding (devanagri) nasal consonant e.g. **கங, சஞ, டண, தந, பம** कङ, चञ, टण, तन, पम;

6. Next four consonants form two pairs like the Devanagari Alphabet. **ய ர, ல வ** य र, ल व; *y r, l v*

7. No Tamil word begins with the last four consonants **ழ, ள, ற, ன**.

8. A Tamil mute or half consonant (with the dot over it) is named by prefixing **இ** *i* इ sound to that consonant. e.g. **க ங ச ... ம ர** = क ङ च ... म र *ka, nga, cha ... ma, ra* etc.;
   க் ங் ச் ... ம் ர் etc. = इक् इङ् इच् ... इम् इर् *ik, ing, ich ... im, ir* etc.;

9. Like Sanskrit and Hindi, when Tamil consonants are doubled they are pronounced more distinctly and strongly than they are done in English. e.g. Tamil : **பட்டணம்** (पट्टणम् *paṭṭanam* City). Sanskrit : पट्टनम् (*paṭṭanam* City); Hindi : पट्टन (*paṭṭan* City); English : butter (बटर).

10. When a word begins with vowel **எ** (*e* ए) or **ஏ** (*ĕ* ऍ), these vowels are sounded like **யே** (ये ye), as in Hindi, vowel ए (e) is sounded like ये (ye). e.g. Tamil : **என்ன** (*yenna,* येन्न What?) **ஏன்** (*yen* येन् Why?); Hindi गए, गये (*gae, gaye* Gone); Sanskrit : येन (*yena* By whom).

NOW YOU ARE READY TO LEARN READING, WRITING and SPEAKING TAMIL.

A PRELIMINARY VOCABULARY OF KEY TAMIL WORDS

EXERCISE : Read, write, understand and remember as many Tamil words possible.

English (हिंदी)	Devnagari	Tamil	Transliteration
I (मैं)	नान्	நான்	*nān*
We (all) (हम	नाम्	நாம்	*nām*
We (all - you)	नांगळ्	நாங்கள்	*nāngaḷ*
You (तू)	नी	நீ	*nī*
You (आप)	नीर्	நீர்	*nīr*
You (all)	नींगळ्	நீங்கள்	*ningaḷ*
He (that boy)	अवन्	அவன்	*avan*
He/she (Respect.able that)	अवर्	அவர்	*avar*
He (this boy)	इवन्	இவன்	*ivan*
He/she (Respectable. this)	इवर्	இவர்	*ivar*
She (that girl)	अवळ्	அவள்	*avaḷ*
She (this girl)	इवळ्	இவள்	*ivaḷ*
Those people	अवर्गळ्	அவர்கள்	*avargaḷ*
These people	इवर्गळ्	இவர்கள்	*ivargaḷ*
It, this thing	इदु	இது	*idu*
That thing	अदु	அது	*adu*
These things	इवै	இவை	*ivai*
Those things	अवै	அவை	*avai*
All	एल्लाम्	எல்லாம்	*ellām*
Each	ओव्वोरुवरुम्	ஒவ்வொருவரும்	*ovvaruvarum*
What?	एन्न	என்ன	*enna*
Which?	एदु	எது	*edu*
Who?	यार्	யார்	*yār*
How many?	एत्तने	எத்த	*ettane*
How, in what manner?	एप्पडि	எப்படி	*eppadi*
How much?	एव्वळवु	எவ்வளவு	*evvaḷavu*
When?	एप्पो	எப்போ	*eppo*
In this manner	इप्पडि	இப்படி	*ippaḍi*
What for?	एदर्काह	எதற்காக	*ippaḍi*
Where?	एंगे	எங்கே	*enge*
Now	इप्प	இப்ப	*ippa*
My	एन्	என்	*en*
Name	पेयर्	பெயர்	*peyar*

LESSON 5

THE BASIC TAMIL NUMERALS

0 பூஜியம் सून्यम् *sūnyam*

1 ஒன்று ओन्रु *onru* One book. ஒரு புத்தகம்

2 இரண்டு इरण्डु *irandu* Two books. இரண்டு புத்தகங்கள்

3 மூன்று मून्रु *mūnru* Three books. மூன்று புத்தகங்கள்

4 நான்கு नान्गु *nāngu*

5 ஐந்து ऐन्दु *aindu*

6 ஆறு आरु *āru*

7 ஏழு एळु *eḷu*

8 எட்டு एट्टु *eṭṭu*

9 ஒன்பது ओन्बदु *onbadu*

10 பத்து पत्तु *pattu*

EXERCISE : Numerals

(1) Read the numbers in Tamil :

1 7 9 4 0 3 2 8 5 6

(2) Read the following Tamil numerals :

மூன்று எட்டு ஏழு பத்து ஒன்று ஆறு ஒன்பது நான்கு பூஜியம் இரண்டு ஐந்து

(3) Read and Write the following Tamil numerals :

நான்கு ஒன்பது சூன்யம் இரண்டு ஐந்து எட்டு ஒன்று பத்து ஏழு மூன்று ஆறு

books-india.com

LESSON 6

HOW TO MAKE YOUR OWN TAMIL SENTENCES

This is the Most Important Chapter in Learning Tamil Properly

PLEASE BE REMINDED OF THE FOLLOWING BEFORE YOU BEGIN

i. When we speak or write, we use words. We use them in meaningful groups to form sentences. Sometimes we form a compound sentence made up of two or more clauses. The order in which we arrange the words in the clauses and sentences is the Syntax.

ii. The sentences are of four kinds :
(a) An Assertive sentence, that makes an Assertion, Declaration or a Statement.
(b) An Interrogative sentence, that asks a Question.
(c) An Imperative statement, that expresses a Request, an Order (request is a polite order).
(d) An Exclamatory sentence, that expresses a strong feeling.

iii. When we make a sentence, we :
(a) Mention a Person or a Thing and say something about him/her/it.
(b) The person or thing about which we say something, is the subject.
(c) What we say about him/her/it is the predicate.

iv. In Tamil, English, Hindi and Sanskrit sentences the Subject comes before the predicate. However, in the imperative sentences we leave the subject out and understood.

v. Each sentence has some action. The action word is Verb. In Tamil, Hindi and Sanskrit sentences we place the verb at the end of the sentence. Whereas, in English the verb comes right after the subject.
The doer of the action is the Subject, which is normally the first word of the sentence. Therefore, Tamil, Hindi and Sanskrit are SOV (Subject-Object-Verb) languages and English is SVO language.

vi. The thing(s) or person(s) on which the verb (action) is performed is(are) the Object(s) in the sentence.

vii. It is often said that *"Tamil is totally independent original language and has no connection with Sanskrit language in its origin and development."* The above study and the following research on the common fibers in these two languages, however, suggests that one language must have come from other, or, if not, influenced the other greatly, for sure. These large scale similarities and interrelationships can not just be a coincidence, or could it?

vii. Again, please DO NOT begin this lesson without finishing previous lessons properly. Review this lesson at least twice. Here we go ...

books-india.com

6.1 TAMIL NOUNS

i. MASCULINE, FEMININE and NEUTER TAMIL GENDER

Like Sanskrit, the Tamil nouns are Masculine, Feminine or Neuter Gender. But, the gender classification is much more systematic in Tamil, than in Sanskrit. In Hindi is it is most erratic.

The Tamil (i) Masculine Nouns include all rational beings (actual and imaginary) such as gods, men and personified males such as the actors in the Panchatantra fables and the Fables of Aesop. Similarly, the (iii) Feminine category includes all goddesses, women and personified females such as the actresses in the fables. The third class then consists of (iii) everything else, which includes inanimate objects and living things such as stones, trees, animals, insects, birds, etc. regardless of their actually being male of female. Again, like Sanskrit, the Tamil verb agrees with its subject.

The gender of a noun is generally indicated by the m◦ f◦ or n◦ termination suffixed to the noun, pronoun and verb. The (Nominative, Singular) Masculine terminations are ன், அன், ஆன் . The Feminine Terminations are ள், இ, ஐ . The Neuter Terminations are து, அது . e.g.

TABLE 8 : GENDER M. F. N. TAMIL TERMINATIONS

	Termination	MASCULINE	FEMININE	NEUTER
Noun	ன் ள் து ள், இ, ஐ து, அது	மகன் महन् *mahan* (Son) மாணவன் माणवन् *māṇavan* (Student)	மகள் महळ् *mahaḷ* (Daughter) மாணவி माणवि *māṇavi* (Student)	மற்றது मट्रदु *matradu* (Not this thing) பந்து पन्दु *pandu* (Ball)
Pronoun	ன், அன், ஆன்	அவன் अवन् *avan* (He)	அவள் अवळ् *avaḷ* (She)	அது अदु *adu* (That thing)
Verb செய் सेय् *sey* (to do)	ன் ள் து	செய்கிறான் सेय्किरान् *seykiran* (He does)	செய்கிறாள் सेय्किराळ् *seykiral* (She does)	செய்கிறது सेय्किरादु *seykiradu* (It/that does)

This Table is developed by Sanskrit Hindi Research Institute for *"Learn Tamil Through English/Hindi"* by Ratnakar Narale.

SOME MASCULINE - FEMININE TAMIL NOUNS

Masculine			Feminine		
English	Tamil	Hindi script	English	Tamil	Hindi script
1. Student	மாணவன்	माणवन्	Student (f)	மாணவி	माणवि
2. Son	மகன்	महन्	Daughter	மகள்	महळ्
3. Friend (m)	சிநேகிதன்	सिनेहिदन्	Friend (f)	சிநேகிதி	सिनेहिदि
4. Uncle	மாமா	मामा	Aunty	மாமி	मामी
5. Milkman	பால்காரன்	पालकारन्	Milkmaid	பால்காரி	पालकरि
6. Actor	நடிகர்	नटिकर	Actress	நடிகை	नटिकै
7. Poet	கவிஞன்	कविरुन्	Poetess	பெண் கவிஞர்	पेण्कविरुन्
8. God	தேவன்	देवन्	Goddess	தேவி	देवि
9. Lion	சிங்கம்	सिंगम्	Lioness	பெண்சிங்கம்	पेण्सिंगम्
10. Tiger	புலி	पुलि	Tigress	பெண்புலி	पेण्पुलि

Let's make simplest Tamil sentences

NOTE : The English articles *a, an* and *the* do not get translated in Tamil (like Hindi and Sanslrit). The numbers (one. two, three etc.) do get translated.

1. A student	மாணவன்	माणवन्	*māṇavan*
2. One student	ஒரு மாணவன்	ओरु माणवन्	*oru māṇavan*
3. The tiger	புலி	पुलि	*puli*
4. One lion	ஒரு சிங்கம்	ओरु सिंगम्	*oru singam*
5. An actor	நடிகர்	नटिकर्	*naṭikar*

ii. SINGULAR and PLURAL TAMIL NUMBER

i. Like Hindi, Tamil has two Numbers, Singular and Plural (Sanskrit has three : Singular, Dual and Plural).

ii. Plural Nominative of a Noun is always formed from a Singular Nominative Noun/pronoun.

iii. It is MOSTLY formed by adding suffix கள் गळ *gaḷ* to singular nominative noun/pronoun.
e.g. Singular புஸ்தகம் पुस्तकम् *pustakam* (Book); Plural புஸ்தகங்கள் पुस्तकंगळ् *pustakangaḷ* (Books). (Note : final ம் म् *m* is dropped before following ங் ङ *ng*).

iv. In some NOUNS and in pronoun அது अदु *adu* (It) , the plural is formed by just changing the final letter ன் न् *n* of the nominative singular to ர் र् *r*..e.g. மனிதன் (Man) मनिदन् *manidan* to மனிதர் (Men) मनिदर् *maindar*

v.. Like Hindi and sometimes Sanskrit too, the Honorific Expressions also mean pluralization and vice versa (see previous section). e.g.

(a) The Second Person short pronoun நீர் नीर् *nīr* (You, तुम, आप), though plural in nature, it is used commonly as an honorific singular, The non-honorific singular being नी *nī* (You तुम, तू). The second person long pronoun நீங்கள் नींगळ् *ningaḷ* is (full form of நீர் नीर् *nīr*) is actually a plural form (आप लोग), but is often used as honorific singular pronoun (आप), more respectful than நீர் नीर् *nīr* (तुम)

(b) The Third Person plural short pronoun அவர் अवर् *avar* (They वे) is more often used as honorific singular, to imply more respect than the Third Person Singular Pronoun அவன் अवन् *avan* (He वह) or அவள் अवळ् *avaḷ* (She वह). The Third Person plural long pronoun அவர்கள் अवर्गळ् *avargaḷ* (They वे) is (full form of அவர் अवर् *avar*) is actually a plural form (वे लोग, वे श्रीमान्), but is often used as honorific singular pronoun (वे), more respectful than அவர் अवर् *avar.*

vi. Like Sanskrit, the Tamil Subject agrees with predicate in person, number, case and gender.

SOME PLURAL TAMIL NOUNS

SINGULAR			PLURAL		
1. Student	மாணவன்	माणवन्	Students	மாணவர்கள்	माणवर्गळ् *
2. Son	மகன்	महन्	Sons	மகன்கள்	महंगळ्
3. Man	மனிதன்	मनिदन्	Men	மனிதர்கள்	मनिदर्गळ्
4. Dog	நாய்	नाय्	Dogs	நாய்கள்	नायगळ्
5. Tree	மரம்	मरम्	Trees	மரங்கள்	मरंगळ, मरङ्गळ् **
6. Flower	பூ	पू	Flowers	பூக்கள்	पूक्कळ् ***
7. Bird	பறவை	परवै	Birds	பறவைகள்	परवैगळ्
8. Cow	மாடு	माडु	Cows	மாடுகள்	माडुगळ्
9. Cat	பூனை	पूनै	Cats	பூனைகள்	पूनैगळ्
10. Basket	கூடை	कूडै	Baskets	கூடைகள்	कूडैगळ्

* See note ii. below, ** See note iii below, *** see note iv below.

IMPORTANT NOTES :

i. The most common plural suffix is கள் *gaḷ* गळ् that is added to a singular noun to make it plural.

ii. * When a Singular Masculine/Feminine Noun ending in ன் *n* न् is PLURALED, the ன் *n* न् is changer to ர் *r* र् before attaching the plural suffix கள் *gaḷ* गळ् to it.

iii. ** When a word ending in ம் *m* म् is followed by a word beginning with க *k* क, the ம் *m* म् is changed to ங் *ng* ङ्

iv. *** When a word ending in a vowel is followed by a word beginning with க, ச, த, ப *k, ch, ta* or *pa*, क, च, त or प, the க, ச, த, ப is (many times) doubled.

Now let's make more simple Tamil constructions with the basics we learned so far

1. The students	மாணவர்கள்	माणवर्हळ्	*māṇavarhaḷ*
2. Two students	இரண்டு மாணவர்கள்	इरण्डु माणवर्हळ्	*iraṇḍu māṇavarhaḷ*
3. Three cats	மூன்று பூனைகள்	मून्रु पूनैगळ्	*munru pūnaigaḷ*
4. Four baskets	நான்கு கூடைகள்	नान्गु कूडैगळ्	*nāngu kūḍaigaḷ*
5. Five actors	ஐந்து நடிகர்கள்	ऐन्दु नटिकर्हळ्	*aindu naṭikarhaḷ*
6. Six birds	ஆறு பறவைகள்	आरु परवैगळ्	*āru paravaigaḷ*
7. Seven Trees	ஏழு மரங்கள்	एळु मरङ्गळ्	*eḷu maraṅgaḷ*
8. Eight cows	எட்டு பசுக்கள்	एट्टु पसुक्कळ्	*eṭṭu pasukkaḷ*
9. Nine flowers	ஒன்பது பூக்கள்	ओन्बदु पूक्कळ्	*Onbadu kpūkkaḷ*
10. Ten men	பத்து மனிதர்கள்	पत्तु मनिदर्हळ्	*pattu manidarhaḷ*
11. Eleven boys	பதினொன்று பையன்கள்	पदिनोन्रु पैयंगळ्	*padinonru paiyaṅgaḷ*
12. Twelve girls	பன்னிரண்டு பெண்கள்	पन्निरण्डु पेण्हळ्	*panniraṇḍu peṇgaḷ*
13. Thirteen horses	பதிமூன்று குதிரைகள்	पदिमून्रु कुदिरैगळ्	*padimunru kudiraigaḷ*
14. Fourteen houses	பதினான்கு வீடுகள்	पदिनान्गु वीडुगळ्	*padināngu vīḍugaḷ*
15. Fifteen fish	பதினைந்து மீன்கள்	पदिनैन्दु मीन्हळ्	*padinaindu mīnhaḷ*
16. Sixteen foxes	பதினாறு நரிகள்	पदिनारु नरिगळ्	*padināru narigaḷ*
17. Seventeen saints	பதினேழு சாதுக்கள்	पदिनेळु सादुक्कळ्	*padineḷu sādukkaḷ*
18. Eighteen days	பதினெட்டு நாட்கள்	पदिनेट्टु नाट्हळ्	*padineṭṭu nāṭhaḷ*
19. Nineteen daughters	பத்தொன்பது மகன்கள்	पत्तोन्बदु महन्हळ्	*pattonbadu mahaṭhaḷ*
20. Twenty women	இருபது பெண்கள்	इरुबदु पेण्हळ्	*irubadu peṇhaḷ*

Now let's make our own simple Tamil sentences using Pronouns

6.2 THE BASIC TAMIL PRONOUNS

i. MASCULINE, FEMININE and NEUTER GENDER

TABLE 9 : BASIC TAMIL PRONOUNS

	Pronoun	Tamil	Devnagari	*Transliteration*	Oblique Case/ Possessive case *
1	I मैं (M.F.)	நான்	नान्	*nān*	एन् என்
2	We (हम) (M.F.)	நாங்கள்	नांगळ्	*naṅgaḷ*	एंगळ् எங்கள்
3	You (तू) (M.F.)	நீ	नी	*nī*	उन् உன்
4	You (आप) (M.F.)	நீர்	नीर्	*nīr*	उम् உம்
5	You (all आप लोग) (M.F.)	நீங்கள்	नींगळ्	*nīngaḷ*	उंगळ् உங்கள்
6	He (that boy) (M)	அவன்	अवन्		अवन्
7	He/she (Resp. That) (M.F.)	அவர்	अवर्		अवर्
8	He (this boy) (M.)	இவன்	इवन्		इवन्
9	He/she (Resp., This) (M.F.)	இவர்	इवर्		इवर्
10	She (that girl) (F.)	அவள்	अवळ्		अवळ्
11	She (this girl) (F.)	இவள்	इवळ्		इवळ्
12	Those people (M.F.)	அவர்கள்	अवर्गळ्		अवर्गळ्
13	These people (M.F.)	இவர்கள்	इवर्गळ्		इवर्गळ्
14	It, this thing (N.)	இது	इदु		इदु
15	That thing (N.)	அது	अदु		अदु
16	These things (N.)	இவை	इवै, इवैगळ्		इवै, इवैगळ्
17	Those things (N.)	அவை	अवै, अवैगळ्		अवै, अवैगळ्
* Oblique case (inflectional base) is used as possesive pronoun such as my, our, your, his, her, their etc.					
This Table is developed by Sanskrit Hindi Research Institute for *"Learn Tamil Through English/Hindi"* by Ratnakar Narale.					

Let's make simple Tamil constructions using common Personal Ponouns

1. That student	அவன் மாணவன்	अवन् माणवन्	*avan māṇavan*
2. Those students	அவர்கள் மாணவர்கள்	अवर्हळ् माणवर्हळ्	*avarhaḷ māṇavargaḷ*
3. This is a cat	இந்த ஒரு பூனை	इन्द ओरु पूनै	*inda oru pūnaị*
4. This cat	இந்த பூனை	इन्द पूनै	*inda pūnaị*
5. These baskets	இவை கூடைகள்	इवै कूडैगळ्	*ivai kūḍaigaḷ*
6. He is an actor	அவன் நடிகன்	अवन् नटिगन्	*avan naṭigan*
7. Those are birds	அவை பறவைகள்	अवै परवैगळ्	*avai paravaigaḷ*

8. Those Trees அவை மரங்கள் अवै मरङ्गळ् *avai marangaḷ*

9. That cow அந்த பசு अद्दु पसु *addu pasu*

10. My dog என் நாய் एन् नाय् *en nāy* *

11. These men இவர்கள் மனிதர்கள் इवर्हळ् मनिदर्हळ् *ivarhaḷ manidarhaḷ*

* NOTE Oblique cases (the inflectional base) shown in the right column of the above table is also used for Possesive Pronouns, such as : my, our, your, his, her, it's, their, etc.

TAMIL INTERROGATIVE PRONOUNS

TABLE 10 : COMMON TAMIL INTERROGATIVE PRONOUNS

	Pronoun	Tamil	Devnagari	*Transliteration*
1	What? (क्या?)	என்ன	एन्न?	*enna*
2	Who? which person (कौन?) (M.F; Sg. Pl.)	யார் ?	यार्?	*yār?*
	Which persons? (कौनसे लोग?) (M.F.)	எவர்கள்	एवर्हळ्	
3	Who? which man (कौन?) (M.)	எவன் ?	एवन्?	*evan?*
4	Who? which woman (कौन?) (F.)	எவள் ?	एवळ्?	*evaḷ?*
5	Who? with respect (कौन?) (M.F.)	எவர்	एवर्?	*evar*
6	Who all? (कौन लोग?) (M.F.)	எவர்கள் ?	एवर्हळ्?	*evarhaḷ?*
7	Which thing? (कौनसी चीज़?) (N)	எது ?	एदु?	*edu?*
	Which things? (कौनसे?) (N)	எவை, எவைகள்	एवै, एवैगळ्	
8	Which one? of many (कौनसा एक?)	எந்த	एन्द	*end*
9	Where? (कहाँ?)	எங்கே ?	एंगे?	*enge?*
10	Why? (क्यों?)	ஏன்	एन्?	*en*
11	When? (कब?)	எப்போ	एप्पो?	*eppo*
12	What for? why (किस लिये? क्यों?)	எதனால் ?	एदनाल्?	*ednāl?*
13	How much? (कितना?)	எவ்வளவு ?	इएव्वलवु?	*evvaḷvu?*
14	How? (कैसे?)	எப்படி	एप्पडि	*eppaḍi*
1	Here (यहाँ)	இங்கு	इंकु	*iṅku*
2	There (वहाँ)	அங்கு	अंकु	*aṅku*
3	Somebody (कोई)	யாரோ	यारो	*yaro*
4	All (सब)	எல்லாரும்	एल्लारुम्	*ellarum*
5	Now (अब)	இப்பொழுது	इप्पोलुदु	*ippoḷudu*
6	When?	எப்பொழுது	एप्पोलुदु	*eppoḷudu*

This Table is developed by Sanskrit Hindi Research Institute for *"Learn Tamil Through English/Hindi"* by Ratnakar Narale.

Let's make simple Tamil constructions <u>using Interrogative Pronouns</u>

REMEMBER : <u>TAMIL SYNTAX IS SAME AS HINDI SYNTAX</u> (but not like English),
In Tamil *is, are* (है, हैं) need not get translated, like Sanskrit.
<u>A Tamil sentence can be translated word for word in Hindi and vice versa</u>.

<u>VOCAB</u> : Name = பெயர் *peyar* पेयर्, Place (गाँव/स्थान) = ஊர் *ūr* ऊर्, Mother tongue (मातृभाषा) = தாய்மொழி *tāymoḷi* तायमोळि, Is not, Not, No = இல்லை *illai* इल्लै.

1. Which student? எந்த மாணவன் एन्द माणवन् *enda māṇvan*

1a. Who is the student? யார் மாணவன் यार् माणवन् *yār māṇvan*

2. Which students? எந்த மாணவர்கள் एन्द माणवर्हळ् *enda māṇavargaḷ*

3. Which book? எந்த புத்தகம் एददु पुत्तहम्? *eḍdu puttaham*

4. Which one? This one. எந்த? இது. एन्द? इदु *end? idu.*

5. What is your name? உங்கள் பெயர் என்ன? उंगळ् पेयर् एन्न? (आपका नाम क्या है?) *ungaḷ peyar enna?*

6. My name is Ratnakar என் பெயர் ரத்னாகரன் एन् पेर् रत्नाकरन् *en per Ratnākaṛan*

7. What is your place name (Where do you live?)? உங்க ஊர் பேர் என்ன उंगन् ऊर् पेर् एन्न? (आपके गाँव का नाम क्या है?) *ungn ūr per enna*

8. My place name is Toronto (I live in Toronto). என் ஊர் பெயர் டொராண்டொ एन् ऊर् पेयर् टोरांटो. (मेरे गाँव का नाम टोरांटो है = मैं टोरांटो में रहता हूँ) *en ūr per Toronto.*

9. Who is she? அவள் யார் अवळ् यार् (वह कौन है?) *avaḷ yār*

10. Who is he? அவன் யார் अवन् यार् (वह कौन है?) *avan yār*

11. Who is that (respectable) person? அவர் யார் अवर् यार् (वे कौन हैं?) *avar yār*

12. I am Indian. நான் இந்தியன் नान् इन्दियन् *nān Indian*

13. She is not Telgu. அவள் தெலுங்கு இல்லை अवळ् तेलुंगु इल्लै *avaḷ Telungu illai*

14. We are Indians. நாங்கள் இந்தியர்கள் नांगळ् इन्दियर्गळ् *nāngaḷ Indiyargaḷ*

15. My mother tongue is Hindi. என் தாய்மொழி இந்தி एन् तायमोळि इन्दि *en tāymoḷi Indi*

16. What is your mother tongue? உங்கள் தாய்மொழி என்ன उंगळ् तायमोळि एन्न? *ungaḷ tāymoḷi enna*

17. My mother tongue is Tamil. என் தாய்மொழி தமிழ் एन् तायमोळि तमिळ् *en tāymoḷi Tamiḷ*

18. Is he* a student? அவன் மாணவனா ? अवन् माणवना? *avan māṇvanā?*

* NOTE : <u>Suffix ஆ *ā* आ is attached to a noun to ask a question</u> (the question that does not begin with any Interrogative adjective such as, what?, which? when? etc). The Suffix ஆ *ā* आ can be attached to any word in a sentence to make a question pointing to that word.

EXERCISE : Translate, Say and Write it in Tamil Answers are given in small font for your help, if you need.

VOCAB : Boy = பையன் *paiyan* पैयन्, Girl/Woman = பெண் *peṇ* पेण्, Man = மனிதன் *manidan* मनिदन्, Friend (m) = சிநேகிதன் सिनेहिदन् *sinehidan*

1. Which boy? எந்த பையன்? एन्द पैयन्? *enda paiyan*
2. Which girl? எந்த பெண்? एन्द पेण्? *enda peṇ*
3. Which man? எந்த மனிதன்? एन्द मनिदन्? *enda manidan*
4. Which woman? எந்த பெண்? एन्द पेण्? *enda peṇ*
5. What is her name? (इसका नाम क्या है?) இவள் பெயர் என்ன? इवळ् पेर् एन्न? *ivaḷ per enna*
6. Her name is Radha. இவள் பெயர் ராதா इवळ् पेयर् रादा *ivaḷ peyar Rādạ̄*
7. Where does she live? (her place name)? இவள் ஊர் பெயர் என்ன
इवळ् ऊर् पेर् एन्न? *ivaḷ ūr per enna*
8. She lives in Madurai. இவள் ஊர் பெயர் மதுரை
इवळ् ऊर् पेयर् मदुरै *ivaḷ ūr peyar Madurai*
9. Who is he? அவன் யார் अवन् यार् *avan yār*
10. He is my friend, Mr. Singh. அவன் என் சினேகிதன் மிஸ்டர் ஸிங்
अवन् एन् सिनेहिदन् मिस्टर सिंग. *avan en sinehidan Mr. Singh*
11. Is he* Telgu? அவன் தெலுங்கா? अवन् तेलुंगा? *avan Telunga?*
12. No. He is not Telgu. இல்லை அவன் தெலுங்கு இல்லை
इल्लै. अवन् तेलुंगु इल्लै *illai. avan Telungu illai*
13. What is his mother tongue? அவர் தாய்மொழி என்ன
अवर् तायमोऴि एन्न? *avar tāymolí enna*
14. His mother tongue is Punjabi. அவர் தாய்மொழி பஞ்சாபி
अवन् तायमोळि पंजाबी. *avan tāymoḷi Panjābī*

EXERCISE : Translate in English or Hindi Answers are given in small font for your help, if you need.

1. உங்க பெயர் என்ன उंग पेर् एन्न? *ung per enna* — What is your name?
2. என் பெயர் ரங்கன் एन् पेर् रंगन् *en per Rangaṇ* — My name is Rangan.
3. உங்க ஊர் பெயர் என்ன उंग ऊर् पेर् एन्न? *ung ūr per enna* — Where do you live?
4. அவள் பெயர் என்ன अवळ् पेर् एन्न? *ivaḷ per enna* — What is her (that girl's) name?
5. அவள் யார் अवळ् यार् *avaḷ yār* — Who is she (that girl)?
6. இவன் ஊர் பெயர் என்ன इवन् ऊर् पेर् एन्न? *ivan ūr per enna* — Where does he live?
7. இவன் ஊர் பெயர் மதுரை इवन् ऊर् पेर् मदुरै *ivan ūr per Madurai* — He lives in Madurai
8. அவன் மாணவனா ? अवन् माणवना? *avan māṇvanā?* — Is he* a student?
8a. அவள் மாணவியா ? अवळ् माणविया? *avaḷ māṇviyā?* — Is she* a student?

THE 'YES/NO' TYPE OF QUESTIONS

i. 'Yes / No' type of questions in Tamil are expressed with the use of the 'question marker' ஆ *ā* आ.

ii. This question marker may be attached to any word of the a sentence, other than to the adjective of the noun. However, the interrogative suffix is attached usually to the last word.

EXAMPLES :

1. Is it a goat? இது ஆடா? *idu āḍā* इदु आडा? இதுவா ஆடு *iduvā āḍu* इदुवा आडु?
2. Is that a parrot? அது கிளியா? *adu kiḷiyā* अदु किळिया? அதுவா கிளி *aduvā kiḷi* अदुवा किळि?
3. Is that a boy? அவன் பையனா? *avan paiyanā* अदु पैयना? அவனா பையன் *avanā piyan* अवना पैयन्?
4. Is it a book? இது புத்தகமா? *idu puttahamā* इदु पुत्तहमा? இதுவா புத்தகம் *iduvā puttaham* इदुवा पुत्तहम्?
5. Is that a Dollar? அது டாலரா? *adu ḍālarā* अदु डालरा? அதுவா டாலர் *aduvā ḍālar* अदुवा डालर्?
6. Is she Indian? அவள் இந்தியனா? *avaḷ indianā* अवळ् इन्दियना? அவளா இந்தியன் *avaḷā indian* अवळा इन्दियन्?
7. Is your mothertongue Tamil? உன் தாய்மொழி தமிழா? *un tāymoḷi tamiḷā* उन् ताय्मोऴि तमिऴा?
8. How many pairs of gloves are these? (எத்தனை *ettanai* एत्तनै = How many? ஜோடி *joḍī* जोडी = Pair; கையுறை *kaiyurai* कैयुरै = Glove) இது எத்தனை ஜோடி கையுறை? *idu ettanai joḍi kaiyurai?* इदु एत्तनै जोडी कैयुरै?
9. Is she your wife? (உம்முடைய *ummuḍaiya* उम्मुडैय = Wife) அவள் உம்முடைய மனைவியா? *avaḷ ummuḍaiya maneviyā* अवळ् उम्मुडैय मनेविया?
10. Howmanieth Prime Mininster is Mr. Manmohan Singh? (திரு *thiru* तिरु = Mister; எத்தனைவது *ettanāivadu* एत्तनैवदु = Howmanieth; பிரதம மந்திரி *piradan mandiri* पिरदम मन्दिरि = Prime Minister) திரு மன்மோஹன் ஸிங் எத்தனைவது பிரதம மந்திரி? *thiru Manmohan Singh ettannāvadu piradan mandiri* तिरु मनमोहन सिंग एत्तन्नावदु पिरदम मन्दिरि? NOTE : This was not a Yes/No type of question, therefore அ suffix is not used.

iii. THE POLITE / FORMAL SPEECH

i. The Honorific Suffix ங்க ङ *ng* is added to the last word of the sentence to show politeness or respect by the speaker to the listner.

NOTE :

(i) If the word ends in ன் न् *n* or ம் म् *m,* the last ன் न् n or ம் म् *m* is dropped before attaching ங்க ङ *ng*

e.g. (i) நீ (You = तू) + ங்க = நீங்க (You Sir/Madam - आप) नी + ङ = नीङ *nī + ṅg = nīṅg*

(ii) வணக்கம் (Hi नमस्ते) वणक्कम् *vaṇakkam* = (Respect) வணக்கங்க (Hello नमस्ते जी) वणक्कङ *vaṇakkaṅg*

(ii) In Tamil, somewhat like Hindi (आप = you = with respect as well as plural), the expression of respect by adding the Honorific Suffix suffix ங்க ङ् *ṅg* to a noun also means expression of plurality of that noun.

e.g. வா vā (come) + ங்க ṅk (Respect) = வாங்க वाङ्ग *vāṅga* (Please come)

(iii) Suffix आर् *ār* may be attached a Singular Noun and suffix मार् *mār* to plural Nouns, to denote respect. e.g. தாய் tāy ताय् (Mother) + ங்க ṅk (Respect) = தாயார் तायार् *tayār* (Mother, with respect)

TERMINATIONS OF RESPECT / PLURAL FOR PRONOUNS

TABLE 11 : TERMINATIONS of RESPECT / PLURAL, for PRONOUNS

PERSON	**HONORIFIC / PLURAL** Pronoun		SINGULAR **Termination**	PLURAL **Termination**
	Singular	Plural	Honorific	Honorific
2nd (You) M.F.	நீர் नीर् *nīr* (आप)	நீங்கள் नींगळ् *niṅgaḷ* (आप लोग)	ஈர் ईर् *īr*	ஈர்கள் ईर्गळ् *īrgaḷ*
3rd (He/She) M..F.	அவர் अवर् *avar* (वे)	அவர்கள் अवर्गळ् *avargaḷ* (वे लोग)	ஆர் आर् *ār*	ஆர்கள் आर्गळ् *ārgaḷ*
3rd (It) N.		அவைகள் अवैगळ् *avaigaḷ* (वे)		அன अन *an*
First Person Pronoun I or We is not used in Honorific Manner in polite talk (for, one does not give respect to himself).				
This Table is developed for Sanskrit Hindi Research Institute for *"Learn Tamil Through English/Hindi"* by Ratnakar Narale.				

IV. MAKING OUR OWN TAMIL SENTENCES WITH ACTION WORDS

1. Speaking PRESENT events

TABLE 12 : Speaking Present Events

	Subject		Verb (Learn கல்)	+ Present Tense Suffix	+ Personal Suffix
1	I	நான் नान् *nān*	கல் कल् *kal*	கிறு, க்கிறு * किरु, क्किरु *kiru, kkiru*	ஏன் ऍन् *ĕn*
2	We	நாங்கள் नांगळ् *nāṅgaḷ*	Same as above	Same as above	ஓம் ओम् *om*
3	You तुम	நீ नी *nī*	Same as above	Same as above	ஆய் आय् *āy*
4	You (hon) आप	நீர் नीर् *nīr*	Same as above	Same as above	ஈர் ईर् *īr*
5	You all (plural) आप लोग	நீங்கள் नींगळ् *nīṅgaḷ*	Same as above	Same as above	ஈர்கள் ईर्हळ् *īrhaḷ*
6	He (m)	அவன் अवन् *avan*	Same as above	Same as above	ஆன் आन् *ān*
7	She (f)	அவள் अवळ् *avaḷ*	Same as above	Same as above	ஆள் आळ् *āḷ*
8	He, She (hon)	அவர் अवर् *avar*	Same as above	Same as above	ஆர் आर् *ār*
9	They (m.f.)	அவர்கள் ** अवर्हळ् *avarhaḷ*	Same as above	Same as above	ஆர்கள் आर्हळ् *ārhaḷ*
10	It (n.)	அது अदु *adu*	Same as above	Same as above	அது अदु *adu*
11	They (n.)	அவைகள் अवैगळ् *avaigal*	Same as above	Same as above	அன अन *ana*

NOTES : * (i) The உ (उ u) of கிறு, க்கிறு drops when personal suffix starting with any vowel is added.
(ii) Sometimes Present Tense suffix கின்து (किन्दु *kindu*) is used in place of கிறு (किरु *kiru*) and க்கிறு (क्किरु *kkiru*)
(iii) ** க between two consonants is pronounced as h (ह).

This Table is developed for Sanskrit Hindi Research Institute for *"Learn Tamil Through English/Hindi"* by Ratnakar Narale.

THUS : The FORMULA for making a sentence in any tense is : **Verb + Tense suffix + Personal suffix.**

EXAMPLES :

NOTE : Like Sanskrit, Tamil language also generally treats Present Habitual and Present continuous tenses as a Simple Present Tense, unless specifically required. Such constructions are explained later.

1. I am learning Tamil / I learn Tamil. **நான் தமிழ் கற்கிறேன்** *nān tamiḷ karkiren* (*kal + kiru + ĕn = kar + kir + ĕn = karkiren*) नान् तमिऴ् कर्किरेन् (कर् + किरु + ऍन् = कर् + किर् + ऍन् = कर्किरेन्

நான் தமிழ் கற்கிறேன் *nān tamiḷ karkiren* (*kar + kiru + ĕn = kar + kir + ĕn = karkiren*) नान् तमिऴ् कर्किरेन् (कर् + किरु + ऍन् = कर् + किर् + ऍन् = कर्किरेन्

NOTES : (i) Again like Sanskrit, the verb "is" (**இரு** इरु *iru,* Sanskrit अस्ति, Hindi है) is actually not written. (ii) Having understood the breakdown in the above example clearly, other Pronouns in other two Tenses of any Verb can easily be figured out in same style, by attaching the Past or Future Tense Suffix to any chosen verb. (iii) Notice the rhyming between the pronoun and its verb.

2. I drink milk. **நான் பால் குடிக்கிறேன்** नान् पाल् कुडिक्किरेन् *nān pāl kuḍikkiren* (कुडि *kuḍi* = drink)

3. She is reading a book. **அவள் புத்தகம் படிகிறாள்** अवळ् पुत्तहम् पडिकिराळ् *avaḷ putthaham paḍikirāḷ.* (पडि *paḍi* = Read)

4. He walks 10 km. **அவன்** 10 k.m. **நடக்கிறான்** अवन् 10 k.m. नडक्किरान् *avan 10 km. naḍakkirān* (नड *naḍa* = Walk)

5. You are sleeping. **நீ தூங்குகிறாய்** नी तूंगुकिराय् *nī tūngukirāy.* (तूंगु *tūngu* = Sleep)

6. They are. **அவர்கள் இருக்கிறார்கள்** अवर्गळ् इरुक्किरार्गळ् *avargaḷ irukkirārgaḷ.* (इरु *iru* = Be)

7. He/she goes. **அவர் போகிறார்** अवर् पोकिरार् *avar pokirār.* (पो *po* = Go)

8. You (all) are giving money. **நீங்கள் பணம் இடுகிறீர்கள்** नींगळ् पणम् इडुकिरीर्गळ् *ningaḷ paṇam idukirīrgaḷ* (ई, इडु *ī, idu* = Give)

9. She takes flowers. **அவள் பூக்கள் எடுத்துக் கொள்ளுகிறாள்** अवळ् पूक्कळ् एडुत्तुक् कोळ्ळुकिराळ् *avaḷ pūkkaḷ eduttuk koḷḷukirāḷ* (कोळ् *koḷ* = Take)

10. I worship. **நான் தொழுகிறேன்** नान् दोऴुकिरेन् *nān doḷukiren.* (दोऴ् *doḷ* = Worship)

EXERCISE : Translate in Tamil (answers are given for your help, if you need)

2. I eat. — நான் உண்கிறேன் नान् उणकिरेन् *nān uṇkiren* (उण् *uṇ* = Eat)
3. She is fighting. — அவள் பொருதுகிறாள் अवळ् पोरुगुकिराळ् *avaḷ porudukirāḷ.* (पोरु *poru* = Fight)
4. He falls. — அவன் விழுகிறான் अवन् विऴुकिरान् *avan viḷukirān* (विऴु *viḷu* = Fall)
5. You do / you are doing. — நீ செய்கிறாய் नी सेयकिराय् *nī seykirāy.* (सेय् *sey* = Do)
6. They die. — அவர்கள் மரிக்கிரார்கள் अवर्गळ् मरिक्किरार्गळ् *avargaḷ marikkirārgaḷ.* (मरि *mari* = Die)
7. He speaks. — அவர் பேசுகிறார் अवर् पेसुकिरार् *avar pesukirār.* (पेसु *pesu* = Speak)
8. You are running. — நீங்கள் ஒடுகிறீர்கள் नींगळ् ओडुकिरीर्गळ् *nīngaḷ oḍukirīrgaḷ* (ओडु *oḍu* = Run)
9. She is writing. — அவள் எழுதுகிறாள் अवळ् एऴुदुकिराळ् *avaḷ eḷudukirāḷ* (एऴुदु *eḷudu* = Write)
10. I trust. — நான் நம்புகிறேன் नान् नंबुकिरेन् *nān nambukiren.* (नंबु *nambu* = Trust)

COMMON TAMIL VERBS, Part I

TABLE 13 : VERB LIST 1

1) Bathe	குளி	कुळि	*kuḷi*	*29)* Keep	வை	वै	*vai*
2) Be	இரு	इरु	*iru*	30) Know	அறி	अरि	*ari*
3) Become	ஆ	आ	*ā*	*31)* Laugh	சிரி	सिरि	*siri*
4) Begin	ஆரம்பி	आरंबि	*ārambi*	*32)* Learn	படி	पडि	*paḍi*
5) Break	உடை	उडै	*uḍai*	*33)* Leave	விடு	विडु	*viḍu*
6) Buy	வாங்கு	वांगु	*vāṅgu*	*34)* Like	விரும்பு	विरुंबु	*virumbu*
7) Come	வா, வரு	वा, वरु	*vā, varu*	*35)* Perish	அழி	अळि	*aḷi*
8) Cry	அழு	अळु	*aḷu*	*36)* Put	போடு	पोडु	*poḍu*
9) Desire	இச்சை	इच्चै	*ichchai*	*37)* Rain	மழை	मऴै	*maḷ́ai*
10) Die	சாவு	सावु	*sāvu*	*38)* Read	படி	पडि	*paḍi*
11) Dislike	வெறு	वेरु	*veru*	*39)* Run	ஒடு	ओडु	*oḍu*
12) Do	செய்	सेय्	*sey*	*40)* Say	சொல்	सोल्	*sol*
13) Drink	குடி	कुडि	*kuḍi*	*41)* See	காண்	काण्	*kāṇ*
14) Eat	உண்	उण्	*uṇ*	42) Sell	விற்	विर्	*vir*
15) Eat	சாப்பிடு	साप्पिडु	*sāppiḍu*	*43)* Sing	பாடு	पाडु	*pāḍu*
16) Enter	புகு	पुकु	*puku*	*44)* Sit	உட்கார்	उड्कार्	*uḍkār*
17) Exist, be	ஆகு	आगु	*āgu*	*45)* Sleep	உறங்கு	उरंगु	*uraṅgu*
18) Exist	உறு	उरु	*uru*	*46)* Sleep	தூங்கு	तूरंगु	*thūṅgu*
19) Fall	விழு	विळु	*viḷu*	*47)* Speak	பேசு	पेसु	*pesu*
20) Fight	பொரு	पोरु	*poru*	*48)* Stand	நில்	निल्	*nil*
21) Get	வாங்கு	वांगु	*vāṅgu*	*49)* Steal	திருடு	थिरुडु	*thiruḍu*
22) Give	இடு	इडु	*iḍu*	*50)* Stop	நிறுத்து	निरुद्दु	*niruddu*
23) Give	கொடு	कोडु	*koḍu*	51) Surrender	பணி	पणि	*paṇi*
24) Give	தா	दा	*dā*	*52)* Take	எடு	एडु	*eḍu*
25) Give	அளி	अळि	*aḷi*	*53)* Talk	கொல்	कोल्	*kol*
26) Go	போ	पो	*po*	*54)* Walk	நட	नड	*nada*
27) Grow	வளரு	वळरु	*vaḷru*	*55)* Wash	கழுவு	कलुवु	*kaḷuvu*
28) Hear	கேள்	केळ्	*keḷ*	*56)* Wear	உடுத்து	उडुत्तु	*uḍuddu*

2. Speaking PAST events

TABLE 14 : Speaking Past Events

	Subject		Verb (Learn கல்)	+ Past Tense Suffixes (see Table 15)	+ Personal Suffix
1	I	நான் नान् *nān*	கல் कल् *kal*	ந்து, த்து, இது* न्दु, द्दु, इदु *ndu, ddu, idu*	ஏன் ऍन् *ĕn*
2	We	நாங்கள் नांगळ् *nāngaḷ*	Same as above	Same as above	ஓம் ओम् *om*
3	You तुम	நீ नी *nī*	Same as above	Same as above	ஆய் आय् *āy*
4	You (hon) आप	நீர் नीर् *nīr*	Same as above	Same as above	ஈர் ईर् *īr*
5	You all आप लोग	நீங்கள் नींगळ् *nīngaḷ*	Same as above	Same as above	ஈர்கள் ईर्गळ् *īrgaḷ*
6	He (m)	அவன் अवन् *avan*	Same as above	Same as above	ஆன் आन् *ān*
7	She (f)	அவள் अवळ् *avaḷ*	Same as above	Same as above	ஆள் आळ् *āḷ*
8	He, She (hon)	அவர் अवर् *avar*	Same as above	Same as above	ஆர் आर् *ār*
9	They (m.f.)	அவர்கள் अवर्गळ् *avargaḷ*	Same as above	Same as above	ஆர்கள் आर्गळ् *ārgaḷ*
10	It (n.)	அது अदु *adu*	Same as above	Same as above	அது अदु *adu*
11	They (n.)	அவைகள் अवैगळ् *avaigal*	Same as above	Same as above	அன अन *ana*

∗ NOTES : (i) The end உ (उ u) drops when personal suffix starting with any vowel is added.

(ii) For detailed list of PAST Tense SUFFIXES, please refer to TABLE 15 given below.

(iii) Change may take place when letter த் *d* द् (Past Tense) is added, as said in earlier chapters.

(iv) For third person Singular as well as Plural, Neuter Subjects the suffixe is உம், க்கும் उम्, or क्कुम् *um, kkum*

This Table is developed for Sanskrit Hindi Research Institute for *"Learn Tamil Through English/Hindi"* by Ratnakar Narale.

EXAMPLES :

NOTE : Like Sanskrit (लङ् Past tense), Tamil language also generally treats Past habitual and Past continuous tenses as a Simple Past Tense. The specific construction is explained later.

1. I was learning Tamil / I learned Tamil. **நான் தமிழ் கற்றேன்** *nān tamiḻ karren* नान् तमिळ् कर्रेन् (कल् + द् + ऍन् = कर् + र + ऍन् = कर्रेन् *kal + d + ĕn = kar + r + ĕn = karren*)

<u>NOTE</u> : As said before, when a word ending in **ல்** ल् *l* is followed by a word beginning with **த்** त् *t*, the final **ல்** ल् *l* becomes **ற்** र् *r*. and the **த்** त् *t* also becomes **ற்** र् *r*. (See the useful Tables 5 and 16)

2. I drank milk. **நான் பால் குடித்தேன்** नान् पाल् कुडित्तेन् *nān pāl kuḍitten* (कुडि *kuḍi* = drink)

3. She was reading a book. **அவள் புத்தகம் படித்தாள்** अवळ् पुत्तहम् पडित्ताळ् *avaḷ putthaham paḍittāḷ.* (पडि *paḍi* = Read)

4. He walked 10 km. **அவன் பத்து** k.m. **நடந்தான்** अवन् पत्तु k.m. नडन्दान् *avan pattu km. naḍandān* (नड *naḍa* = Walk)

5. You were sleeping. **நீ தூங்கினாய்** नी तूंगिनाय् *nī tūṅgināy.* (तुंगु *tuṅgu* = Sleep) (तुंगु + इनु + आय् = तुंग् + इन् + आय् = तुंगिनाय् *tuṅgu + inu + āy = tuṅg + in + āy = tuṅgināy;* see Table 15 below)

TABLE 15 : PRESENT, PAST and FUTURE Tense SUFFIXES

TENSES ↓	VERBS ENDING IN						
	आ **ஆ** *ā*	इ, ऐ, य् *i, ai, y*	उ **உ** *u*	ण्, न् *ṇ, n*	र्, ऴ् **ழ்** *r, ḻ*	ल्, ळ् **ள்** *l, ḷ*	Other
Present	**க்கிறு** क्किरु *kkiru*	**க்கிறு** क्किरु *kkiru*	i. Verbs ending in two short syllables **க்கிறு** क्किरु *kkiru* ii. Other verbs **கிறு** किरु *kiru*	**கிறு** किरु *kiru*	**கிறு** किरु *kiru*	**கிறு** किरु *kiru*	**க்கிறு, கிறு** क्किरु, किरु *kkiru,kiru*
Past	**ந்த்** न्द् *nd*	**ந்த்** न्द् *nd*	i. Verbs ending in two short syllables. **ந்த்** न्द् *nd* ii. Other. **இன்** इन् *nd*	**த், ட், ற்** द्, ट्, र् *d, ṭ, r* *	**ந்த்** न्द् *nd*	**த், ன்ற், ண்ட்** द्, न्र्, ण्ट् *nd, nr, ṇṭ* **	**ந்த்** न्द् *nd*
Future	**ப்** प् *p* ***	i. Intransitive **ப்** प् *p* ii. Transitive **வ்** व् *v*	i. Intransitive **ப்** प् *p* ii. Transitive **வ்** व् *v*	**ப்** प् *p*	**உ + வ்** उ + व् *u + v*	**வ்** व् *v*	**வ், று + வ்** व्, रु + व् *v, ru + v*

* A word ending in **ண** *ṇ* ण् if followed by **த** *d* द्, the **த** *d* द् changes to **ட்** *ṭ* द् See Tables 5, 16

** **ல்** + **த்** = **ன்ற்** ल् + द् = न्र *l + d = nr* ; **ள்** + **த்** = **ண்ட்** ळ् + द् = ण्ट् *ḷ + d = ṇṭ* See Tables 5, 16

*** When a word ending in any vowl is followed by consonant क्, च्, त्, or प्, *k, ck, t,* or *p* that consonant is <u>doubled</u>.

This Table is developed for Sanskrit Hindi Research Institute for *"Learn Tamil Through English/Hindi"* by Ratnakar Narale.

6. They were. அவர்கள் இருந்தார்கள் अवर्गळ् इरुन्दार्गळ् *avargaḷ irundārgaḷ*. (इरु *iru* = Be)

7. He/she went. அவர் போனார் अवर् पोनार् *avar ponār.* (पो *po* = Go)

8. You (all) are giving money. நீங்கள் பணம் கொடுக்கிறீர்கள் नींगळ् पणम् कोडुक्कीर्गळ् *ningaḷ paṇam koḍukkīrgaḷ* (ई, इडु *ī, idu* = Give)

9. She took flowers. அவள் பூக்களை எடுத்தாள் अवळ् पूक्कळ् एडुत्ताळ् *avaḷ pūkkaḷ eḍuttaḷ* (एडु *eḍu* = Take) See Table 16

10. I worshipped. நான் தொழுதேன் नान् दोऴदेन् *nān doḷden.* (दोळु *doḷu* = Worship)

EXERCISE : Translate in Tamil (answers are given for your help, if you need)

2. I ate.	நான் உண்டேன் नान् उण्डेन् *nān uṇḍen* (उण् *uṇ* = Eat)
3. She was fighting.	அவள் பொருவினாள் अवळ् पोरुविनाळ् *avaḷ poruvināḷ.* (पोरु *poru* = Fight)
4. He fell.	அவன் விழுந்தான் अवन् विळुन्दान् *avan viḷundān* (विळु *viḷu* = Fall)
5. You did / you were doing.	நீ செய்தாய் नी सेय्दाय् *nī seydāy.* (सेय् *sey* = Do)
6. They died.	அவர்கள் மரித்தார்கள் अवर्गळ् मरित्तार्गळ् *avargaḷ mariththārgaḷ.* (मरि *mari* = Die)
7. He spoke.	அவர் பேசினார் अवर् पेसिनार् *avar pesinār.* (पेसु *pesu* = Speak)
8. You were running.	நீங்கள் ஓடுகிறீர்கள் नींगळ् ओडुगिरीर्गळ् *nīngaḷ odugirīrgaḷ* (ओडु *oḍu* = Run)
9. She was writing.	அவள் எழுதினாள் अवळ् एळुदिनाळ् *avaḷ eḷudināḷ* (एळुदु *eḷudu* = Write)
10. I trusted.	நான் நம்பினேன் नान् नंबिनेन् *nān nambinen.* (नंबु *nambu* = Trust)

श्री HINDI श्री
SANSKRIT RESEARCH
श्री INSTITUTE श्री

TABLE 16 : ADVANCED CONSONANT- CONSONANT COMPOUNDING (see Table 5 for common)

THIS ↓	Initial	Mute	Double	AFTER ங்	ஞ்	ட்	ண்	ம்	ர்	ல்	ள்	ற்	ன்	Between two Conso.	Last letter	Other places
க	क k	क k	क k	ग g		क k	ग g द्क ṭk	ङ ng	ग g	र्क rk	ट्क ṭk	क k	र्क rk	ह h	ग g	ग* g
ச	स s		च ch		ज j	च ch	ट्च tch	ञ्च* ñch		र्च rch	ट्च tch	च ch	र्च rch			स s श sh
ட		ट ṭ	ट ṭ													ड ḍ
த	त t थ th	त t थ th	त t थ th				ण्ट ṇt	न्द nd		न्र nr ऱ् rr	ट्ट ṭṭ ण्ड ṇḍ		न्र nr ऱ् rr			द d
ந							ण्ण ṇṇ	न्न nn		न्न nn	ण्ण ṇṇ ण् ṇ		न्न nn			
ப	प p	प p	प p							र्प rp	ट्प ṭp		र्प rp			ब b
ம										न्म	ण्म					
ண																
ற	ट् ṯ	ट् ṯ	ट् ṯ									ण्ड्र ṇḍr				ऱ् ṟ

* (i) When a word ending in ம் is followed by a word beginning with a hard/soft consonant, ம் is sometimes dropped, and the hard consonant is doubled.

(ii) When letter க comes between two consonants, the க sounds like ह *h.*

This Table is developed by Sanskrit Hindi Research Institute for *"Learn Tamil Through English/Hindi"* by Ratnakar Narale.

3. Speaking FUTURE events

TABLE 17 : Speaking Future Events

	Subject		Verb (Learn கல்)	+ Future Tense Suffixes (see Table 15)	+ Personal Suffix
1	I	நான் नान् *nān*	கல் कल् *kal*	ப்பு *ppu* (Strong, Intr.)* பு पु *pu* (for verbs with nasal ending) வு वु *vu* (Weak, Trans.)	ஏன் ऍन् *ĕn*
2	We	நாங்கள் नांगळ् *nāngal*	Same as above	Same as above	ஓம் ओम् *om*
3	You तुम	நீ नी *nī*	Same as above	Same as above	ஆய் आय् *āy*
4	You (hon) आप	நீர் नीर् *nīr*	Same as above	Same as above	ஈர் ईर् *īr*
5	You all आप लोग	நீங்கள் नींगळ् *nīngal*	Same as above	Same as above	ஈர்கள் ईर्गळ् *īrgal*
6	He (m)	அவன் अवन् *avan*	Same as above	Same as above	ஆன் आन् *ān*
7	She (f)	அவள் अवळ् *aval*	Same as above	Same as above	ஆள் आळ् *āl*
8	He, She (hon)	அவர் अवर् *avar*	Same as above	Same as above	ஆர் आर् *ār*
9	They (m.f.)	அவர்கள் अवर्गळ् *avargal*	Same as above	Same as above	ஆர்கள் आर्गळ् *ārgal*
10	It (n.)	அது अदु *adu*	Same as above	Same as above	உம், க்கும் उम्, क्कुम् *um, kkum* *
11	They (n.)	அவைகள் अवैगळ् *avaigal*	Same as above	Same as above	உம், க்கும் उम्, क्कुम् *um, kkum* *

* NOTES : (i) The end உ (उ u) of the suffix drops when personal suffix starting with any vowel is added.

(ii) Weak verbs form Present tense with suffix கிறு किरु *kiru* and Future with வு वु *vu.*

(ii) Strong verbs form Present tense with suffix க்கிறு क्किरु *kkiru,* Past with த்த् त् *tt* and Future with ப்ப् प्प् *pp*

(iii) For Third Person Neuter Subjects (Singular as well as Plural), the suffixe is உம் or க்கும் उम्, क्कुम् *um, kkum*

This Table is developed for Sanskrit Hindi Research Institute for *"Learn Tamil Through English/Hindi"* by Ratnakar Narale.

EXAMPLES :

NOTE : Like Sanskrit (लृट् Future tense), Tamil language also generally treats most of the future actions as Simple Future Tense, unless specifically required. Such specific actions will be explained later.

1. I will learn Tamil. நான் தமிழ் கற்பேன் नान् तमिळ् कर्पेन् (कल् + प् + ऍन् = कर् + प + ऍन् = कर्पेन् *kal + pa + ĕn = kar + p + ĕn = karpen*)

NOTE : As said before, when a word ending in ல் ल् *l* is followed by a word beginning with ப் प् *p*, the final ல் ल् *l* becomes ற் र् *r*. (See the useful Tables 5 and 16)

2. I will drink milk. நான் பால் குடிப்பேன் नान् पाल् कुडिप्पेन् *nān pāl kuḍippen* (कुडि *kuḍi* = drink)

3. She will read a book. அவள் புத்தகம் படிப்பாள் अवळ् पुत्तहम् पडिप्पाळ् *avaḷ putthaham paḍippāḷ.* (पडि *paḍi* = Read)

4. He will walk 10 km. அவன் பத்து k.m. நடப்பான் अवन् पत्तु k.m. नडप्पान् *avan pattu km. naḍappān* (नड *naḍa* = Walk)

5. You were sleeping. நீ தூங்குவாய் नी तूंगुवाय् *nī tūṅguvāy.*

TABLE 18 : FUTURE Tense SUFFIXES

TENSES ↓	VERBS ENDING IN						
	आ	इ, ऐ, य्	उ	ण्, न्	र्, ळ् ழ்	ल्, ळ् ள்	Other
Future Tense	ப் प् *p* *	i. Intransitive ப் प् *p* ii. Transitive வ் व् *v*	i. Intransitive ப் प् *p* ii. Transitive வ் व् *v*	ப் प् *p*	உ + வ் उ + व् *u + v*	வ் व् *v*	வ், று + வ் व्, रु + व् *v, ru + v*
* When a word ending in any vowl is followed by consonant क्, च्, त्, or प्, *k, ck, t,* or *p* that consonant is <u>Doubled</u>.							
This Table is developed for Sanskrit Hindi Research Institute for *"Learn Tamil Through English/Hindi"* by Ratnakar Narale.							

6. They will. அவர்கள் இருப்பார்கள் अवर्गळ् इरुप्पार्गळ् *avargaḷ iruppārgaḷ.* (इरु *iru* = Be)

7. He/she will go. அவர் போவார் अवर् पोवार् *avar povār.* (पो *po* = Go)

8. You (all) will give money. நீங்கள் பணம் இடுவீ ர்கள் नींगळ् पणम् इडुवीर्गळ् *ningaḷ paṇam iduvīrgaḷ* (ई, इडु *ī, idu* = Give)

9. She will take flowers. அவள் பூக்களை எடுத்துக் கொள்வாள் अवळ् एडुत्तुक् पूक्कोळवाळ् *avaḷ eduttuk pūkkoḷvāḷ* (एडु *eḍu* = Take) See Table 16

10. I will worship. நான் தொழுவேன் नान् दोळ्वेन् *nān doḷven.* (दोळु *doḷu* = Worship)

EXERCISE : Translate in Tamil (answers are given for your help, if you need)

2. I will eat.	நான் உண்பேன் नान् उण्पेन् *nān uṇpen* (उण् *uṇ* = Eat)
3. She will fight.	அவள் பொருதுவாள் अवळ् पोरुदुवाळ् *avaḷ poruduvāḷ.* (पोरु *poru* = Fight)
4. He will fall.	அவன் விழுவான் अवन् विळुवान् *avan viḷuvān* (विळु *viḷu* = Fall)
5. You will do.	நீ செய்வாய் नी सेय्वाय् *nī seyvāy.* (सेय् *sey* = Do)
6. They will die.	அவர்கள் மரிப்பார்கள் अवर्गळ् मरिप्पार्गळ् *avargaḷ marppārgaḷ.* (मरि *mari* = Die)
7. He will speak.	அவர் பேசுவார் अवर् पेसुवार् *avar pesuvār.* (पेसु *pesu* = Speak)
8. You (all) will run.	நீங்கள் ஓடுவீர்கள் नींगळ् ओडुवीर्गळ् *niṅgaḷ oduvīrgaḷ* (ई, ओडु *oḍu* = Run)
9. She will write.	அவள் எழுதுவாள் अवळ् एळुदुवाळ् *avaḷ eḷuduvāḷ* (एळुदु *eḷudu* = Write)
10. I will trust.	நான் நம்புவேன் नान् नंबुवेन् *nān nambuven.* (नंबु *nambu* = Trust)

EXAMPLES : Third Person Neuter Gender Future Tense

REMEMBER :

(i) For Third Person Singular <u>as well as</u> Plural, Neuter Subjects, the Future Tense suffixe is உம் or க்கும் उम्, क्कुम् *um, kkum* (see Table 14). Same suffix for singular and pluraal both.

(ii) The verbs that take கிறு किरु *kiru* in Present tense, take உம் उम् *um* in Furure tense

(iii) The verbs that take க்கிறு क्किरु *kkiru* in Present tense, take க்கும் क्कुम् *kkum* in Furure tense

1. I will eat.	நான் உண்பேன் नान् उण्पेन् *nān uṇpen* (उण् *uṇ* = Eat)
2. The dog will eat bone.	நாய் எலும்பு உண்ணும் नाय् एलुम्बु उण्णुम् *nāy elumbu uṇnum* (एलुम्बु, अस्थि *elumbu, asthi* = Bone)
3. He will fall.	அவன் விழுவான் अवन् विळुवान् *avan viḷuvān* (विळु *viḷu* = Fall)
4. I walk.	நான் நடக்கிறேன் नान् नडक्किरेन् *nān naḍkkiren* (नड *naḍ* = Walk)
5. The elephant will walk.	யானை நடக்கும் यानै नडक्कुम् *yānai naḍakkum* (यानै *yānai* = Elephant)

LESSON 7

USING PRE-MADE TAMIL SENTENCES, Part I

PLEASE BE AWARE OF THIS, BEFORE YOU BEGIN

i. When you are able make your own sentences, your power is infinite. And, you know why each sentence is made this way. Only pre-made sentences is not the right way to learn Tamil.

ii. If you learn Tamil (or any language) through the common practice of learning through pre-made sentences, you are learning blindly, without knowing why the sentence is made this way. It's a lame job. HOWEVER, if you first learn how to make your own sentences <u>and then</u> look at pre-made phrases and sentences, you polish your learning.

iii. Therefore, please finish Lesson 6 properly, with confidence, before taking up this lesson.

iv. So far we have learned how to make our own sentences in Simple Present, Past and Future tenses of the VERBS. Thus in this lesson we will limit our scope to what we have learned so far.

v. In the next lesson we will learn how to use such English prepositions of the NOUNS such as : to, with, by, for, from, in, on, at ...etc. in Tamil sentences and make a better speech. In the following lesson we will first use these affixes again to make OWR OWN sentences, and then study more pre-made sentences.

vi. In this lesson we will increase our VOCABLARY with the use of a Picture Dictionary of Nouns. We will use this knowledge in the next lesson.

vii. Those who know Hindi, please remember that Hindi uses ने *ne* suffix for Transitive actions of any Perfect tense. But THERE IS NO ने *ne* suffix (or equivalent) IN TAMIL. e.g. Hindi मैने खाया will be in Tamil simply मैं खाया (नान् उण्डेन्).

viii. Make sure you have mastered TABLES 13 and 15. Mastering these is the key to make your own sentences in three tenses.

ix. With this book, even though you can learn Tamil without learning the Tamil script, **<u>I highly recommend that you learn Tamil through Tamil Script only. Please use the English and Hindi script for help and verification purpose only.</u>**

PRE-MADE ENGLISH-TAMIL SENTENCES
Part I

NOTE : At this stage you may not understand every part of all sentences given below, but as we make more of our own sentences in the following chapters, you will see them clearly if you revise this again.

1. Hi! Hello! नमस्ते = வணக்கம் वणक्कम् *vaṇakkam.*

2. How are you? आप कैसे हैं? = எப்படி இருக்கிறீர்கள் एप्पडि इरुक्किरीर्गळ् *eppadi irukkirīrgaḷ.*

3. How are you? क्या हाल है? = நலமா नलमा? *nalmā.*

4. Good morning! Goodnight! नमस्ते = வணக்கம் वणक्कम् *vaṇakkam.*

5. I am ok! मैं ठीक हूँ! = நான் நல்லா யிருக்கேன் नान् नल्ला यिरुक्केन् *nallā yirukken*

6. Thanks! धन्यवाद, शुक्रिया = நன்றி ननरि *nanri.*

7. Would you like to have tea? चाय पीएँगे? = தேநீர் குடிக்கிறீங்களா तेनीर कुडिक्किरींगळा? *thenir kuḍikkirīngaḷā* (தேநீர் तेनीर *thenīr* = Tea)

8. Certainly! For sure! अवश्य, बेशक = நிச்சயமாய் निच्चयमाय् *nichchamāy* (सं. निश्चयमाय्, निश्चयम्)

9. That's all बस ठीक है = போதும் पोदुम् *podum.*

10. No नहीं = இல்லை इल्लै *illai.*

11. Yes हाँ = ஆம், ஆமாம், ஓம் आम्, आमाम्, ओम् *ām, āmām, om.* (रां. आम्)

12. Truly सच = உண்மையாய், உள்ளபடி उण्मैयाय्, उळ्ळपडि *uṇmaiyāy, uḷḷapaḍi.*

13. What is the news क्या खबर है? = என்ன சமாசாரம் एन्न समाचारम् *enna samāchāram*

14. Don't worry कोई बात नहीं = பரவா-யில்லை परवा इल्लै *parvā illai*

15. Please! कृपया = பிரீதியா पिरीतिया *pirīthiyā.* (सं. प्रीत्या), தயவுசெய்து दयवुसेयदु *dayavuseudu*

16. Please listen जरा सुनिये = அதைக் கேளுங்கள் इदैक् केळुंगळ् *idaik keḷungaḷ.* (கேள் = Listen)

17. Excuse me! क्षमा कीजिये = மன்னியுங்கள் मन्नि-युंगळ् *manni-yungaḷ.*

18. What is this यह क्या है = இது என்ன इदु एन्न *idu enna.*

19. What happened? क्या हुआ = என்ன ஆயிற்று एन्न आयिट्रु *enna āyiṭru.* NOTE : When two ற்ற *rr* ऱ्ऱ come in a row, they are pronounced as ட்ற tr ट्र (see Table 16).

20. Nothing! कुछ नहीं = ஒன்றுமில்லை ओन्रुमिलै *onrumillai.*

21. Definitely जरूर, अवश्य = சரி सरि *sari.*

22. A little bit थोड़ा थोड़ा = கொஞ்சம் कोंजम् *konjam.*

23. When did it happen? यह कब हुआ = இது எப்போது நடந்தது इदु एप्पोदु नडन्ददु *idu eppodu naḍandadu.*

24. Yesterday monring. कल सवेरे = நேற்று காலை नेट्रु कालै *netru kālai.*

25. Since when? कब से? = எப்போதிலிருந்து एप्पोदिलिरुंदु *eppodilirundu.*

26. Just now. अभी = இப்போதுதான் इप्पोदुदान् *ippodudān.*

27. What will happen now? अब क्या होगा = இனி என்ன ஆகும் इनि एन्न आगुम् *ini enna āgum.*

28. Beautiful! सुंदर! = அழகியது अऴगियदु *alġiyadu.*

29. Of course अवश्य = அவசியம் अवश्यम् *avashyam.*

30. Thank Goodness! बस ठीक है = கடவுளுக்கு நன்றி कड़वुळुक्कु नन्रि *kaḍvuḷkku nanri.*

31. Good अच्छा, उत्तम = நல்ல, உத்தமம், நன்மை नल्ल, उत्तमम्, नन्मै *naLLa, uttamam, nanmai*

32. Say! बोलिये = சொல்லுங்கள் सोल्लुंगळ् *sollungaḷ.*

33. You are welcome स्वागत है = நல்வரவு नल्वरवु *aḷgiyadu.*

34. Why not? क्यों नहीं = ஏன் கூடாது एन् कूडादु *en kūḍāḍu.*

35. Where are you going? = நீங்கள் எங்கே செல்கிறீர்கள் नींगळ् एंगे सेल्हिरीर्हळ् *nīngaḷ enge selhirīrhaḷ.*

36. I am going to Chennai = நான் சென்னைக்குப் போகிறேன் नान् चेन्नैक्कुप् पोहिरेन् *nān Chennaikkup pohiren*

37. I can speak English मुझे अंग्रेज़ी आती है = எனக்கு ஆங்கிலம் பேசவரும் एनक्कु आंगिलम् पेसवरुम् *enakku Angilam pesvarum*

38. I know a little bit of Tamil = எனக்கு கொஞ்சம் தமிழ் தெரியும் एनक्कु कोंचम् तमिळ् तेरियुम् *enakku koncham Tamiḷ teriyum*

39. No! He does not understand Tamil = இல்லை, அவனுக்கு தமிழ் தெரியாது इल्लै, अवनुक्कु तमिऴ् तेरियादु *illai, avanakku Tamiḷ teriyādu*

40. What's your native language? = உங்கள் தாய்மொழி என்ன उंगळ् तायमोऴि एन्न *ungaḷ tāymoḷi enna*

41. My mothertongue is Hindi = என் தாய்மொழி இந்தி एन् तायमोऴि इन्दि *en tāymoḷi indi*

42. Do you know Tamil? = உங்களுக்கு தமிழ் புரியுமா उंग तमिऴ् पुरियुमा *ung Tamiḷ puriyumā*

43. I don't know Tamil = எனக்கு தமிழ் புரியாது एनक्कु तमिऴ् पुरियादु *enakku Tamiḷ puriyādu*

44. How do you say it in Tamil? = இதை தமிழில் எப்படிக்கூறுவது इदै तमिऴिल् एप्पडिक्कूरुवदु *idai Tamiḷil eppaḍikkūruvadu*

45. What does it mean? = அப்படி என்றால் என்ன एप्पडि एन्राल् एन्न *eppaḍi enrāl ennạ.*

46. Do you want coffee? = காப்பி வேணுமா? काप्पी वेणुमा *kappi veṇumā?*

47. No, I want tea = இல்லை, எனக்கு தேநீர் வேணும் इल्लै, एनक्कु तेनीर् वेणुम् *illai, enakku thenīr veṇum.* (வேணும் or வேண்டும்)

LESSON 8

TAMIL DICTIONARY OF

COMMON NOUNS
பொதுவான பெயர்ச்சொற்கள்
Potuvā<u>n</u>a peyarcco<u>r</u>kaḷ

TABLE 19 :

INDEX சுட்டு Cuṭṭu

8.1 ANIMALS, **Domestic / Farm** வீட்டு விலங்குகள் Vīṭṭu Vilaṅkukaḷ

8.2 ANIMALS, Wild காட்டு விலங்குகள் Kāṭṭu Vilaṅkukaḷ

8.3 INSECTS பூச்சிகள் Pūccikaḷ

8.4 BIRDS பறவைகள் Pa<u>r</u>avaikaḷ

8.5 THE BODY PARTS உடல் பாகங்கள் Uṭal pākaṅkaḷ

8.6 AILMENTS and BODY CONDITIONS வியாதிகளுக்கு மற்றும் உடல் நிலை Viyātikaḷukku Ma<u>r</u><u>r</u>um Uṭal nilai

8.7 CLOTHING, DRESS etc. ஆடை, உடை Āṭai, Uṭai

8.8 RELATIONS உறவுகள் U<u>r</u>avukaḷ

8.9 HOUSEHOLD THINGS வீட்டு உபயோக ப்பொருட்களுக்கு Vīṭṭu upayōka pporuṭkaḷukku

8.10 TOOLS உபகரணங்கள் Upakaraṇaṅkaḷ

8.11 FLOWERS பூக்கள் Pūkkaḷ

8.12 FRUITS பழங்கள் Pa<u>l</u>aṅkaḷ

8.23 VEGETABLES காய்கறிகள் Kāyka<u>r</u>ikaḷ

8.14 PLANTS தாவரங்கள் Tāvaraṅkaḷ

8.15 FOOD STUFF உணவு பொருள் Uṇavu poruḷ

8.16 SPICES மசாலா Macālā

8.17 MINERALS, METALS and JEWELS தாதுக்கள், உலோகங்கள் மற்றும் நகைகள் Tātukkaḷ, ulōkaṅkaḷ ma<u>r</u><u>r</u>um nakaikaḷ

8.18 MUSIC இசை Icai

8.19 PROFESSIONS தொழில்கள் To<u>l</u>ilkaḷ

8.20 BUSINESS வணிகம் Vaṇikam

8.21 WARFARE எதிரியின் மீது போர் தொடுத்தல் Etiriyi<u>n</u> mītu pōr toṭuttal

8.1 ANIMALS, Domastic / Farm

வீட்டு விலங்குகள் Vīṭṭu Vilaṅkukaḷ

Bitch	பெண் நாய் Peṇ nāy
Buffalo	எருமை Erumai
Bull, Bullock	எருது Erutu
Calf	கன்றுக்குட்டி Kaṉṟukkuṭṭi
Camel	ஒட்டகம் Oṭṭakam
Cat	பூனை Pūṉai
Colt	குதிரைக்குட்டி kutiraikkuṭṭi
Cow	பசு Pasu
Dog	நாய் Nāy
Donkey	கழுதை Kaḻutai
Ewe	பெண்ஆடு Peṇāṭu
Goat	வெள்ளாடு Veḷḷāṭu
Hare	குழி முயல் Kuḻi muyal
Horse	குதிரை Kutirai
Kitten	பூனை க்குட்டி Pūṉai kkuṭṭi
Lamb	செம்மறி ஆட்டு க்குட்டி Cem'maṟi āṭṭu kkuṭṭi
Lizard	பல்லி Palli
Mare	பெண்குதிரை Peṇkutirai
Mouse	சுண்டெலி Cuṇṭeli
Mule	கோவேறு கழுதை Kōvēṟu kaḻutai
Ox	எருது Erutu
Pig	பன்றி Paṉṟi
Puppy	நாய்க்குட்டி Nāykkuṭṭi
Rabbit	குழி முயல் Kuḻi muyal
Ram	ஆட்டுக்கடா āṭṭukkaṭā
Rat	எலி Eli

.

8.2 ANIMALS, Wild

காட்டு விலங்குகள் Kāṭṭu vilaṅkukaḷ

Alligator	முதலை Mutalai
Bat	வௌவால்Vauvāl

Bear	கரடி Karaṭi
Beast	மிருகம் Mirukam
Boa	மலை பாம்பு Malai pāmpu
Boar	கரடி Karaṭi
Cobra	நல்ல பாம்பு Nalla pāmpu, நாகம் Nākam
Crocodile	முதலை Mutalai
Deer	மான் Māṉ
Elephant	யானை Yāṉai
Fawn	இளமஞ்சள் Iḷamañcaḷ
Fish	மீன் Mīṉ
Fox	நரி Nari
Frog	தவளை Tavaḷai
Hippo	நீர்யானை Nīryāṉai
Jackal	குள்ளநரி Kuḷḷanari
Leopard	சிறுத்தை ப்புலி Ciṟuttai ppuli
Lion	சிங்கம் Ciṅkam
Mongoose	கீரி ப்பிள்ளை Kīri ppiḷḷai, கீரி Kīri
Monkey	குரங்கு Kuraṅku
Mosquito	கொசு Kocu
Panther	சிறுத்தை Ciṟuttai
Porcupine	முள்ளம்பன்றி Muḷḷampaṉṟi
Rhino	காண்டாமிருகம் Kāṇṭāmirukam
Snake	பாம்பு Pāmpu
Squirrel	அணில் Aṇil
Stag	ஆண் கலைமான் Āṇ kalaimāṉ
Tiger	புலி Puli
Turtle	கடல் ஆமை Kaṭal āmai
Wolf	ஓநாய் Ōnāy
Zebra	வரி க்குதிரை Vari kkutirai

.

8.3 INSECTS

பூச்சிகள் Pūccikaḷ

Ant	எறும்பு Eṟumpu

Bedbug	மூட்டைப்பூச்சி Mūṭṭaippūcci
Bee	தேனீ Tēṉī
Bookworm	புத்தகப்புழு Puttakappuḻu
Bug	பிழை Piḻai
Butterfly	வண்ணாத்தி பூச்சி Vaṇṇātti pūcci
Centipede	பூரான் போன்ற, பல கால்கள் உள்ள பூச்சி. Pūrāṉ pōṉṟa, pala kālkaḷ uḷḷa pūcci
Cockroach	கரப்பான் பூச்சி Karappāṉ pūcci
Crab	நண்டு Naṇṭu
Cricket	சிள்வண்டு Silvaṇṭu, சிள் வண்டு Ciḷ vaṇṭu
Earthworm	மண்புழு Maṇpuḻu
Flea	தெள்ளுபூச்சி Theḷḷupūcc i
Fly	ஈ ī
Glow worm	மின்மினி Minmini
Grasshopper	வெட்டுக்கிளி Veṭṭukkiḷi
Honey bee	தேனீ Tēṉī
Hornet	குளவி Kuḷavi
Insect	பூச்சி Pūcci
Locust	வெட்டுக்கிளி Veṭṭukkiḷi
Millipede	மரவட்டை Maravaṭṭai
Moth	தூசு Tūcu
Oyster	சிப்பி Cippi
Scorpion	தேள் Tēḷ
Silk worm	பட்டு ப்புழு Paṭṭu ppuḻu
Snail	நத்தை Nattai
Spider	சிலந்தி பூச்சி Cilanti pūcci
Termite	கறையான் Kaṟaiyāṉ
Worm	புழு Puḻu

.

8.4 BIRDS

பறவைகள் Paṟavaikaḷ

Blackbird	பிளாக்பேர்ட் Piḷākpērṭ (கருப்பு பறவை Karuppu paṟavai)
Blue bird	நீல ப்பறவை Nīla ppaṟavai

books-india.com

Chicken	கோழிக்குஞ்சு Kōl̲ikkuñcu
Cock	சேவல் Cēval
Crane	கொக்கு Kokku
Crow	காக்கை Kākkai
Dove	புறா Pur̲ā
Duck	வாத்து Vāttu
Eagle	கழுகு Kal̲uku
Flamingo	நாரை Nārai
Goose	வாத்து Vāttu
Hawk	பருந்து paruntu
Hen	பெட்டை க்கோழி Peṭṭai kkōl̲i
Heron	குருகு Kurugu,
Kite	பருந்து, கழுகு Paruntu, Kal̲uku
Owl	ஆந்தை Āntai
Parrot	கிளி Kiḷi
Partridge	கௌதாரி Kautāri
Pigeon	புறா Pur̲ā
Peacock	பெண் மயில் Peṇ mayil
Rooster	சேவல் Cēval
Sparrow	சிட்டு க்குருவி Ciṭṭu kkuruvi
Swan	அன்ன ப்பறவை An̲n̲a ppar̲avai
Woodpecker	மரங்கொத்தி Maraṅkotti

8.5 THE BODY PARTS

உடல் பாகங்கள் Uṭal pākaṅkaḷ

Abdomen	அடிவயிறு Aṭivayir̲u
Ankle	கணுக்கால் Kaṇukkāl
Anus	அபானம் Apān̲am, மலம் கழியும் வாய் Malam kal̲iyum vāy
Arm	கை Kai
Armpit	கக்கம் Kakkam
Artery	தமனி, நாடி taman̲i, nāḍī
Back	பின்புறம் pinpuram
Bald	வழுக்கை Val̲ukkai

Beak	பறவையலகு Paṟavaiyalaku
Beard	தாடி Tāṭi
Belly	உதரம் Utaram
Bellybutton	தொப்புள் Toppuḷ
Blood	இரத்தம் Irattam
Blood vessel	இரத்த க்குழல் Iratta kkuḻal
Bosom	மார்பகம் Mārpakam
Body	உடல் Uṭal
Brain	மூளை Mūḷai
Breath	சுவாசம் Cuvācam
Breast	மார்பகம் Mārpakam
Cadaver	சவம் Cavam, பிணம் Piṇam
Cartilage	குருத்தெலும்பு Kuruttelumpu
Cheek	கன்னம் Kaṉṉam
Chest	நெஞ்சு Neñcu
Chin	மோவாய்க்கட்டை Mōvāykkaṭṭai
Corpse	சவம் Cavam, பிணம் Piṇam
Egg	முட்டை Muṭṭai
Ear	காது Kātu
Elbow	முழங்கை Muḻaṅkai
Eye	கண் Kaṇ
Eyebrow	புருவம் Puruvam
Eyelash	கண்ணிமை Kaṇṇimai
Eyelid	கண்மடல் Kaṇmdal
Face	முகம் Mukam
Feather	இறகு Iṟaku
Feet	அடி Aṭi
Finger	விரல் Viral
Fist	முட்டி muṭṭi
Foetus	கரு Karul
Fore-finger	சுட்டு விரல் suṭṭu viral

Forehead	நெற்றி Neṟṟi, neṭṭi
Gum	முரசு murasu
Hair	மயிர் Mayir, உரோமம் uromam, கேசம் kesam
Hand	கை Kai
Head	தலை Talai
Heart	இதயம் Itayam
Heel	குதிக்கால் Kutikkāl
Hip	இடுப்பு Iṭuppu
Hoof	குளம்பு Kuḷampu
Horn	கொம்பு kompu
Index-finger	சுட்டு விரல் Cuṭṭu viral
Intestine	குடல் Kuṭal
Jaw	தாடை Tāṭai
Joint	பூட்டு Pūṭṭu, கூட்டு Kūṭṭu
Kidney	சிறுநீரகம் Ciṟunīrakam
Knee	முழங்கால் மூட்டு Muḻaṅkāl mūṭṭu
Knot	முடிச்சு Muṭiccu
Lap	மடி madi
Life	உயிர் Uyir
Limb	அங்கம் Aṅkam
Lip	உதடு Utaṭu
Little-finger	சிற்று விரல் Ciṟu viral
Liver	கல்லீரல் Kallīral
Lungs	நுரையீரல்கள் Nuraiyīralkaḷ
Marrow	பலம் Palam
Meat	இறைச்சி Iṟaicci
Menses	மாதவிடாய் Mātaviṭāy, பூப்பு pūppu
Middle-finger	நடு விரல் Naṭu viral
Moustaches	மீசைகள் Mīcaikaḷ

Mouth	வாய் Vāy
Muscle	தசை Tacai
Nail	**நகம்** Nagam
Navel	தொப்பூழ் Toppūḻ, தொப்பள் Toppaḷ
Neck	கழுத்து Kaḻuttu
Nerve	நரம்பு Narampu
Nipple	முலைக்காம்பு Mulaikkāmpu
Nose	மூக்கு mukku
Nostril	நாசித்துவாரம் Nācittuvāram
Palm	உள்ளங்கை Uḷḷaṅkai
Penis	ஆண்குறி Āṇkuṟi
Ponytail	குதிரைவால் Kutiraivāl
Poo	மலம் Malam
Pore	நுண் துளை Nuṇ tuḷai
Pulse	நாடித்துடிப்பு Nāṭittuṭippu
Rib	விலா எலும்பு Vilā elumpu
Ring-finger	மோதிர விரல் Mōtira viral
Rump	பிட்டம் Piṭṭam
Saliva	உமிழ் நீர் Umiḻ nīr, எச்சில் Eccil
Semen	விந்து Vintu
Shoulder	தோள் Tōḷ
Sight	பார்வை Pārvai
Skeleton	எலும்பக்கூடு Elumpakkūṭu
Skin	தோல் Tōl
Skull	மண்டையோடு Maṇṭaiyōṭu
Sole	தனித்த Taṉitta
Soul	ஆத்மா Ātmā
Spine	முதுகெலும்பு Mutukelumpu
Spit	உமிழ் நீர் Umiḻ nīr
Stomach	இரைப்பை Iraippai

Tail	வால் Vāl	
Tears	கண்ணீர் Kaṇṇīr	
Teeth	பற்கள் Paṟkaḷ	
Testicle	அண்டம் Aṇṭam, விதை Vitai	
Thigh	தொடை Toṭai	
Throat	தொண்டை Toṇṭai	
Thumb	கட்டைவிரல் Kaṭṭaiviral	
Tongue	நாக்கு Nākku	
Trunk	முண்டம் Muṇṭam	
Uterus	கருப்பை Karuppai	
Vagina	உறை Uṟai, யோனி Yōṇi, பெண்ணுறுப்பு Peṇṇuṟuppu	
Vein	நரம்பு Narampu	
Vision	பார்வை Pārvai	
Waist	இடுப்பு Iṭuppu	
Wool	பலனற்ற பேச்சு Palaṉaṟṟa pēccu	
Womb	கருப்பை Karuppai	
Wrist	மணிக்கட்டு Maṇikkaṭṭu	

8.6 AILMENTS and BODY CONDITIONS
வியாதிகளுக்கு மற்றும் உடல் நிலை Viyātikaḷukku Maṟṟum Uṭal nilai

Acidity	அமிலத்தன்மை Amilattaṉmai	
Asthma	ஆஸ்துமா Āstumā	
Baldness	வழுக்கை Vaḻukkai	
Belching	ஏப்பம் Ēppam	
Bleeding	இரத்தம் வழிதல் Irattam vaḻital	
Blindness	குருட்டுத்தன்மை Kuruṭṭuttaṉmai	
Boil	கட்டி Kaṭṭi	
Bone	எலும்பு Elumpu	
Burns	தீக்காயங்கள் Tīkkāyaṅkaḷ	
Cancer	புற்றுநோய் Puṟṟunōy	

Chill	குளிர் Kuḷir
Constipation	மலச்சிக்கல் Malaccikkal
Cough	இருமல் Irumal
Craze	மதிமாற்றம் Matimāṟṟam
Diabetes	நீரிழிவு நோய் Nīriḻivu nōy
Diarrhoea	வயிற்றுப்போக்கு Vayiṟṟuppōkku
Disease	நோய் Nōy
Dwarf	குள்ள Kuḷḷa
Dysentry	வயிற்றுளைச்சல் Vayiṟṟuḷaiccal
Eczema	சிரங்கு Ciraṅku
Epilepsy	வலிப்பு Valippu
Giddiness	மயக்கம் Mayakkam
Headache	தலை வலி Talai vali
Health	உடல்நலம் Uṭalnalam
Heart stroke	இதய ஸ்ட்ரோக் Itaya sṭrōk, இதய பக்கவாதம் Itaya pakkavātam
Hiccup	விக்கல் Vikkal
Hunchback	கூன் முதுகு Kūṉ mutuku
Hurt	காயம் Kāyam, காயப்படுத்த Kāyappaṭutta
Indigestion	அஜீரணம் Ajīraṇam
Influenza	குளிர் கபசுரம் Kuḷir kapacuram
Injury	காயம் Kāyam
Insomnia	தூக்கம் இன்மை Tūkkam iṉmai
Itching	அரிப்பு Arippu
Jaundice	மஞ்சட் காமாலை நோய் Mañcaṭ kāmālai nōy
Leprosy	பெருவியாதி Peruviyāti, தொழுநோய் Toḻunōy, குஷ்டம் kuṣṭam
Lunacy	பைத்தியம் Paittiyam
Madness	பித்து பிடித்தவர் Pittu piṭittavar
Obese	பருமனான Parumaṉāṉa
Pain	வலி Vali
Paralysis	முடக்கு வாதம் Muṭakku vātam

Pimple	பரு Paru
Piles	மூல வியாதி Mūla viyāti
Plague	கொள்ளை நோய் Ko||ai nōy
Pneumonia	கபவாதம் Kapavātam
Pus	சீழ் Cīḻ
Rheumatism	கீல் வாதம் Kīl vātam
Sickness	வியாதி Viyāti
Sleeplessness	தூக்கமற்ற Tūkkamaṟṟa
Sleepy	மந்தமான Mantamāṉa
Sneeze	தும்மல் dummal
Sore	புண் Puṇ
Sprain	சுளுக்கு Cuḷukku
Stool	மலம் Malam
Sweat	வியர்வை Viyarvai
Swelling	வீக்கம் Vīkkam
Tears	கண்ணீர் Kaṇṇīr
Thirst	தாகம் Tākam
Tuberculosis	க்ஷயரோகம் Kṣayarōkam
Urine	சிறுநீர் Ciṟunīr
Vomit	வாந்தி Vāndhi
Wart	மறு maru, பாலுண்ணி Pāluṇṇi
Wound	காயம் Kāyam
Yawn	கொட்டாவி Koṭṭāvi

8.7 CLOTHING, DRESS etc.
ஆடை, உடை Āṭai, Uṭai

Belt	அரைக்கச்சு Araikkaccu
Blanket	போர்வை Pōrvai, துப்பட்டி Tuppaṭṭi
Button	பொத்தான் Pottāṉ
Cap	தொப்பி Toppi

Cloth	துணி Tuṇi
Coat	மேல்சட்டை Mēlcaṭṭai
Colour	நிறம் Niṟam
Cotton	பருத்தி Parutti
Glove	கையுறை Kaiyuṟai
Gown	பெண்களின் மேலாடை Peṇkaḷiṉ mēlāṭai
Hat	தொப்பி toppi
Jacket	மேலுறை Mēluṟai, மேல்சட்டை Mēlcaṭṭai
Lace	பின்னற்பட்டி Piṉṉaṟpaṭṭi
Measurement	அளவு Aḷavu
Needle	ஊசி Ūci
Pocket	சட்டைப்பை Caṭṭaippai
Scarf	உத்திரியம் Uttiriyam
Sheet	தாள Tāḷ
Shirt	சட்டை Caṭṭai
Silk	பட்டு Paṭṭu
Size	அளவு Aḷavu
Skirt	பாவாடை Pāvāṭai
Sleeve	சட்டையின் கை Caṭṭaiyiṉ kai
Style	பாங்கு Pāṅku
Thread	நூல் Nūl
Towel	துடைக்கும் துணி Tuṭaikkum tuṇi
Turban	தலைப்பாகை Talaippākai
Uniform	சீருடை Cīruṭai
Wool	கம்பளி Kampaḷi
Yarn	நூல் Nūl

8.8 RELATIONS

உறவுகள் Uṟavukaḷ

Adopted	தத்தெடுத்த Tatteṭutta

books-india.com

Aunt	அத்தை Attai, மாமி Māmi, சித்தி Citti
Brother	தம்பி Tampi, சகோதரன் Cakōtaraṉ
Brother, younger	தம்பி tampi
Brother, elder	அண்ணண் Aṇṇan
Brotherhood	சகோதரத்துவம் Cakōtarattuvam
Brother' son	அண்ணன் மகன் Aṇṇaṉ makaṉ
Brother's daughter	சகோதரனின் மகள் Cakōtaraṉiṉ makaḷ
Brother's wife	சகோதரனின் மனைவி Cakōtaraṉiṉ maṉaivi, அண்ணி aṇṇi
Couple	ஜோடி Jōṭi
Daughter	மகள் Makaḷ
Daughter-in-law	மருமகள் Marumakaḷ
Family	குடும்பம் Kuṭumpam
Father	தந்தை Tantai
Fatherhood	தந்தை Tantai
Fatherly	அப்பாவுக்குரிய Appāvukkuriya
Father-in-law	மாமனார் Māmaṉār
Father's brother	தந்தையின் சகோதரர் Tantaiyiṉ cakōtarar
Father's father	தந்தையின் தந்தை Tantaiyiṉ tantai; தாத்தா Tāttā
Father's mother	தந்தையின் அம்மா Tantaiyiṉ am'mā, பாட்டி Pāṭṭi
Father's sister	தந்தையின் சகோதரி Tantaiyiṉ cakōtari
Forefathers	முன்னோர்கள் Muṉṉōrkaḷ
Friend	நண்பர் Naṇpar
Grand-daughter	பெயர்த்தி Peyartti
Grandson	பெயரன் Peyaraṉ
Husband	கணவன் Kaṇavaṉ
Husband's brother	கணவரின் அண்ணன் Kaṇavariṉ aṇṇaṉ
Husband's sister	கணவரின் சகோதரி Kaṇavariṉ cakōtari
Lord	கடவுள் Kaṭavuḷ
Love	அன்பு Aṉpu
Lover	(m. boyfriend) காதலன் Kātalaṉ, (f. girlfriend) காதலி Kātali

books-india.com

Mistress	வீட்டு எஜமானி Vīṭṭu ejamāṉi, வைப்பாட்டி Vaippāṭṭi
Mother	தாய் Tāy
Motherhood	தாய்மை Tāymai
Motherly	தாய்க்குரிய Tāykkuriya
Mother-in-law	மாமியார் Māmiyār
Mother's brother	தாயின் சகோதரர் Tāyiṉ cakōtarar, மாமன்Māman
Mother's mother	அம்மா அம்மா Am'mā am'mā, பாட்டி Pāṭṭi
Mother's sister	தாயின் சகோதரி Tāyiṉ cakōtari, அன்னம்மா Annamma
Neighbor	அண்டை வீட்டுக்காரர் Aṇṭai vīṭṭukkārar
Niece	மகள் Makaḷ, தம்பி மகள் Tampi makaḷ, தங்கை மகள் Taṅkai makaḷ
Pupil	மாணவன் Māṇavaṉ
Relation	உறவு Uṟavu
Relative	உறவினர் Uṟaviṉar
Sister	சகோதரி Cakōtari
Sister's son	அக்காள் மகன் Akkāḷ makaṉ
Sister-in-law	மைத்துனி Maittuṉi
Sisterly	சகோதரி போன்ற Cakōtari pōṉṟa
Sister's husband	சகோதரியின் கணவர் Cakōtariyiṉ kaṇavar
Son	மகன் Makaṉ
Son-in-law	மருமகன் Marumakaṉ
Stranger	அந்நியன் Anniyaṉ
Wife	மனைவி Maṉaivi

8.9 HOUSEHOLD THINGS

வீட்டு உபயோக ப்பொருட்களுக்கு Vīṭṭu upayōka pporuṭkaḷukku

Bag	பை Pai
Basket	கூடை Kūṭai
Bed	படுக்கை Paṭukkai
Blanket	துப்பட்டி Tuppaṭṭi
Bottle	புட்டி Puṭṭi

Bowl	கிண்ணம்	Kiṇṇam
Box	பெட்டி	Peṭṭi
Broom	துடைப்பம்	Tuṭaippam
Brush	துலக்கி Tulakki, துரிகை	Turikai
Bucket	இறைசால்	Iṟaicāl
Button	பொத்தான்	Pottāṉ
Candle	மெழுகுவர்த்தி	Meḻukuvartti
Chair	நாற்காலி	Nāṟkāli
Comb	சீப்பு	Cīppu
Cot	கட்டில்	Kaṭṭil
Cup	கிண்ணம்	Kiṇṇam
Dictionary	அகராதி	Akarāti
Dish	வட்டில்	Vaṭṭil
Fuel	எரிபொருள்	Eriporuḷ
Furniture	மரச்சாமான்	Maraccāmāṉ
Glass	கண்ணாடி	Kaṇṇāṭi
Glue	பசை	Pacai
Hearth	அடுப்பு	Aṭuppu
Key	சாவி Cāvi, திறப்பு	thirappu
Knife	கைப்பிடியுள்ள கத்தி	Kaippiṭiyuḷḷa katti
Lamp	விளக்கு	Viḷakku
Lock	குஞ்சம் Kuñcam, பூட்டு	Pūṭṭu
Mat	பாய்	Pāy
Mirror	கண்ணாடி Kaṇṇāṭi ஆடி	Āṭi
Needle	ஊசி	Ūci
Oven	அடுப்பு	Aṭuppu
Paper	காகிதம்	Kākitam
Pen	பேனா	Pēṉā
Pillow	தலையணை	Talaiyaṇai
Plate	வட்டில் Vaṭṭil தட்டு	Taṭṭu

Pot	பாத்திரம் Pāttiram, பானை Pāṉai
Rope	கயிறு Kayiṟu
Soap	சோப்பு Cōppu
Spoon	கரண்டி Karaṇṭi
Stove	அடுப்பு Aṭuppu
String	நூல் Nūl
Swing	ஊஞ்சல் ūñcal
Table	மேசை Mēcai
Thread	நூல் Nūl
Umbrella	குடை Kuṭai
Wire	கம்பி Kampi
Wok	வோக்கில் Vōkkil
Yarn	நூல் Nūl

8.10 TOOLS
உபகரணங்கள் Upakaraṇaṅkaḷ

Anvil	பட்டறைக்கல் Paṭṭaṟaikkal
Awl	குத்தூசி Kuttūci
Axe	கோடாரி Kōṭāri
Blade	ப்ளேடு Pḷēṭu
Chisel	உளி Uḷi
Clamp	படி பற்ற Paṭi paṟṟa
Compass	திசை காட்டி Ticai kāṭṭi
Drill	துறப்பணம் Tuṟappaṇam
Hammer	சுத்தி Cutti
Knife	கத்தி Katti
Plough	ஏர் Ēr, உழு Uḻu
Razor	சவரக்கத்தி Cavarakkatti
Saw	ஈர்வாள் Irval
Scissors	கத்தரிக்கோல் Kattarikkōl

books-india.com

Spade மண்வெட்டி Maṇvetṭi

Syringe இறை Iṟai

8.11 FLOWERS

பூக்கள் Pūkkaḷ

Bud மொட்டு Moṭṭu

Chrysanthemum சாமந்தி Cāmanti, செவ்வந்தி Cevvanti

Flower பூ Pū

Fragrance நறுமணம் Naṟumaṇam

Jasmine மல்லிகை Mallikai

Lotus தாமரை Tāmarai

Marigold மேரிகோல்டு Mērikōlṭu, சாமந்தி Cāmanti

Nectar அமிழ்தம் Amiḻtam, தேன் Tēṉ

Night Jasmine இரவு மல்லிகை Iravu Mallikai

Petal பூவிதழ் Pūvitaḻ

Pollen மகரந்த தூள் Makaranta tūḷ

Rose ரோஜா Rōjā

Sunflower சூரியகாந்தி Cūriyakānti

8.12 FRUITS

பழங்கள் Paḻaṅkaḷ

Almond பாதாம் Pātām

Apple ஒரு பழம் Oru paḻam, ஆப்பிள் Āppiḷ

Banana வாழை Vāḻai

Chestnut கஷ்கொட்டை Kaṣkoṭṭai

Coconut தேங்காய் Tēṅkāy

Figs அத்தி Atti

Grapes திராட்சை Tirāṭcai

Guava கொய்யா Koyyā

Lemon எலுமிச்சை Elumiccai

Mango	மாங்கனி Māṅkaṉi
Melon	முலாம்பழம் Mulāmpaḻam
Mulberry	முசுக்கட்டடை செடி Mucukkaṭṭaṭai ceṭi, முசுக்கொட்டை Mucukkoṭṭai
Orange	நாரத்தை Nārattai, ஆரஞ்சு பழம் Āravcu paḻam
Papaya	பப்பாளிப்பழம் Pappāḷippaḻam
Pineapple	அன்னாசி Aṉṉāci
Plum	பிளம் Piḷam
Pomegranate	மாதுளை பழம் Mātuḷai paḻam
Tamarind	புளி Puḷi
Walnut	வாதுமை கொட்டை வகை Vātumai koṭṭai vakai
Watermelon	முலாம் பழம் Mulām paḻam, தர்பூசணி Tarpūcaṇi

8.13 VEGETABLES
காய்கறிகள் Kāykaṟikaḷ

Beans	அவரை Avarai
Bittergourd	பாகற்காய் Pākaṟkāy
Cabbage	முட்டை கோசு Muṭṭai kōcu
Carrot	முள்ளங்கி போன்ற கிழங்கு Muḷḷaṅki pōṉṟa kiḻaṅku, கேரட் Kēraṭ
Cashew	முந்திரி Muntiri
Cauliflower	பூ க்கோசு Pū kkōcu
Celentro	கொத்துமல்லி Kottumalli
Chilli pepper	மிளகாய் Miḷakāy
Coconut	தேங்காய் Tēṅkāy
Coriander	கொத்துமல்லி Kottumalli
Cucumber	வெள்ளரிக்காய் Veḷḷarikkāy
Eggplant	கத்திரிக்காய் Kattirikkāy
Garlic	பூண்டு Pūṇṭu
Gourd	சுரைக்காய் Curaikkāy
Jackfruit	பலாப்பழம் Palāppaḻam
Lemon	எலுமிச்சை Elumiccai

Lotus root	தாமரை	Tāmarai
Mint	புதினா	Putiṉā
Okra	வெண்டைக்காய்	Veṇṭaikkāy
Onion	வெங்காயம்	Veṅkāyam
Peanuts	வேர்கடலை	Vērkaṭalai
Peas	பட்டாணி	Paṭṭāṇi
Potato	உருளைக்கிழங்கு	Uruḷaikkiḻaṅku
Pumpkin	பரங்கி க்காய்	Paraṅki kkāy
Radish	முள்ளங்கி கிழங்கு	Muḷḷaṅki kiḻaṅku
Spinach	பசலை கீரை	Pacalai kīrai
Sugarcane	கரும்பு	Karumpu
Tomato	தக்காளி	Takkāḷi
Turnip	நூல்கோல்	Nūlkōl
Vegetables	காய்கறிகள்	Kāykaṟikaḷ

8.14 PLANTS
தாவரங்கள் Tāvaraṅkaḷ

Bamboo	மூங்கில்	Mūṅkil
Banyan	ஆலமரம்	Ālamaram
Bark	மரப்பட்டை	Marappaṭṭai
Branch	கிளை	Kiḷai
Bud	மொட்டு	Moṭṭu
Bulb	கிழங்கு	Kiḻaṅku
Chlorophyll	(இலைப்) பச்சையம்	(Ilaip) paccaiyam
Climber	படரும் கொடி	Paṭarum koṭi
Creeper	படரும் கொடி	Paṭarum koṭi
Farm	பண்ணை	Paṇṇai
Flower	பூ	Pū
Forest	காடு	Kāṭu
Grass	புல்	Pul

Green	பசுமையான Pacumaiyāṉa
Guava	கொய்யா Koyyā
Gum	கோந்து Kōntu
Juice	சாறு Cāṟu
Leaf	இலை Ilai
Lemon	எலுமிச்சை Elumiccai
Mango	மாங்கனி Māṅkaṉi
Palm	பனை Paṉai, தென்ன Teṉṉai
Peel	பழத்தோல் Paḻattōl
Pine	தேவதாரு Tēvatāru
Plant	தாவரம் Tāvaram
Pollen	மகரந்த தூள் Makaranta tūḷ
Root	வேர் Vēr
Seed	விதை Vitai
Shade	நிழல் Niḻal
Stem	காம்பு Kāmpu
Tamarind	புளி Puḷi
Teak	தேக்கு மரம் Tēkku maram
Thorn	முள் Muḷ
Tree	மரம் Maram
Tuber	கிழங்கு Kiḻaṅku
Vine	படரும் கொடி Paṭarum koṭi
Wood	மரம் Maram

8.15 FOOD STUFF
உணவு பொருள் Uṇavu poruḷ

Barley	வாற்கோதுமை Vāṟkōtumai
Beverage	பானம் Pāṉam
Bread	ரொட்டி Roṭṭi
Butter	வெண்ணெய் Veṇṇey
Butter ghee	நெய் Ney

Buttermilk	மோர்	Mōr
Cheese	பாலாடைக்கட்டி	Pālāṭaikkaṭṭi
Chickpeas	சுண்டல்	Cuṇṭal
Coffee	காபி	Kāpi
Corn	நவதானியம்	Navatāṉiyam
Cream	பாலேடு	Pālēṭu
Drink	பானம்	pāṉam
Flour	மாவு	Māvu
Food	உணவு	Uṇavu
Grain	விதை	Vitai
Honey	தேன்	Tēṉ
Ice	பனி, பனிக்கட்டி	Paṉi, Paṉikkaṭṭi
Kidney beans	மொச்சா	Mocca
Kitchen	சமையல் அறை	Camaiyal aṟai
Lentil	துவரம் பருப்பு, அவரை வகை	Tuvaram paruppu, Avarai vakai
Marmalade	ஆரஞ்சு பழ பாகு	Ārañcu paḷa pāku
Meat	இறைச்சி	Iṟaicci
Milk	பால்	Pāl
Mung green	பச்சை பயிறு	Paccai payiṟu
Oil	எண்ணெய்	Eṇṇey
Paddy	நெல்	Nel
Peas	பட்டாணி	Paṭṭāṇi
Pickle	ஊறுகாய்	Ūṟukāy
Rice	அரிசி	Arici
Salt	உப்பு	Uppu
Samosa	சமோசா	Camōcā
Sorghum	சோள பயிர் வகை	Cōḷa payir vakai
Sugar	சர்க்கரை	Carkkarai
Sweets	இனிப்பு	Iṉippu
Vinegar	காடி	Kāṭi

Wheat	கோதுமை Kōtumai
Water	தண்ணீர் Taṇṇīr
Wine	மது Matu, சாராயம் Cārāyam
Yougrt	தயிர் Tayir

8.16 SPICES
மசாலா Macālā

Anise	சோம்பு Cōmpu
Asafoetida	பெருங்காயம் Peruṅkāyam
Basil	ஓமம Ōmam
Betel-nut	பாக்கு Pākku
Cardamom	ஏலக்காய் Ēlakkāy
Cinnamon	இலவங்க பட்டை Ilavaṅka paṭṭai
Clove	லவங்கம் Lavaṅkam
Coriander	கொத்துமல்லி Kottumalli
Cumin	சீரகம் Cīrakam
Garlic	பூண்டு Pūṇṭu
Ginger	இஞ்சி Iñci
Hot spice	காரமான மசாலா Kāramāṉa macālā
Linseed	ஆளி விதை Āḷi vitai
Mango powder	மா Mā poṭi
Mint	புதினா Putiṉā
Mustard	கடுகு Kaṭuku
Nutmeg	ஜாதிக்காய் Jātikkāy
Parsley	வோக்கோச
Pepper	மிளகு Miḷaku
Pepper, black	கருப்பு மிளகு Karuppu miḷaku
Spice	மசாலா macālā
Saffron	குங்குமப்பூ Kuṅkumappū
Salt	உப்பு Uppu

Sugar சர்க்கரை Carkkarai

Tamarind புளி Puḷi

Turmeric மஞ்சள் Mañcaḷ

Walnut வாதுமை கொட்டை வகை Vātumai koṭṭai vakai

8.17 MINERALS, METALS and JEWELS

தாதுக்கள், உலோகங்கள் மற்றும் நகைகள் Tātukkaḷ, ulōkaṅkaḷ maṟṟum nakaikaḷ

Coal நிலக்கரி Nilakkari

Coral பவழம் Pavaḻam

Brass பித்தளை Pittaḷai

Copper தாமிரம் Tāmiram, செம்பு Cempu

Diamond வைரம் Vairam

Gold தங்கம் Taṅkam

Iron இரும்பு Irumpu

Jade பச்சை மாணிக்க கல் Paccai māṇikka kal

Jewel ஆபரணம் Āparaṇam

Lead தலைமை Talaimai

Marble சலவைக்கல் Calavaikkal

Mercury பாதரசம் Pātaracam

Mica அபிரகம் Apirakam

Mine சுரங்கம் Curaṅkam

Mineral தாது Tātu, கனிய Kaṉiya

Opal ஒருவகை மாணிக்ககல் Oruvakai māṇikkakal

Pearl முத்து Muttu

Ruby கெம்பு Kempu, மாணிக்கம் Māṇikkam

Sapphire நீல கல் Nīla kal

Silver வெள்ளி Veḷḷi

Soil மண் Maṇ

Sulphur கந்தகம் Kantakam

Tin தகரம் Takaram

Topaz புஷ்பராகம் Puṣparākam

Zinc துத்தநாகம் Tuttanākam

8.18 MUSIC
இசை Icai

Ascending ஏறுமுகம் Ēṟumukam

Bell மணி Maṇi

Bugle ஊதுகுழல் Ūtukuḻal

Conch சங்கு Caṅku

Cymbal ஜாலரா Jālarā

Descending இறங்கு Iṟaṅku

Devotional song ஆன்மீக கீதம் Āṉmīka Kītam

Drum தபலா Tapalā, முரசு Muracu

Flute புல்லாங்குழல் Pullāṅkuḻal

Guitar indian வீணை Vīṇai

Melody இன்னிசை Iṉṉicai

Note குறிப்பு Kuṟippu

Prayer பிரார்த்தனை Pirārttaṉai

Rhythm தாளம் Tāḷam

Song கீதம் Kītam

Tambourine டாம்பரின் Ṭāmpariṉ

Tempo போக்கு Pōkku

Violin பிடில் Piṭil, வயலின் Vayaliṉ

Whistle ஊதல் Ūtal

8.19 PROFESSIONS
தொழில்கள் Toḻilkaḷ

Actor நடிகன் Naṭikaṉ

Actress நடிகை Naṭikai

Advocate வழக்கறிஞர் Vaḻakkaṟiñar

Artist ஓவியன் Ōviyaṉ

Assassin கொலைபாதகன் Kolaipātakaṉ, கொலையாளி Kolaiyāḷi

Barber நாவிதன் Nāvitaṉ

Blacksmith கருமான் Karumāṉ

Boatman படகோட்டி Paṭakōṭṭi

Broker தரகன் Tarakaṉ

Butcher கசாப்புக்காரன் Kacāppukkāraṉ

Butler உக்கிராணக்காரன் Ukkirāṇakkāraṉ

Carpenter தச்சன் Taccan, மரவேலை செய்வோன் Maravēlai ceyvōṉ

Cashier பணம் வாங்கவும் கொடுக்கவும் செய்பவர் Paṇam vāṅkavum koṭukkavum ceypavar

Chemist ரசவாதி Racavāti

Clerk எழுத்தர் Eḻuttar

Confectioner மிட்டாய் செய்பவர் Miṭṭāy ceypavar

Constable காவலர் Kāvalar

Cook சமையற்காரர் Camaiyaṟkārar

Dancer நடன கலைஞர் Naṭaṉa kalaiñar

Dentist பல் மருத்துவர் Pal maruttuvar

Doctor வைத்தியர் vaittiyar

Editor ஆசிரியர் Āciriyar

Engineer பொறியாளர் Poṟiyāḷar

Examiner பரீட்சிப்பவர் Parīṭcippavar

Farmer விவசாயி Vivacāyi

Fisherman மீனவர் Mīṉavar

Florist பூ வியாபாரி Pū viyāpāri

Gardener தோட்டக்காரன் Tōṭṭakkāraṉ

Goldsmith தட்டான் Taṭṭāṉ

Guard காவலன் Kāvalaṉ

Inspector காவல் துறை மேலாளர் Kāval tuṟai mēlāḷar

Jeweler நகை வணிகர் Nakai vaṇikar

Lawyer	வழக்குரைஞர்	Vaḻakkuraiñar
Magician	வித்தைக்காரர்	Vittaikkārar
Manager	மேலாளர்	Mēlāḷar
Mason	கொல்லத்து காரர்	Kollattu kārar
Merchant	வியாபாரி	Viyāpāri
Messenger	தூதன்	Tūtaṉ
Midwife	மருத்துவச்சி	Maruttuvacci
Milkman	பால்காரர்	Pālkārar
Novelist	நாவலாசிரியர்	Nāvalāciriyar
Nurse	செவிலி	Cevili
Painter	ஓவியர்	Ōviyar
Peon	வேலையாள்	Vēlaiyāḷ
Photographer	நிழற் படம் எடுப்பவர	Niḻaṟ paṭam eṭuppavar
Physician	மருத்துவர்	Maruttuvar
Poet	கவிஞன்	Kaviñaṉ
Police	காவல்துறை Kāvaltuṟai, போலீஸ்	Pōlīs
Politician	அரசியல்வாதி	Araciyalvāti
Postman	தபால்காரர்	Tapālkārar
Priest	மதகுரு	Matakuru
Printer	அச்சுப்பொறி	Accuppoṟi
Publisher	பிரசுரிப்பவர்	Piracurippavar
Retailer	சில்லறை விற்பனையாளர்	Cillaṟai viṟpaṉaiyāḷar
Sailor	மாலுமி Mālumi, கப்பலோட்டி	Kappalōṭṭi,
Sculptor	சிற்பி	Ciṟpi
Shopkeeper	கடைக்காரர்	Kaṭaikkārar
Sorcerer	மந்திரவாதி	Mantiravāti
Student	மாணவர்	Māṇavar
Surgeon	அறுவை சிகிச்சை திபுணர்	Aṟuvai cikiccai nibunar
Tailor	தையற்காரர்	Taiyaṟkārar
Teacher	ஆசிரியர்	Āciriyar

Treasurer	பொக்கிஷதாரர்	Pokkiṣatārar
Washerman	துணி வெளுப்பவர்	Tuṇi veḷuppavar
Weaver	நெசவாளர்	Necavāḷar

8.20 BUSINESS
வணிகம் Vaṇikam

Account	கணக்கு	Kaṇakku
Accountant	கணக்கர்	Kaṇakkar
Advancement	உயர்வு	Uyarvu
Advantage	நன்மை	Naṉmai
Adverse	விரோதமான	Virōtamāṉa
Advertisement	விளம்பரம்	Viḷamparam
Annual	வருடாந்திர	Varuṭāntira
Annuity	ஆண்டு சந்தா	Āṇṭu cantā
Annulment	இல்லாததாக செய்தல்	Illātatāka ceytal
Application	விண்ணப்பம்	Viṇṇappam
Assistant	உதவியாளர்	Utaviyāḷar
Average	சராசரி	Carācari
Bank	வங்கி	Vaṅki
Bankrupt	திவாலான Tivālāṉa, ஓட்டாண்டி	Ōṭṭāṇṭi
Broker	தரகன்	Tarakaṉ
Brokerage	தரகு	Taraku
Business	வேலை	Vēlai
Businessman	தொழிலதிபர்	Toḻilatipar
Buyer	விலைக்கு வாங்குபவர்	Vilaikku vāṅkupavar
Capital	மூலதனம்	Mūlataṉam
Cash	பணம்	Paṇam
Charges	கட்டணங்கள்	Kaṭṭaṇaṅkaḷ
Clerk	எழுத்தர்	Eḻuttar
Coin	நாணயம்	Nāṇayam

Commerce	வர்த்தகம்	Varttakam
Court	நீதிமன்றம்	Nītimaṉṟam
Customer	வாடிக்கையாளர்	Vāṭikkaiyāḷar
Company	நிறுவனம்	Niṟuvaṉam
Consumer	நுகர்வோர்	Nukarvōr
Customer	வாடிக்கையாளர்	Vāṭikkaiyāḷar
Credit	கடன்	Kaṭaṉ
Creditor	கடன் கொடுத்தவர்	Kaṭaṉ koṭuttavar
Current	தற்போதைய	Taṟpōtaiya
Currency	நாணய	Nāṇaya
Daily	தினசரி	Tiṉacari
Debt	கடன்	Kaṭaṉ
Demand	தேவை	Tēvaiya
Deposit	வைப்பு	Vaippu
Depreciation	மதிப்பிறக்கம் தேய்மானம்	Matippiṟakkam tēymāṉam
Discount	தள்ளுபடி	Taḷḷupaṭi
Document	பத்திரம்	Pattiram
Draft	வரைவு	Varaivu
Duty	வரி	Vari
Earnings	சம்பாத்தியம்	Campāttiyam
Economy	பொருளாதாரம்	Poruḷātāram
Electricity	மின்சாரம்	Miṉcāram
Employee	பணியாளர்	Paṇiyāḷar
Employer	முதலாளி	Mutalāḷi
Endowment	நன்கொடை நிறுவல்	Naṉkoṭai niṟuval
Exchange	பரிவர்த்தனை	Parivarttaṉai
Expense	செலவு	Celavu
Export	ஏற்றுமதி	Ēṟṟumati
Factory	தொழிற்சாலை	Toḻiṟcālai
Finance	நிதி	Niti

books-india.com

Financier	நிதியாளர் Nitiyāḷar
Fixed	நிலையான Nilaiyāṉa
Foreign	வெளியுறவு Veḷiyuṟavu
Fraud	மோசடி Mōcaṭi
Freight	சரக்கு Carakku
Fund	நிதி Niti
Goods	சரக்கு Carakku
Gross	மொத்த Motta
Import	இறக்குமதி Iṟakkumati
Income	வருமானம் Varumāṉam
Industry	தொழில் துறை Toḻil tuṟai
Inflation	பணவீக்கம் Paṇavīkkam
Insurance	காப்புறுதி Kāppuṟuti
Job	வேலை Vēlai,
Labour	உழைப்பு Uḻaippu
Labourer	உழைப்பாளி Uḻaippāḷi
Land	நிலம் Nilam
Ledger	பேரேடு Pērēṭu
Legal	சட்ட Caṭṭa
Letter	கடிதம் Kaṭitam
Loan	கடன் Kaṭaṉ
Lock	பூட்டு Pūṭṭu
Locker	பெட்டகம் Peṭṭakam
Loss	இழப்பு Iḻappu
Management	மேலாண்மை Mēlāṇmai
Manipulation	கையாளுதல் Kaiyāḷutal
Market	அங்காடி Aṅkāṭi
Merchandise	சரக்கு Carakku, வியாபார சரக்கு Viyāpāra carakku
Merchant	வியாபாரி Viyāpāri, பெருவணிகர் Peruvaṇikar
Mint	நாணய சாலை Nāṇaya cālai, தங்க சாலை taṅka cālai

Money பணம் Paṇam, தனம் Taṉam

Monthly மாதாந்த Mātānta

Net நிகர Nikara

Notice அறிவிப்பு Aṟivippu, விளம்பரம் Viḷamparam

Occupation பதவி Patavi

Office அலுவலகம் Aluvalakam

Officer அதிகாரி Atikāri

Owner உடைமையாளர் Uṭaimaiyāḷar

Partner கூட்டாளி Kūṭṭāḷi

Phone தொலைபேசி Tolaipēci

Price விலை Vilai

Private பிரத்யேக Piratyēka

Profit ஆதாயம் Ātāyam

Public பொது மக்கள் Potu makkaḷ

Publication வெளியிடுதல் Veḷiyiṭutal

Rate வரிவீதம் Varivītam

Receipt பற்றுச்சீட்டு Paṟṟuccīṭṭu

Rent குடிக்கூலி Kuṭikkūli, வாடகை Vāṭakai

Sale விற்பனை Viṟpaṉai

Savings சேமிப்பு Cēmippu

Seal முத்திரை Muttirai

Secretary காரியதரிசி Kāriyatarici

Servant வேலைக்காரன் Vēlaikkāraṉ

Shop கடை Kaṭai

Sign அடையாளம் Aṭaiyāḷam

Signature கையொப்பம் Kaiyoppam

Stamp விற்பனை Viṟpaṉai

Stock பங்கு Paṅku

Store, shop கடை Kaṭai

Store, warehouse கிடங்கு Kiṭaṅku

books-india.com

Trade	வாணிகம்	Vāṇikam
Telephone	தொலைபேசி	Tolaipēci
Treasury	காருவூலம்	Karuvooḷam
Warehouse	கிடங்கு	Kiṭaṅku
Wholesale	மொத்த வியாபாரம்	Motta viyāpāram
Work	வேலை	Vēlai

8.21 WARFARE

எதிரியின் மீது போர் தொடுத்தல் Etiriyiṉ mītu pōr toṭuttal

Aggression	ஆக்கிரமிப்பு	Ākkiramippu,
Aggressor	ஆக்கிரமிப்பாளர்	Ākkiramippāḷar
Airforce	விமானப்படை	Vimāṉappaṭai
Archery	வில்வித்தை	Vilvittai
Arms	ஆயுதங்களை	Āyutaṅkaḷai
Armless	ஆயுதமில்லாத	Āyutamillāta
Army	படை	Paṭai;
Armament	போர் தளவாடங்கள்	Pōr taḷavāṭaṅkaḷ
Armour	போர் கவசம்	Pōr kavacam
Arrow	அம்பு	Ampu
Atom bomb	அணுகுண்டு	Aṇukuṇṭu
Attack	தாக்குதல்	Tākkutal
Battle	யுத்தம்	Yuttam
Battle field	போர்க்களம்	Pōrkkaḷam
Blockade	முற்றுகை	Muṟṟukai
Bomb	வெடி குண்டு	Veṭi kuṇṭu
Bloodshed	குருதி சிந்துதல் Kuruti cintutal, கொலை	Kolai
Blunder	தவறு	Tavaṟu
Brave	தைரியமுள்ள	Tairiyamuḷḷa
Bullet	துப்பாக்கி குண்டு	Tuppākki kuṇṭu
Campaign	பிரச்சாரம்	Piraccāram

Cannon	பீரங்கி	Pīraṅki
Cartridge	துப்பாக்கி வெடி மருந்து	Tuppākki veṭi maruntu
Cavalry	குதிரை படை	Kutirai paṭai
Chariot	ரதம்	Ratam
Civil war	உள்நாட்டு போர்	Uḷnāṭṭu pōr
Colonel	படைத்தலைவர்	Paṭaittalaivar
Colony	குடியேற்ற நாடு	Kuṭiyēṟṟa nāṭu
Combat	போராடு	Pōrāṭu
Combatant	போராளி	Pōrāḷi
Command	கட்டளை	Kaṭṭaḷai
Commander	தளபதி	Taḷapati
Death	இறப்பு	Iṟappu
Defeat	தோற்கடி	Tōṟkaṭi
Defence	பாதுகாப்பு	Pātukāppu
Democracy	குடியரசு	Kuṭiyaracu
Dictator	சர்வாதிகாரி	Carvātikāri
Enemy	பகைவன்	Pakaivaṉ
Expedition	பயணம்	Payaṇam
Fight	சண்டை	Caṇṭai
Fist fight	ஃபிஸ்ட் சண்டை Hpisṭ caṇṭai, கைப்பிடி சண்டை	Kaippiṭi caṇṭai
Foot soldier	கால் சிப்பாய்	Kāl cippāy
Fort	கோட்டை	Kōṭṭai
Fortification	வலுவூட்டல்	Valuvūṭṭal
Freedom	சுதந்திரம்	Cutantiram
Gun	துப்பாக்கி	Tuppākki
Gunpowder	வெடி மருந்து	Veṭi maruntu
Helmet	தலைக்கவசம்	talaikkavaca
Hostage	பிணை	Piṇai
Indemnity	முன் காப்பீடு	Muṉ kāppīṭu
Mariner	மாலுமி	Mālumi

books-india.com

Maritime	கப்பலோட்டம் சார்ந்த	Kappalōṭṭam cārnta
Medal	வெகுமான பதக்கம்	Vekumāṉa patakkam
Melee	கைகலப்பு	Kaikalappu
Mutiny	கீழ்ப்படிய மறுத்தல்	Kīḻppaṭiya maṟuttal
Navy	கடற்படை	Kaṭaṟpaṭai
Peace	அமைதி	Amaiti
Prisoner of war	போர் கைதி	Pōr kaiti
Recruit	புது சிப்பாய்	Putu cippāy
Secret	இரகசியமான	Irakaciyamāṉa
Service	சேவை	Cēvai
Ship	கப்பல்	Kappal
Signal	சமிக்ஞை	Camikñai
Shot	துப்பாக்கி	Tuppākki
Siege	முற்றுகை	Muṟṟukai
Slaughter	வதை Vatai, கொலை	Kolai
Strategy	உத்தி Utti, மூலோபாயம்	Mūlōpāyam
Spear	ஈட்டி	Īṭṭi
Spy	உளவாளி	Uḷavāḷi
Sword	வாள்	Vāḷ
Traitor	காட்டிக்கொடுப்பவன்	Kāṭṭikkoṭuppavaṉ
Treaty	உடன்படிக்கை	Uṭaṉpaṭikkai
Trechery	துரோகம்	Turōkam
Trench	அகழி	Akaḻi
Troops	துருப்புக்கள்	Turuppukkaḷ
Victory	வெற்றி	Veṟṟi
War	போர்	Pōr
World war	உலக போர்	Ulaka pōr

books-india.com

LESSON 9

Tamil Imperative and Negative Sentences

1. Requests and Orders

i. The Requests (formal) and orders (informal) imperatives are made to the Second Person 'you' only. The pronoun you, as the subject, may actually be mentioned or only understood.

(ii) In Tamil, as said earlier, subject 'you' could be (i) singular (நீ *nī* तू), non-honorific; (ii) singular honorific (நீர் *nī nīr* आप, तुम), technically a plural form but used as singular; or (iii) the plural (நீங்கள் *nīṅgaḷ* आप, तुम लोग, आप लोग), courteously used as singular honorific (आप) or used as plural non-honorific (तुम लोग, आप लोग).

(iii) In Tamil, similar to Hindi and Sanskrit, pronoun நீ *nī* नी (नी = तू) is used for addressing inferiors, children or very intimate people, In this case, the pure form of the root verb (without any suffix) is used as imperative (order) form as well. e.g. (Thou, you) study! (तू पढ़!) (நீ) படி! (*nī paḍi* नी पडि).

(iv) Pronoun நீர் *nīr* निर् (नीर् = तुम)) is used for addressing similar people or friends. Technically this pronoun is plural of singular non-honorific pronoun (तू → तुम), but is used as semi-honorific singular. In this case, the imperative (request) suffix உம் *um* उम् is added to the pure form of the root verb. e.g. (you please) study! (तुम पढ़ो, आप पढ़ो!) (நீர்) படியும்! (*nīr paḍiyum* नीर् पडियुम्).

(iii) Pronoun நீங்கள் *nīṅgaḷ* निंगळ् (नींगळ् = आप, आप लोग) is used for addressing someone formally with respect. Technically this pronoun is also plural of singular pronoun (आप → आप लोग), but is also used as formal honorific singular. In this case, plural suffix கள் *gaḷ* गळ् is added to the singular imperative suffix உம் *um* उम् . This compound oblique suffix உங்கள் *ungaḷ* उँगळ् is then added to the pure form of the root verb. e.g. (you Sir please) study! (आप पढ़िये!) (நீங்கள்) படியுங்கள்! (*nīngaḷ paḍiyuṅgaḷ* नींगळ् पडियुंगळ्).

TABLE 20 : IMPERATIVE Request or ORDER (verb example படி *paḍi* पडि Read)

You	Verb Read	Imperative suffix	= Request / Order : You (please) read.
நீ नी *nī*	படி *paḍi* पडि	No suffix	(நீ) படி! (*nī paḍi* नी पडि) You read.
நீர் नीर् *nīr*	படி *paḍi* पडि	உம் *um* उम्	(நீர்) படியும்! (*nīr paḍiyum* नीर् पडियुम्)
நீங்கள் नींगळ् *nīṅgaḷ*	படி *paḍi* पडि	உங்கள் *ungaḷ* उँगळ्	(நீங்கள்) படியுங்கள்! (*nīngaḷ paḍiyuṅgaḷ* नींगळ् पडियुंगळ्) You (all) please read.

EXERCISE : IMPERATIVE **ஏவல்** (ORDER or REQUEST)

Translate into Tamil
(Remember, Tamil syntax is same as Hindi. Answers are given for your help, if you need.)

NOTE : Like Hindi and Sanskrit, you need not say "Please" in every Tamil sentence. The Polite Imperative suffix already includes 'please'in it, but you can still add 'please' to it. It's your choice.

1) Please! कृपया, कृपा करके! (Doing = **செய்து**, Mercy = **தயவு**) தயவுசெய்து *dayavuseydụ* दयवुसेय्दु
2) Please come in अंदर आयिये (In = **உள்ளே**) உள்ளே வாருங்கள் *uḷḷe vāruṅgaḷ* उळ्ळे वारुंगळ्
3) Please have a seat. बैठिये! (Sit = **உட்கார்**) உட்காருங்கள் *uṭkāruṅkaḷ* उट्कारुंगळ्
4) Sit. बैठो! बैठ! बैठ जा! உட்காரு *uṭkārụ* उट्कारु
5) Please come again. फिर पधारें (Again = **மீண்டு**) மீண்டும் வாருங்கள் *minḍum vāruṅgaḷ* मिंडुम् वारुंगळ्
6) Say yes! हाँ कहो! (Yes = **ஆம், ஒம்**) நீர் ஆம் சொல்லவும் *nīr ām sollavum* नीर् आम् सोल्लवुम्
7) Please order me. आज्ञा दीजिये! (Order = **உத்தரவிடு**) உத்தரவிடுங்கள் *uttarviḍuṅgaḷ* उत्तरविडुंगळ्
8) Please excuse me. क्षमा कीजिये (Excuse = **மன்னி**) மன்னியுங்கள் *manniyuṅgaḷ* मन्नियुंगळ्
9) Please wait. प्रतिक्षा करें, कृपया रुकें (Wait a while = **பொறு**) சற்றுப்பொறுங்கள் *saṭrupporuṅgaḷ* सट्रुप्पोरुंगळ्
10) Please be quite. शांत रहिये! (Quiet = **சாந்தம்**) சாந்தமா யிருங்கள் *shānthamā yīruṅgaḷ* शांतमा यिरुंगळ्
11) Please think. सोचिये (Think = **சிந்தனை**) சிந்தனை செய்யுங்கள் *chinthanai seyyuṅgaḷ* चिंतनै सेयुंगळ्
12) Once more. और एक बार (No. of times = **முறை**) மீண்டும் ஒரு முறை *mīṇḍum oru muraị* मीडुम् ओरु मुरै
13) Give a bit more! (Demanding 'more' = **இன்னும்**) இன்னும் கொஞ்சம் *innum konjam* इन्नुम् कोंजम्
14) Say! कहिये! (Say = **சொல்**) சொல்லுங்கள் *solluṅgaḷ* सोल्लुंगळ्
15) Stop it! Enough! रहने दो! बस! (Stop! = **நிறுத்து, போதும்**) போதும் *podum* पोदुम्
16) Hurry up! जल्दी कर! (Rush = **சீக்கிரம்** सं.शीघ्रम्) சீக்கிரம் செய் *sikkiram sẹy* सीक्किरम् सेय्
17) Open the door! दरवाजा खोलो! (Open = **திற**) கதவை த்திற *ukadvai thir* कदवै तिर
18) Shut the window. खिड़की खेलिये (Shut = **மூடு**) ஜன்னலை மூடு *jannalai mūḍu* जन्नलै मूडु
19) Come soon. जल्दी आओ சீக்கிரம் வா *sikkiram sẹy* सीक्किरम् वा
20) Be ready. तैयार रहो! (Ready = **தயார்**) தயாராக இரு *tayārāk iru* तयाराक इरु
21) Wait. Please wait. रुक. रुकिये! (Wait = **நில்**) நில்லு, நில்லுங்கள் *nill. nilluṅgaḷ* निल्लु. निलुंगळ्
22) Please come here. इधर आइये! (Here = **இங்கே**) இங்கே வாருங்கள் *iṅge vāruṅgaḷ* इंगे वारुंगळ्
23) Please give permission. अनुमति दीजिये! (Bestow = **அளி**) அனுமதியளியுங்கள் *anumadiyaḷiyuṅgaḷ* अनुमदियळियुंगळ्
24) Please pick it up. इसको उठाओ. (Pick up = **தூக்கு**) இதைத்தூக்கு *idaiddūkkụ* इदैद्दूक्कु
25) Please sit. बैठिये! உட்காருங்கள் *uṭkāruṅkaḷ* उट्कारुंगळ्

MORE TAMIL VERBS, Part II

TABLE 21 : VERB LIST 2

1) Add	கூட்டு	कूट्टु	*kūṭṭu*	29) Love	நேசி	नेसि	*nesi*
2) Agree	உடன்படு	उटन्पु	*uṭanpu*	30) Make	பண்ணு	पण्णु	*paṇṇu*
3) Ask	கேள்	केळ्	*keḷ*	31) Open	திற	तिर	*tir*
4) Bathe	குளி	कुळि	*kuḷi*	32) Pick up	தூக்கு	तूक्कु	*tūkku*
5) Become	ஆகு	आकु	*āku*	33) Place	இடு	इडु	*iḍu*
6) Bite	கடி	कडि	*kaḍi*	34) Plant	நடு	नडु	*naḍu*
7) Bloom	பூ	पू	*pū*	35) Play	விளையாடு	विळैयाडु	*viḷaiyāḍu*
8) Burn	எரி	एरि	*eri*	36) Punish	தண்டி	दंडि	*daṇḍi*
9) Catch	பிடி	पिडि	*piḍi*	37) Remove	நீக்கு	नीक्कु	*nīkku*
10) Control	அடக்கு	अडक्कु	*aḍakku*	38) Rub	தேய்	तेय्	*tey*
11) Count	எண்ணு	एण्णु	*eṇṇu*	39) Save	மீள்	मीळ्	*mīḷ*
12) Cover	மூடு	मूडु	*mūḍu*	40) Say	சொல்லு	सोल्लु	*sollu*
13) Create	படை	पडै	*padai*	41) Shake	ஆட்டு	आड्डु	*āḍḍu*
14) Cut	வெட்டு	वेड्डु	*veḍḍu*	42) Show	காட்டு	काड्डु	*kāḍḍu*
15) Dance	ஆடு	आडु	*āḍu*	43) Shut	மூடு	मूडु	*mūḍu*
16) Desire	ஆசை	आसै	*āsai*	44) Sing	பாடு	पाडु	*pāḍu*
17) Die	மாளு	माळु	*māḷu*	45) Sit	உட்காரு	उटकारु	*uṭakāru*
18) Drive	ஓட்டு	ओड्डु	*oḍḍu*	46) Stop	நிறுத்து	निरुद्दु	*niruddu*
19) Feed	மேய்	मेय्	*mey*	47) Strike	அடி	अडि	*aḍi*
20) Get	வாங்கு	वांकु	*v̇nku*	48) Study	படி	पडि	*paḍi*
21) Happen	நேரிடு	नेरिडु	*neriḍu*	49) Swallow	விழுங்கு	विळुंकु	*viḷúnku*
22) Have	கொள்ளு	कोळ्ळु	*koḷḷu*	50) Swim	நீந்து	नींदु	*nīndu*
23) Heal	ஆறு	आरु	*āru*	51) Think	எண்ணு	एण्णु	*eṇṇu*
24) Hold	பிடி	पिडि	*piḍi*	52) Tie	கட்டு	कड्डु	*kaḍḍu*
25) Hope	நம்பு	नंबु	*nambu*	53) Touch	தொடு	तोडु	*toḍu*
26) kill	கொல்ல	कोल्ल्	*koll*	54) Trust	நம்பு	नंबु	*nambu*
27) Learn	கல்	कल्	*kaḷ*	55) Wait	நில்	निल्	*nil*
28) Leave	விடு	विडु	*viḍu*	56) Worship	தொழு	तोळु	*toḷu*

2. Making Verbal Nouns or Infinitives from Verbs

i. Many Hindi teachers, grammarians, authors and thus the students, have a general misunderstanding that ***pīnā*** **(पीना to drink),** ***khāna*** **(खाना to eat),** ***ānā*** **(आना to come),** ***jānā*** **(जाना to go)...** are verbs. They are not verbs. They are Infinitives or verbal nouns. In these infinitives or verbal nouns, only the *pī, khā, ā, jā ...etc.* पी, खा, आ, जा are verbs (or verb-stems), and nā (ना) is infinitive (or noun) forming suffix. Tamil grammarians are clear about verbs and the infinitive mood, as Sanskrit.

ii. In Tamil, an infinitive (or verbal noun) is formed by adding அ *a* अ or க்க *kk* क्क to the verb roots. (a) அ *a* अ is added to the Type 1 verbs that form Present tense with suffix கிறு *kiru* किरु, and (b) க்க *kk* क्क is added to the Type 2 verbs that form Present tense with suffix க்கிறு *kkiru* क्किरु (See Tables 12, 14 and 17 Tense Suffixes). e.g.

(a) Type 1 verb Eat : Verb Eat (Hindi खा) Tamil உண் *uṇ* उण् ; Tense suffix கிறு *kiru* किरु, (First Person Singular Present tense will be உண்கிறேன் *uṇikiren* उण्किरेन्). Therefore, Verb உண் *uṇ* उण् + Infinitive type 1 suffix அ *a* अ = உண்ண* *uṇṇ* उण्ण = To Eat (खाना) or Eating (खाना). Similarly verb Say என் *en* एन् will be என்ன* *enna* एन्न To Say or Saying.

* REMEMBER THE IMPORTANT RULE : If a word ending in mute (half) consonant is joined (संधि) with a word starting with a vowel, the mute consonant doubles. e.g. Verb ending in short consonant உண் *uṇ* उण् + vowel அ *a* अ = உண்ண, the short consonant ண் *ṇ* ण s doubled ண்ண *ṇṇ* ण्ण.

(b) Type 2 verb Read/Learn : Verb Read (Hindi पढ़) Tamil படி *padi* पडि ; Tense suffix க்கிறு *kkiru* क्किरु, (Present tense படிக்கிறேன் *padikkiren* पडिक्किरेन्). Thus, Verb படி *padi* पडि + Infinitive type 2 suffix க்க *kka* क्क = படிக்க *padikka* पडिक्क = To Read (पढ़ना) or Reading (पढ़ना).

TABLE 22 : INFINITIVES or VERBAL NOUNS

Type	Verb Type1/Type2	Present Tense	Iifinitive / V. Noun
1	Become ஆ आ *ā* (हो)	ஆகிறேன் आकिरेन् *ākiren* (मैं होता हूँ)	ஆ आ *ā* (*honā* होना)
2	Create படை *paḍai* पडै	படைக்கிறேன் पडैकिरेन् *paḍaikkiren*	படைக்க पडैक्क *paḍaikka*
1	Get அடை अडै *aḍai*	அடைகிறேன் अडैकिरेन् *aḍaikiren*	அடைய अडैय *aḍaiya*
2	Walk நட नड *naḍ* (आ)	நடக்கிறேன் नडक्किरेन् *naḍkkiren*	நடக்க नडक्क *naḍakka*
1	Come வா वा *vā*	வருகிறேன் वरुकिरेन् *varukiren*	வருகை वरुगै *varugai* (*ānā* आना)
2	Love நேசி नेसि *nesi*	நேசிக்கிறேன் नेसिक्किरेन् *nesikkiren*	நேசிக்க नेसिक्क *nesikka*
1	Do செய் सेय् *sey* (कर)	செய்கிறேன் सेय्किरेन् *seykiren*	செய सेय *seya* (*karnā* करना)
2	Drink குடி कुडि *kuḍi*	குடிக்கிறேன் कुडिक्किरेन् *kuḍikkiren*	குடிக்க कुडिक्क *kuḍikka*

books-india.com

3. Negative Expressions

i. As we have seen earlier, 'No' and 'Not' is **இல்லை** *illai* इल्लै In Tamil. 'No' is an adverb and 'not' is an indeclinable negative finite verb. The other words for 'no' are **அல்ல** *alla* अल्ल, **அன்று** *anru* अन्रु, **இன்று** *inru* इन्रु and some people use **இல்லை** *illai* इल्लै .

ii. The negative of a 'yes-no' type of question is replied in three ways using **இல்லை** *illai* इल्लै.

(a) Question : Is it true? (True, truth = **நிசம்** *nijam* निजम्, **உண்மை** *uṇmai* उण्मै).

Answer : No **இல்லை** *illai* इल्लै. Negative answer.

(b) Q : Is it true? (क्या यह सच है?) A: <u>No, it is not true</u>. **இல்லை, அது உண்மை இல்லை** *illai, adu uṇmai illai.* इल्लै, अदु उण्मै इलै. A: Negating what is asked by the speaker.

(c) Q : Is it true? A: <u>No, it is false</u>. **இல்லை, அது பொய்** *illai, adu poy* इल्लै अदु पोय्. (False = **பொய்** *poy* पोय्). Telling what is correct.

Another set of examples : Where the question itself is negative.

(d) Q : Isn't Vishvanathan a Punjabi? A: <u>No</u> **இல்லை** *illai* इल्लै. Negative answer.

(e) Isn't Vishvanathan a Punjabi? A: <u>No, he is not a Punjabi</u>. **இல்லை, அவன் பஞ்சாபி இல்லை.** *illai, avan pañjābi illai.* इल्लै, अवन् पंजाबि इलै. A: Negating what is asked.

(f) A: <u>No, *Vishvanāthan* is Tamilian</u>. **இல்லை, விஷ்வநாதன் தமிழன்** *illai, vishvanāthan tamiḻan.* इल्लै, विश्वनाथन् तमिऴन्.

iii. In Tamil negative is often expressed in 'negative forms' of the verbs. The Universal/Present Habitual negative verb is formed by simply attaching the required personal suffix (see Table 12) to the verb. The pronoun suffix shows the person, gender and number of the -ve verb. e.g. +ve I drink → -ve I do not drink. The three tenses (present, past and future) are formed similarly. (seen chapter 9).

TABLE 23 : Negative Verb : e.g. Drink **குடி** *kuḍi* कुडि

PRONOUN	Personal Suffix	verb + personal suffix = negative verb	meaning
I நான் नान् *nān*	ஏன் एन् *ĕn*	குடியேன் कुडियेन् *kudiyen*	I don't drink
We தாங்கள் नांगळ् *nāṅgaḷ*	ஒம், ஓம் ओम् *om*	குடியோம் कुडियोम् *kudiyom*	We don't drink
You நீ नी *nī*	ஆய் आय् *āy*	குடியாய் कुडियाय् *kudiyāy*	You don't drink
You நீர் नीर् *nīr*	ஈர் ईर् *īr*	குடியீர் कुडियीर् *kudiyīr*	You don't drink
You நீங்கள் नींगळ् *nīṅgaḷ*	ஈர்கள் ईर्गळ् *īrgaḷ*	குடியீங்கள் कुडियींगळ् *kudiyīṅgaḷ*	You don't drink
He அவன் अवन् *avan*	ஆன் आन् *ān*	குடியான் कुडियान् *kudiyān*	He doesn't drink
She அவள் अवळ् *avaḷ*	ஆள் आळ् *āḷ*	குடியாள் कुडियाळ् *kudiyāḷ*	She doesn't drink
They அவர்கள் अवर्गळ् *avargaḷ*	ஆர்கள் आर्गळ् *ārgaḷ*	குடியார்கள் कुडियार्गळ् *kudiyārgaḷ*	They don't drink
It அது अदु *adu*	அது अदु *adu*	குடியாது कुडियादु *kudiyādu*	It doesn't drink

3. Prohibitive (-ve) and Polite Imperatives

i. The Tamil Prohibitive or the Negative Imperative sentences are made by adding the -ve Singular suffix ஆயும் *ādeyum* आदेयुम् or -ve plural suffix ஆதேயுங்கள் *ādeyuṅgaḷ* आदेयुंगळ् to the verb. e.g.

TABLE 24 : Prohibitive : Don't (Don't come) (Don't go)

PRONOUN	Negative Imperative SUFFIX	verb 'come' வா *vā* वा	verb 'go' போ *po* पो
You நீ नी *nī*	ஆதே *āde* आदे	வராதே वरादे *varāde*	போகாதே पोगादे *pogāde*
You நீர் नीर् *nīr*	ஆதேயும் *ādeyum* आदेयुम्	வராதேயும் वरादेयुम् *varādeyum*	போகாதேயும் पोगादेयुम् *pogādeyum*
You நீங்கள் नींगळ् *nīṅgaḷ*	ஆதேயுங்கள் *ādeyuṅgaḷ* आदेयुंगळ्	வராதேயுங்கள் वरादेयुंगळ् *varādeyuṅgaḷ*	போகாதேயுங்கள் पोगादेयुंगळ् *pogādeyuṅgaḷ*

This Table is developed for Sanskrit Hindi Research Institute for *"Learn Tamil Through English/Hindi"* by Ratnakar Narale.

ii. The polite imperative can also be formed by adding the உம் *um* उम् suffix to the Infinitive (see Table 22) of the verb. e.g.

TABLE 25 : Polite Imperative : 'Please do' (Please come) (Please go)

PRONOUN	Negative Imperative	verb 'come' வா *vā* वा	verb 'go' போ *po* पो
You நீர் नीर् *nīr*	உம் *um* उम्	வாரும் वारुम् *vārum*	போக்கும் पोम् *pom*
You நீங்கள் नींगळ् *nīṅgaḷ*	உங்கள் *uṅgaḷ* उंगळ्	வாருங்கள் वारुंगळ् *vāruṅgaḷ*	போங்கள் पोंगळ् *poṅgaḷ*

This Table is developed for Sanskrit Hindi Research Institute for *"Learn Tamil Through English/Hindi"* by Ratnakar Narale.

LESSON 10

Making Complex Tamil Sentences

We have seen how to Make our Own Basic Tamil sentences in all three tenses (lesson 6). We have seen interesting tables, basic Tamil verbs (Tables 13 & 21) and a Pictorial Tamil Dictionary (Table 19. We also briefly saw how to make imperatives, interrogatives and negative expressions, which we will use extensively in the following lessons.

Let's now see how to make a bit complex Tamil sentences with the use of several 'Postpositions' (case suffixes). Similar to the tenses (Lesson 6), this is another very important chapter. Please make sure you understand its every word properly. Again, do not start this lesson without finishing previous lessons well. Review this lesson at least twice. So we begin ...

BEFORE GOING AHEAD PLEASE UNDERSTAND THE FOLLOWING

i. As we learned before (Lesson 6.1), the Tamil nouns are divided into three genders. (i) all human male noun words are Masculine Gender, (ii) the human female noun words are Female Gender, and (iii) all other words are Neuter Gender.

ii. Masculine and Feminine noun words are together called the Rational Nouns. The Neuter noun words are called Irrational nouns.

iii. In grammatical mumbo-jumbo, the '**form**' taken by a noun (or pronoun) to show its 'relationship' in the sentence is called the '**case**' of that word. Big deal.

iv. The noun (or pronoun) itself (singular or plural), without any modification and without attaching any suffix to it, is called the 'Nominative' case of that noun. This case is reserved for the doer ('subject') of the action (verb) in sentence.

v. In addition to this Nominative relationship, there are seven more relationships or 'cases' of the nouns and pronouns. As said in previous point, the Nominative nouns do not require any modification, it means the other cases do need some kind of modification before attaching the case suffix to them. This modified form of any noun (or pronoun) is called the 'Oblique' case or the 'Inflectional Base' of that noun.

vi. The addition of any of the eight case suffixes to the oblique/inflectional base of a noun is called Declension of that noun.

vi. The Plural Nominative is always formed by attaching the 'Plural' Tamil suffix to the Singular Nominative. Most common plural suffix is **கள்** *kaḷ* कळ् The plural Inflectional base of a noun (but may not be of some pronoun) is always same as its Plural Nominative.

vii. All Tamil noun end only in one of the six vowels (ஆ, இ, ஈ, உ, ஊ, ஐ) or in one of the eight consonants (**ண், ம், ய், ர், ல், ழ், ள், ன்**). Tamil nouns do not end in any other Tamil character.

viii. Depending on which letter the noun ends, all Tamil nouns are divided into FOUR GROUPS, for the purpose of attaching corresponding case suffixes (i.e. declension). The four groups are as follows :

(a) The First Group : masculine nouns ending in ன் *n* न्.

(b) The Second Group : (neuter) nouns ending in அம் *am* अम्.

(c) The Third Group : nouns ending in டு or று *du* or *ru* डु or रु

(d) The Fourth Group : the remaining nouns.

ix. For the benefit of those who need a review, or have forgotten or have not learned the English Case prepositions (Hindi कारक, Sanskrit विभक्ति), below is a Table designed to help you with the basics of this lesson.

TABLE 26 : Case Identification

Case No.	English Inflection	Hindi Name	English prepositions	Details
1	Nominative	कर्ता	-	the Doer of the action (the subject)
2	Accusative	कर्म	to	the direct Object of the action (indirect obj. : Dative case)
3	Instrumental	करण	with/by	the Instrument or Means with/by which the action is done
4	Dative	संप्रदान	to/for	the object To or For which the indirect action is done.
5	Ablative	अपादान	from	the place From where the action starts
6	Possessive	अधिकरण	of	the Relationship of the the object in the sentence
7	Locative	सम्बंध	in/on/at/with	the Location of the object.
8	Vocative	संबोधन	Oh!	the Address or a Call
NOTE : These suffixes are actually pre-positions in English, but they are post-positions in Tamil, like Sanskrit.				
This Table is developed for Sanskrit Hindi Research Institute for *"Learn Tamil Through English/Hindi"* by Ratnakar Narale.				

x The case suffixes are Pre-positions in English, but they are Post-positions in Tamil (similar to Hindi and Sanskrit). In other words, in English these word particles come before the NOUN (e.g. To home), but in Tamil (Hindi and Sanskrit) they come after the Noun (e.g. Home to घर को)

xi. Any of these eight Case Suffixes are attached ONLY to nouns or pronouns. They are NEVER attached to the verbs. The verbs take only the Tense Suffixes. The tense suffixes are never attached to the nouns or pronouns. The ADVERBS take NO suffixes of any kind. Tamil Adjectives are also indeclinable and are placed (without any suffix) before the noun. Only the noun takes suffix.

books-india.com

THE GENERAL TAMIL CASE SUFFIXES

TABLE 27 : The GENERAL CASE SUFFIXES for Nouns and Pronouns

Case No.	English Name	Hindi Name (कारक)	English (हिंदी) prefix/suffix	COMMON TAMIL SUFFIXES Singular	Plural
1	Nominative	कर्ता	–	No suffix	கள் *haḷ* हळ्
2	Accusative*	कर्म	to (को)	ை *ai* ऐ *	களை *kalai* हळै *
3	Instrumental	करण	1.with/by (से) 2. together with (के साथ)	ஆல் *āl* आल् ஒடு *oḍu* ओडु உடன் *uḍan* उडन्	களால் *haḷāl* हळाल् களோடு *haḷoḍu* हळोडु களுடன் *haḷuḍan* हळुडन्
4	Dative	संप्रदान	1. to (को) 2. for (के लिये)	க்கு *kku* क्कु *** உக்கு *ukku* उक्कु க்காக *kkāk* क्काक	களக்கு *haḷakku* हळकु களுக்கு *haḷukku* हळुकु கள்க்காக *haḷakāk* हळ्क्काक
5	Ablative	अपादान	from (से)	இல் *il* इल् இலிருந்து *ilirundu* इलिरुंदु	களில் *haḷil* कळिल् களிலிருந்து *haḷilirundu* कळिलिरुंदु
6	Possessive	अधिकरण	of (का)	இன் *in* इन् உடைய *uḍaiya* उडैय	களின் *haḷin* कळिन् களுடைய *haḷuḍaiya* हळुडैय
7	Locative	सम्बंध	1. in/at (में, पर) 2. on (पर) 3. with (पर)	இல் *il* इल् இடம் *iḍam* इडम् ** மேல் *mel* मेल् இடத்தில் *iḍattil* इडत्तिल्	களில் *haḷil* कळिल् களிடம் *haḷiḍam* कळिडम् ** கள்மேல் *haḷel* हळ्मेल् களிடத்தில் *haḷiḍattil* कळिडत्तिल्
8	Vocative	संबोधन	Oh (हे!)	ே *e* ए	களே *haḷe* हळे

NOTES : (i) A case suffix is attached to the oblique form of a noun/pronoun. For oblique pronouns see TABLE 9
(ii) * this suffix is optional, if the object is neuter gender.
(iii) ** this suffix is for masculine and feminine nouns/pronouns only. e.g. In me என்னிடம் एन्निडम् *ennidam*
(iv) *** Suffix க்கு (*kku* क्कु) is added to the noun base ending in இ, ஈ or ஐ *i, ī ai* इ, ई, ऐ, and the suffix உக்கு (*ukku* उक्कु) is added to all noun inflexional endings.

This Table is developed for Sanskrit Hindi Research Institute for *"Learn Tamil Through English/Hindi"* by Ratnakar Narale.

books-india.com

TWO IMPORTANT NOTES : WHILE ADDING THE SUFFIXES Please remember,

(i) When a word ending in இ, ஈ or ஐ *i, ī* or *ai* इ, ई or ऐ is connected to a word beginning with any vowel, letter ய் *y* य् is inserted between these two connecting vowels.

(ii) When a word ending in ஆ, ஊ, எ, ஏ, ஒ, ஓ or ஔ *ā, ū, e, ĕ, o, ŏ,* or *au* आ, ऊ, ए, ऍ, ओ, ऑ or औ is followed by a word beginning with a vowel, letter வ் *v* व् is inserted between the two vowels

THE FOUR GROUPS OF DECLENSIONS

10.1 THE FIRST GROUP

Masculine nouns ending in ன் *n* न्.

i. Masculine Nouns such as மனிதன் *manidan* मनिदन् (Man), பையன் *paiyan* पैयन् (Boy), மகன் *mahan* महन् (Son), மைத்துனன் *maittunan* मैत्तुनन् (Brother-in-law), பேரன் *peran* पेरन् (Grandson), அண்ணன் *aṉṉan* अण्णन् (Elder brother), சகோதரன் *sagodaran* सगोदरन् (Brother) etc. ending in ன் *n* न् fall in 1st group.

ii. In this group the Nominative and the Inflectional base are both same. e.g. மனிதன் *manidan* मनिदन् (Man), This form is often used for Possessive case also. e.g. மனிதன் *manidan* मनिदन् (Of a man or man's),

iii. The Plurals is formed by adding ர் *r* र् (optionally *rkaḷ* र्कळ्) to the Singular. e.g. மனிதர் *manidar* मनिदर् or optionally மனிதர்கள் *manidarkaḷ* मनिदर्कळ् (Men)

TABLE 28 : EXAMPLE of Cases of the first type of nouns, like மனிதன் *manidan* मनिदन् (Man)

case	English हिंदी	GROUP 1 NOUN + CASE SUFFIXES Singular	Plural
nom 1	Man आदमी	மனிதன் *manidan* मनिदन्	மனிதர் *manidar* मनिदर् or மனிதர்கள் *manidarhaḷ* मनिदर्हळ्
acc. 2	to a man आदमी को	மனிதனை *manidanai* मनिदनै	மனிதரை *manidarai* मनिदरै or மனிதர்களை *manidarhalaị* मनिदर्हळै
inst. 3	by a man आदमी से, आदमी के साथ	மனிதனால் *manidanāl* मनिदनाल् or மனிதனோடு *manidanoḍu* मनिदनोड्डु	மனிதரால் *manidarāḷ* मनिदराल् or மனிதரோடு *manidaroḍu* मनिदरोड्डु or மனிதர்களால் *manidarhḷāl* मनिदर्हळाल् or மனிதர்களோடு *manidarhḷoḍu* मनिदर्हळोड्डु

dat. 4	to a man आदमी को –के लिये	மனிதனுக்கு *manidanukku* मनिदनुक्कु or மனிதனுக்காக *manidanukkāk* मनिदनुक्काक	மனிதருக்கு *manidarukku* मनिदरुक्कु or மனிதருக்காக *manidarukkāk* मनिदरुक्काक or மனிதர்களுக்கு *manidarhaḷukku* मनिदर्हळुक्कु or மனிதர்களுக்காக *manidarhaḷukkāk* मनिदर्हळुक्काक
abl. 5	from a man आदमी से	மனிதனில் *manidanil* मनिदनिल् or மனிதனினின்று *manidanininru* मनिदनिनिन्रु or மனிதனிலிருந்து *manidanilirundu* मनिदनिलिरुन्दु	மனிதரில் *manidaril* मनिदरिल् or மனிதர்களில் *manidarhaḷil* मनिदर्हळिल् or மனிதரினின்று *manidarininru* मनिदरिनिन्रु or மனிதர்களினின்று *manidarhaḷininru* मनिदर्हळिनिन्रु or மனிதரிலிருந்து *manidarilirundu* मनिदरिलिरुन्दु, மனிதர்களிலிருந்து *manidarhaḷilirundu* मनिदर्हळिलिरुन्दु
poss 6	of a man आदमी का	மனிதனின் *manidanin* मनिदनिन् or மனிதனுடைய *manidanuḍaiya* मनिदनुडैय	மனிதரின் *manidarin* मनिदरिन् or மனிதர்களின் *manidarhḷin* मनिदर्हळिन् or மனிதரினுடைய*manidarinuḍaiya* मनिदरिनुडैय or மனிதர்களுடைய *manidarhaḷuḍaiya* मनिदर्हळुडैय or மனிதர்களினுடைய *manidarhaḷinuḍaiya* मनिदर्हळिनुडैय
loc. 7	in a man आदमी में	மனிதனிடத்தில் *manidanidattil* मनिदनिडत्तिल् or மனிதனில் *manidanil* मनिदनिल्	மனிதரிடத்தில் *manidaridattil* मनिदरिडत्तिल् or மனிதர்களிடத்தில் *manidarhaḷiḍattil* मनिदर्हळिडत्तिल् or மனிதரில் *manidaril* मनिदरिल् or மனிதர்களில் *manidarhaḷil* मनिदर्हळिल्
voc. 8	Oh man हे आदमी!	மனிதனே *manidane* मनिदने!	மனிதர்களே *manidarhaḷe* मनिदर्हळे!

EXERCISE : USE OF CASES with First Group of nouns : (Remember, Tamil syntax is same as Hindi Syntax)
Translate into Tamil : Answers are given for your help, if you need
NOTE : For possessive case of pronouns (e.g. my, your, his), please refer to the last cloumn of Table 9.

1. A letter to <u>my</u> brother — என் அண்ணனுக்கு கடிதம் *en aṇṇanukku kaḍidam* एन् अण्णनुक्कु कडिदम्
2. The boy is with a man — பையன் மனிதனுடன் இருக்கிறான் *paiyan manidanuḍan irikkirān* पैयन् मनिदनुडन् इरुक्किरान्
3. A man is with the boy — மனிதன் பையனுடன் இருக்கிறான் *manidan paiyanuḍan irikkirān* मनिदन् पैयनुडन् इरुक्किरान्

The pencil of my son(my son's pencil) — என் மகன் பென்சில் *en makan paecil* एन् मकन् पेंसिल

4. O Grandson! — பேரனே! *perane* पेरने!
5. In my brother — என் சகோதரனில் *en sagodaranil* एन् सगोदरनिल्
6. From my brother-in-law — என் மைத்துனனில் *en maittunanil* एन् मैत्तुननिल्

10.2 THE SECOND GROUP

Neuter nouns ending in ending in அம் *am* अम्

i. Neuter Nouns such as **மரம்** *maram* मरम् (Tree), **படம்** *pḍam* पडम् (Picture), **புத்தகம்** *puttaham* पुत्तहम् (Book), **தேசம்** *desam* देसम् (Country), **ஒட்டகம்** *oṭṭgam* आरुट्टगम् (Camel), **பட்டம்** *paṭṭam* पट्टम् (Kite), **காகம்** *kāgam* कागम् (Crow) etc. ending in **அம்** *am* अम् fall in 2nd group.

ii. The notable thing about this group is that the end **ம்** *m* म्.of the noun is changed to **த்த்** *dd* द्द् before attaching the case suffixes (other than in Nominative and Vocative cases).

TABLE 29 : EXAMPLE of Cases of the 2nd type of nouns, like **மரம்** *maram* मरम् (Tree)

case	English हिंदी	GROUP 2 NOUN + CASE SUFFIXES Singular	Plural
nom 1	Tree पेड़	**மரம்** *maram* मरम्	**மரங்கள்** *maraṅgaḷ* मरंगळ्
acc. 2	to a tree पेड़ को	**மரத்தை** *maraththai* मरत्तै	**மரங்களை** *maraṅgaḷai* मरंगळै
inst. 3	by a tree पेड़ से	**மரத்தால்** *maraththāl* मरत्ताल् or **மரத்தோடு** *marattoḍu* मरत्तोडु	**மரங்களால்** *maraṅgaḷāl* मरंगळाल् or **மரங்களோடு** *maraṅgaḷoḍu* मरंगळोडु
dat. 4	to a tree पेड़ को	**மரத்துக்கு** *marattukku* मरत्तुक्कु	**மரங்களுக்கு** *maraṅgaḷukku* मरंगळुक्कु
abl. 5	from a tree पेड़ से	**மரத்தில்** *marattil* मरत्तिल् or **மரத்தினின்று** *marattininru* मरत्तिनिन्रु or **மரத்திலிருந்து** *marattilirundu* मरत्तिलिरुन्दु	**மரங்களில்** *maraṅgaḷil* मरंगळिल् or **மரங்களினின்று** *maraṅgaḷininru* मरंगळिनिन्रु or **மரங்களிலிருந்து** *maraṅgaḷilirundu* मरंगळिलिरुन्दु
poss 6	of a tree पेड़ का	**மரத்தின்** *marattin* मरत्तिन् or **மரத்துடைய** *marattuḍaiya* मरत्तुडैय **மரத்தினுடைய** *marattinuḍaiya* मरत्तिनुडैय *	**மரங்களின்** *maraṅgaḷin* मरंगळिन् or **மரங்களுடைய** *maraṅgaḷuḍaiya* मरंगळुडैय or **மரங்களினுடைய** *maraṅgaḷinuḍaiya* मरंगळिनुडैय *
loc. 7	in a tree पेड़ में	**மரத்தில்** *marattil* मरत्तिल् or **மரத்திடத்தில்** *marattiḍattil* मरत्तिडत्तिल्	**மரங்களில்** *maraṅgaḷil* मरंगळिल् or **மரங்களிடத்தில்** *maraṅgaḷiḍattil* मरंगळिडत्तिल्
voc. 8	Oh tree! हे पेड़!	**மரமே** *marame* मरमे!	**மரங்களே** *maraṅgaḷe* मरंगळे!

NOTE : There is no strict rule which suffix should be used, except that **இன்** *in* इन् should not be used with the pronouns.

This Table is developed for Sanskrit Hindi Research Institute for *"Learn Tamil Through English/Hindi"* by Ratnakar Narale.

books-india.com

EXERCISE : USE OF CASES with Second Group of nouns ending in அம் *am* अम्

Translate into Tamil : Answers are given for your help, if you need

1. In the city (நகரம் *naaram* नगरम् = City) — அந்த நகரில் *and nagaril* अन्द नगरिल्
2. The bird on the tree — மரத்தில் பறவை *marattil parvai* मरत्तिल् परवै
3. Money for the picture — படத்துக்கு பணம் *padattukku panam* पडत्तुक्कु पणम्
4. Page of the book (பக்கம் *pakkam* पक्कम् = Page) — புத்தகத்தின் பக்கம் *puttakattin pakkam* पुत्तहत्तिन् पक्कम्
5. People of the country (மக்கள் *makkal* मक्कळ् = People) — தேசத்துடைய மக்கள் *desattudaiya makkal* देसत्तुडैय मक्कळ्
6. The hump on the camel (திமில் thimil तिमिल् = Hump) — ஒட்டகத்தின் திமில் *ottakattil thimil* ओट्टकत्तिल् तिमिल्
7. Colour of the kite (வர்ணம் *varnam* वर्णम् = Colour) — பட்டத்தின் வர்ணம் *patttin varnam* पट्टत्तिन् वर्णम्
8. Beak of the crow — காகத்தின் அலகு *kāgattin alagu* कागत्तिन् अलगु

10.3 THE THIRD GROUP

nouns ending in டு or று *du* or *ru* डु or रु

i. Nouns such as வீடு *vīdu* वीडु (House), காடு *kādu* काडु (Forest), ஆறு *āru* आरु (River), நண்டு *nandu* नण्डु (Crab), கிணறு *kinaru* किणरु (A well), பூட்டு *puttu* पुट्टु (Lock), *vandu* वण्डु (Bumble bee) etc. ending in து or று *du* or *ru* डु or रु fall in 3rd group.

ii. The notable thing about this group is that the consonant in the end syllable is doubled before attaching singular the case suffix. e.g. டு or று *du* or *ru* डु or रु → ட்டு or ற்று *ddu* or *tru* ड्डु or ट्रु

TABLE 30-A : FIRST EXAMPLE of Cases of the 3rd type of nouns, like வீடு *vīdu* वीडु (House)

case	English हिंदी	GROUP 3 NOUN + CASE SUFFIXES Singular	Plural
nom	House घर	வீடு *vīdu* वीडु	வீடுகள் *vīdukal* वीडुकळ्
acc.	to a house घर को	வீட்டை *vīddai* वीड्डै	வீடுகளை *vīdukalai* वीडुकळै
inst.	by a house घर से	வீட்டால் *vīddāl* वीड्डाल् or வீட்டோடு *vīddodo* वीड्डोडु	வீடுகளால் *vīdukalāl* वीडुकळाल् or வீடுகளோடு *vīdukalodu* वीडुकळोडु
dat.	to home घर को	வீட்டுக்கு *vīddukku* विड्डुक्कु	வீடுகளுக்கு *vīdukalukku* वीडुकळुक्कु
abl.	from home घर से	வீட்டில் *vīddil* वीड्डिल् or வீட்டினின்று *vīddininru* वीड्डिनिन्रु or வீட்டிலிருந்து *vīddilirundu* वीड्डिलिरुन्दु	வீடுகளில் *vīdukalil* वीडुकळिल् or வீடுகளினின்று *vīdukalininru* वीडुकळिनिन्रु or வீடுகளிலிருந்து *vīdukalilirundu* वीडुकळिलिरुन्दु

poss	of a house घर का	வீட்டின் *vīḍḍin* वीड्डिन् or வீட்டினுடைய *vīḍḍinuḍaiya* वीड्डिनुडैय	வீடுகளின் *vīḍukaḷin* वीडुकळिन् or வீடுகளினுடைய *vīḍukaḷinuḍaiya* वीडुकळिनुडैय
loc.	in a house घर में	வீட்டில் *vīḍḍil* वीड्डिल्	வீடுகளில் *vīḍukaḷil* वीडुकळिल् or வீடுகளிடத்தில் *vīḍukaḷiḍattil* वीडुकळिडत्तिल्
voc.	O House! हे घर!	வீடே *vīḍe* वीडे	வீடுகளே *vīḍukaḷe* वीडुकळे!
This Table is developed for Sanskrit Hindi Research Institute for *"Learn Tamil Through English/Hindi"* by Ratnakar Narale.			

TABLE 30-B : SECOND EXAMPLE of Cases of the 3rd type of nouns, like ஆறு *āru* आरु (River)

case	English हिंदी	GROUP 3 NOUN + CASE SUFFIXES Singular	Plural
nom	River नदी	ஆறு *āru* आरु	ஆறுகள் *ārukaḷ* आरुकळ्
acc.	to a river नदी को	ஆற்றை *āṭrai* आट्रै *	ஆறுகளை *ārukaḷai* आरुकळै
inst.	by a river नदी से	ஆற்றால் *āṭrāl* आट्राल् or ஆற்றோடு *āṭroḍo* आट्रोडु	ஆறுகளால் *ārukaḷāl* आरुकळाल् or ஆறுகளோடு *ārukaḷoḍu* आरुकळोडु
dat.	to a river नदी को	ஆற்றுக்கு *āṭrukku* आट्रुक्कु	ஆறுகளுக்கு *ārukaḷukku* आरुकळुक्कु
abl.	from a river नदी से	ஆற்றில் *āṭril* आट्रिल् or ஆற்றினின்று *āṭrininru* आट्रिनिन्रु or ஆற்றலிருந்து *āṭrilirundu* आट्रिलिरुन्दु	ஆறுகளில் *ārukukaḷil* आरुकळिल् or ஆறுகளினின்று *ārukaḷininru* आरुकळिनिन्रु or ஆறுகளிலிருந்து *ārukaḷilirundu* आरुकळिलिरुन्दु
poss	of a river नदी का	ஆற்றின் *āṭrin* आट्रिन् or ஆற்றினுடைய *āṭrinuḍaiya* आट्रिनुडैय	ஆறுகளின் *ārukaḷin* आरुकळिन् or ஆறுகளினுடைய *ārukaḷinuḍaiya* आरुकळिनुडैय
loc.	in a river नदी में	ஆற்றில் *āṭril* आट्रिल्	ஆறுகளில் *ārukaḷil* आरुकळिल् or ஆறுகளிடத்தில் *vīḍukaḷiḍattil* आरुकळिडत्तिल्
voc.	O River! हे नदी!	ஆறே *āre* आरे	ஆறுகளே *ārukaḷe* आरुकळे!
NOTE : * When a suffix is added to a singular word ending in று *ru* रु, the ற் *r* र् is doubled and pronounced as *tr* ट्र			

EXERCISE : USE OF CASES with third Group of nouns ending in டு or று *du* or *ru* डु or रु

1. Translate into Tamil : — Answers are given for your help, if you need
2. My house — என் வீடு *en vīḍu* एन् वीडु
3. Trees in the forest — காட்டில் மரங்கள் *kāṭṭil maraṅgaḷ* काट्टिल् मरंगळ्
4. I swin in the river — நான் ஆற்றில் நீந்துகிறேன் *nān āṭril nīndukireṇ* नान् आट्रिल् नीन्दुकिरेन्

books-india.com

5. He eats crabs (वह केकड़ों को खाता है) அவன் நண்டுகளை உண்கிறான் *avan naṇḍukḷai uṇkirāṉ* अवन् नण्डुकलै उण्किरान्

6. There is water in the well (தண்ணீர் *taṇṇīr* तण्णीर् = Water) கிண்ற்றில் தண்ணீர் இருக்கிறது *kiṇṭril thaṇṇīrirukkirdu* किण्ट्रिल् तण्णिर् इरुक्किरदु

7. There are bumble bees on the trees மரங்களில் வண்டுகள் இருக்கின்றன *maraṅgaḷil vaṇḍukaḷ irikkinraṉ* मरंगिलल् वण्डुकल् इरुक्किन्नन

10.4 THE FOURTH GROUP
The remaining nouns

i. Nouns such as பிதா *pithā* पिता (Father), மாதா *māthā* माता (Mother), பெண் *peṇ* पेण (Woman), குரு *guru* गुरु (Guru), மீன் *mīn* मीन् (Fish), தம்பி *thambi* तंबि (Brother), நரி *nari* नरि (Fox), இராஜா *irājā* इराजा (King), ஈ *ī* ई (Fly), பூ *pū* पू (Flower), கல் *kal* कल् (Stone), etc. and any other noun which does not fall in first three gorups, falls all in the 4th group by default.

ii. This group includes any noun that DOES NOT end in அம் *am* अम्, து *du* डु or று *ru* रु and masculine nouns nouns ending in ன் *n* न्.

TABLE 31 : EXAMPLE of Cases of the 4th type of nouns, like நரி *nari* नरि (Fox)

case	English हिंदी	GROUP 4 NOUN + CASE SUFFIXES	
		Singular	Plural
nom	Fox लोमड़ी	நரி *nari* नरि	நரிகள் *narikaḷ* नरिकळ्
acc.	to a fox लोमड़ी को	நரியை *nariyai* नरियै	நரிகளை *narikaḷai* नरिकलै
inst.	by a fox लोमड़ी से	நரியால் *nariyāl* नरियाल्	நரிகளால் *narikaḷāl* नरिकलाल्
dat.	to a fox लोमड़ी को	நரிக்கு *narikku* नरिक्कु	நரிகளுக்கு *narikaḷukku* नरिकलुक्कु
abl.	from a fox लोमड़ी से	நரியில் *nariyil* नरियिल्	நரிகளில் *narikaḷil* नरिकलिल्
poss	of a fox लोमड़ी का	நரியின் *nariyin* नरियिन्	நரிகளின் *narikaḷin* नरिकलिन्
loc.	in a fox लोमड़ी में	நரியில் *nariyil* नरियिल्	நரிகளில் *narikaḷil* नरिकलिल्
voc.	Oh Fox! हे लोमड़ी!	நரியே *nariye* नरिये!	நரிகளே *narikaḷe* नरिकले!
NOTE : There are exceptions to the common format shown above.			

EXERCISE : USE OF CASES with third Group of nouns ending in டு or று *du* or *ru* डु or रु

Translate into Tamil :

Answers are given for your help, if you need them

1. My Dog
   எ ன் நாய் *en nāy* एन् नाय्

2. The flowers on the tree
   மரத்தில் பூக்கள் *marattil pūkkaḷ* मरत्तिल् पूक्कल्

3. The fox lives in the forest. நரி காட்டில் வாழ்கிறார் *nari kāṭril vaḷkirār* नरि काट्रिल् वाळकिरार्

4. She bathes in the river அவள் ஆற்றில் குளிக்கிறாள் *avaḷ āṭṭril kuḷikkirāḷ* अवळ् आट्रिल कुळिक्किराळ्

5. There is no water in the well கிணற்றில் தண்ணீர் இல்லை *kiṇṭril thaṇṇīr illai* किण्ट्रिल् तण्णिर् इलै

6. He is my teacher அவர் என் குரு *avar en guru* अवर् एन् गुरु

7. Ram and Sita (pls. See note below). ராமனும் சீதையும் *rāmnum sītaiyum* रामनुम् सीतैयुम्

NOTE : In Sanskrit the 'and' (च) goes after each word of the group or at after the last word, but in Tamil construction the 'and' conjunction is placed after each word or after the last word. The last word takes case suffix and உம் *um* उम् as termination. Also remember, when உம் *um* उम् is placed after a single word, it has meaning of : also, too, even, only. For the English word 'or,' the Tamil word is அல்லது *alladu* अल्लदु.

9. Ram and Sita (pls. See note above). இராமனும் சீதையும் *irāmanum sītaaiyum* इरामनुम् सीदैयुम्

10. A goat and the cows. ஆடும் பசுக்களும் *āḍum pasukaḷum* आडुम पसुकलुम्

11. I or you நான் அல்லது நீர் *nān alladu nīr* नान् अल्लदु नीर्

12. Mine and your's எனதும் உனதும் *enathum unmyum* एनत्तुम् उनदुम्

13. Mine or your's எனதும் அல்லது உனதும் *enathumu alladu unmyumu* एनदुम् अल्लदु उनदुम्

14. Please call Seetha. சீதாவைக் கூப்பிடு *sīthāvaik kūppiḍu* सीतावैक् क्कूप्पिडु

15. Go with her. வளுடன் போ *vaḷuḍan po* वळुडन् पो

16. Which one is your home? உங்களுடைய வீடு எது *ungaḷuḍaiya vīḍu edu* ऊँगलुडैय वीडु एदु

17. Turn the light on. (ஏற் *er* एर् = Turn on) விளக்கு ஏற்று *viḷakku eṭru* विळक्कु एॅट्रु

SUMMARY OF SUFFIXES COMMON FOR ALL FOUR NOUN GROUPS

TABLE 32 : CASE SUFFIXES COMMON FOR ALL FOUR GROUPS

Case No.	Case name	English	हिंदी	Singular suffix	Plural suffix
1	Nominative	-	– , ने	-	கள் *kaḷ* कळ्
2	Accusative	to	को	ை *ai* ऐ	களை *kaḷai* कळै
3	Instrumental	with, by	से	ால் *āl* आल्	களால் *kaḷāl* कळाल्
4	Dative	to, for	को, के लिये	க்கு *kku* क्कु	களுக்கு *kaḷukku* कळुक्कु
5	Ablative	from	से	இல் *il* इल्	களில் *kaḷil* कळिल्
6	Possessive	of	का, की, के	இன் *in* इन्	களின் *kaḷin* कळिन्
7	Lacative	in, on, at, with	में, पर	இல் *yil* इल्	களில் *kaḷil* कळिल्
8	Vocative	Oh!	हे!	ே *e* ए!	களே *kaḷe* कळे!

This Table is developed for Sanskrit Hindi Research Institute for *"Learn Tamil Through English/Hindi"* by Ratnakar Narale.

10.5 THE CASES OF THE PRONOUNS

i. The cases of the pronouns are produced the same way as the general format of the nouns.
ii. The oblique cases of pronouns, that is the base for forming cases, is shown in Table 9
iii. As said earlier, when a word ending in a vowel is followed by a word beginning with க, ச, த, ப *k, ch, ta* or *pa*, क, च, त or प, the க, ச, த, ப is doubled.
iv. Also remember, when ற் *r* ऱ् is doubled, it is pronounced as *ṭr* ट्र or *ṭṭ* ट्ट (See Table 16)
v. Below is Table 33-A showing cases of pronouns in Tamil script. For the same data in English *Transliterated* script please see Table 33-B. And, for this info. in Devanagari (Hindi) script, please see Table 33-C presented below.
vi. Hindi equivalents of each pronoun inflection is provided in each table for your clear understanding.

TABLE 33-A : CASE SUFFIXES FOR PRONOUNS in TAMIL Script

1	2	3	4	5	6	7
Nom.	**Accusative**	**Instrumental**	**Dative**	**Ablative**	**Possessive**	**Locative**
	to ை	**with/by ால்**	**to/for க்கு**	**from இல்**	**of இன்**	**in/on/at இல்**
I मैं	**to me** मुझे	**w./by me** मुझसे	**to/for me** मुझे	**from me** मुझसे	**my** मेरा, मेरी	**in/on/at me** मुझमें
நான்	என்னை	என்னால் என்னோடு	எனக்கு எனக்காக	என்னில் என்னினின்று என்னிலிருந்து	என் * எனது என்னின் என்னுடைய	என்னில் என்னிடத்தில் என்னிடம் # (# see Table 27)
We हम	**to us** हमें	**with/by us** हमसे	**to/for us** हमें	**from us** हमसे	**our** हमारा, हमारी	**in/on/at us** हममें
நாங்கள்	எங்களை	எங்களால் எங்களோடு	எங்களுக்கு	எங்களில் எங்களிலிருந்து	எங்கள் * எங்களது எங்களின் எங்களுடைய	எங்களில் எங்களிடத்தில்
You तू	**to you** तुझे	**w./by you** तुझसे	**to/for you** तुझे	**from you** तुझसे	**your** तेरा, तेरी	**in/on/at you** तुझमें
நீ	உன்னை	உன்னால் உன்னோடு	உனக்கு உனக்காக	உன்னில் உன்னிலிருந்து	உன் * உனது உன்னின் உன்னுடைய	உன்னில் உன்னிடத்தில்
You आप	**to you** आपको	**w./by you** आपसे	**to you** आपको	**from you** आपसे	**your** आपका, आपकी	**in/on you** आपमें
நீர்	உம்மை	உம்னால் உம்னோடு	உமக்கு உமக்காக	உம்மில் உம்மிலிருந்து	உம் * உமது உம்முடைய	உம்மில் உம்மிடத்தில்
You all	**to you** आपको	**w./by you** आपसे	**to you** आपको	**from you** आपसे	**your** आपका, आपकी	**in/on you** आपमें
நீங்கள்	உங்களை	உங்களால் உங்களோடு உங்களுடன் # (# See Table 27)	உங்களுக்கு உங்களுக்காக	உங்களில் உங்களிலிருந்து	உங்கள் * உங்களது உங்களுடைய	உங்களில் உங்களிடத்தில்
He वह	**to him** उसे	**w./by him** उससे	**to/for him** उसे	**from him** उससे	**his** उसका, उसकी	**in/on/at him** उसमें
அவன்	அவனை	அவனால் அவனோடு	அவனுக்கு அவனுக்காக	அவனில் அவனிடத்திலி ருந்து	அவன் * அவனது அவனுடைய	அவனில் அவனிடத்தில்

She वह	**to her** उसे	**w./by her** उससे	**to/for her** उसे	**from her** उससे	**her** उसका, उसकी	**in/on/at her** उसमें
அவள்	அவளை	அவனால் அவனோடு	அவளுக்கு அவளுக்காக	அவளில் அவளிடத்திள்	அவள் * அவளது அவளுடைய	அவளில் அவளிடத்தில்
They वे	**to them** उन्हें	**w./by them** उनसे	**to them** उन्हें	**from them** उनसे	**Their** उनका, उनकी	**in/on/at them** उनमें
அவர்	அவரை	அவரால் அவரோடு	அவருக்கு அவருக்காக	அவரில் அவரிலிருந்து	அவர் * அவரது அவருடைய	அவரில் அவரிடத்தில்
They वे	**to them** उन्हें	**w./by them** उनसे	**to them** उन्हें	**from them** उनसे	**Their** उनका	**in/on/at them** उनमें
அவர்கள்	அவர்களை	அவர்களால் அவர்களோடு	அவர்களுக்கு அவர்களுக்காக	அவர்களில் அவர்களிலிருந்து	அவர்கள் * அவர்களது அவர்களுடைய	அவர்களில் அவர்களிடத்தில்
That वह	**to that** उसे	**w./by that** उससे	**to/for that** उसे	**from that** उससे	**Of that** उसका	**in/on/at that** उसमें
அது ***	அதை அதனை	அதால் அதனால் அதினால் அதோடு அதானோடு	அதிற்கு அதற்கு அதுக்கு அதனுக்கு அதற்க்காக	அதில் அதனில்	அதின் * அதன் * அதினது அதத்து அதினுடைய அதனுடைய	அதில் அதினிடத்தில் அதனிடத்தில்
Those वे	**to those** उन्हें	**w./by those** उनसे	**to those** उन्हें	**from those** उनसे	**Of those** उनका	**in/on those** उनमें
அவை அவைகள் அதுகள்	அவைகளை அவற்றை	அவைகளால் அவைகளோடு	அவைகளுக்கு அவைகளுக்காக அவற்றிற்கு	அவைகளில் அவற்றில்	அவைகள் * அவற்றின் அவைகளுடைய அவற்றினுடைய	அவைகளில் அவற்றில்
It यह **	**to it** इसे	**w./by it** इससे	**to/for it** इसे	**from it** इससे	**It's** इसका	**in/on/at it** इसमें
இது ***	இதை இதனை	இதால் இதனால் இதினால் இதோடு இதினோடு	இதிற்கு இதற்கு இதுக்கு இதனுக்கு இதற்க்காக	இதில் இதனில்	இதின் * இதன் * இதினது இதத்து இதினுடைய இதனுடைய	இதில் இதினிடத்தில் இதனிடத்தில்
These ये	**to these** इन्हें	**w./by these** इनसे	**to these** इन्हें	**from these** इनसे	**Of these** इनका	**in/on/at these** इनमें
இவை இவைகள் இதுகள்	இவைகளை இவற்றை	இவைகளால் இவைகளோடு	இவைகளுக்கு இவைகளுக்காக இவற்றிற்கு	இவைகளில் இவற்றில்	இவைகள் * இவற்றின் இவைகளுடைய இவற்றினுடைய	இவைகளில் இவற்றில்

NOTES : (i) * This form of Possessive case is used as Oblique case (inflectional base) to form other cases.

(ii) ** It यह **இது is the (neuter) object that is closer and That** वह **அது is the object that is farther.**

(iii) * The words (pronouns and nouns) begining with letter அ *a* अ that denote fartherness, denote nearness when the initial அ *a* अ is replaced with இ *i* इ.**

This Table is developed for Sanskrit Hindi Research Institute for *"Learn Tamil Through English/Hindi"* by Ratnakar Narale.

THE CASES OF THE PRONOUNS
in English Transliteration
PLEASE FOLLOW THE TAMIL TABLE
Use this table only for reference and varification

TABLE 33-B : CASE SUFFIXES FOR PRONOUNS in English *Transliteration*

1	2	3	4	5	6	7
Nom.	**Accusative**	**Instrumental**	**Dative**	**Ablative**	**Possessive**	**Locative**
I मैं	**to me** मुझे	**w./by me** मुझसे	**to/for me** मुझे	**from me** मुझसे	**my** मेरा	**in/on/at me** मुझमें
	to = *ai*	**with/by** = *āl*	**to/for =** *kku*	**from =** *il*	**of =** *in*	**in/on/at =** ***il***
nān	***ennai***	***ennāl*** ***ennoḍu***	***enakku*** ***enakkāga***	***ennil*** ***enninınru*** ***ennilirundu***	***en*** * ***enadu*** ***ennin*** ***ennuḍaiya***	***ennil*** ***enniḍattil*** ***enniḍam*** # **(# see Table 27)**
We हम	**to us** हमें	**with/by us** हमसे	**to/for us** हमें	**from us** हमसे	**our** हमारा	**in/on/at us** हममें
nāṅgaḷ	***eṅgaḷai***	***eṅngaḷāl*** ***eṅngaḷoḍu***	***eṅngaḷukku***	***eṅngaḷil*** ***eṅgaḷililirundu***	***eṅngaḷ*** * ***eṅngaḷadu*** ***eṅngaḷin*** ***eṅngaḷuḍaiya***	***eṅngaḷil*** ***eṅngaḷiḍattil***
You तू	**to you** तुझे	**w./by you** तुझसे	**to/for you** तुझे	**from you** तुझसे	**your** तेरा	**in/on/at you** तुझमें
nī	***unnai***	***unnāl*** ***unnoḍu***	***unakku*** ***unakkāga***	***unnil*** ***unnininru*** ***unnilirundu***	***un*** * ***unadu*** ***unnin*** ***unnuḍaiya***	***unnil*** ***unniḍattil***
You आप	**to you** आपको	**w./by you** आपसे	**to you** आपको	**from you** आपसे	**your** आपका	**in/on you** आपमें
nīr	***ummai***	***ummāl*** ***ummoḍu***	***umakku*** ***umakkāga***	***ummil*** ***ummilirundu***	***um*** * ***umadu*** ***ummuḍaiya***	***ummil*** ***ummiḍattil***
You all	**to you** आपको	**w./by you** आपसे	**to you** आपको	**from you** आपसे	**your** आपका	**in/on you** आपमें
nīṅgaḷ	***uṅgaḷai***	***uṅgaḷāl*** ***uṅgaḷoḍu*** ***uṅgaḷuḍan*** # **(See Table 27)**	***uṅgaḷukku*** ***uṅgaḷukkāga***	***uṅgaḷil*** ***uṅgaḷililirundu***	***uṅgaḷ*** * ***uṅgaḷadu*** ***uṅgaḷuḍaiya***	***uṅgaḷil*** ***uṅgaḷiḍattil***
He वह	**to him** उसे	**w./by him** उससे	**to/for him** उसे	**from him** उससे	**his** उसका	**in/on/at him** उसमें
avan	***avanai***	***avanāl*** ***avanoḍu***	***avanukku*** ***avanukkāga***	***avanil*** ***avaniḍattilirundu***	***avan*** * ***avanadu*** ***avanuḍaya***	***avanil*** ***avaniḍattil***
She वह	**to her** उसे	**w./by her** उससे	**to/for her** उसे	**from her** उससे	**her** उसका	**in/on/at her** उसमें
avaḷ	***avaḷai***	***avaḷāl*** ***avaḷoḍu***	***avaḷukku*** ***avaḷukkāga***	***avaḷil*** ***avaḷiḍattilirundu***	***avaḷ*** * ***avaḷadu*** ***avaḷuḍaya***	***avaḷil*** ***avaḷiḍattil***

They वे	**to them** उन्हें	**w./by them** उनसे	**to them** उन्हें	**from them** उनसे	**Their** उनका	**in/on/at them** उनमें
avar	***avarai***	***avarāl*** ***avaroḍu***	***avarukku*** ***avarukkāga***	***avaril*** ***avariḍattilirundu***	***avar**** ***avaradu*** ***avaruḍaya***	***avaril*** ***avariḍattil***
They वे	**to them** उन्हें	**w./by them** उनसे	**to them** उन्हें	**from them** उनसे	**Their** उनका	**in/on/at them** उनमें
avargaḷ	***avargaḷai***	***avargaḷāl*** ***avargaḷoḍu***	***avargaḷukku*** ***avargaḷukkā*** ***ga***	***avargaḷil*** ***avargaḷilirundu***	***avargaḷ**** ***avargaḷadu*** ***avargaḷuḍaya***	***avargaḷil*** ***avargaḷiḍattil***
That वह	**to that** उसे	**w./by that** उससे	**to/for that** उसे	**from that** उससे	**Of that** उसका	**in/on/at that** उसमें
adu ***	***adai*** ***adanai***	***adāl*** ***adanāl*** ***adināl*** ***adoḍu*** ***adanoḍu***	***adaṭku*** ***adiṭku*** ***adukku*** ***adanukku*** ***adaṭkāga***	***adil*** ***adanil***	***adin**** * ***adan*** * ***adinadu*** ***adanadu*** ***adinuḍaiya*** ***adanuḍaiya***	***adil*** ***adiniḍattil*** ***adaniḍattil***
Those वे	**to those** उन्हें	**w./by those** उनसे	**to those** उन्हें	**from those** उनसे	**Of those** उनका	**in/on those** उनमें
avai ***avaigaḷ*** ***adugaḷ***	***avaigaḷai*** ***avaṭṭai***	***avaigaḷāl*** ***avaigaḷoḍu***	***avaigaḷukku*** ***avaigaḷukkāga*** ***avaṭṭiku***	***avaigaḷil*** ***avaṭril***	***avaigaḷ**** ***avaṭrin*** ***avaigaḷuḍaiya*** ***avaṭrinudaiya***	***avaigaḷil*** ***avaṭril***
It यह **	**to it** इसे	**w./by it** इससे	**to/for it** इसे	**from it** इससे	**It's** इसका	**in/on/at it** इसमें
idu ***	***idai*** ***idanai***	***idāl*** ***idanāl*** ***idināl*** ***idoḍu*** ***idanoḍu***	***idaṭku*** ***idiṭku*** ***idukku*** ***idanukku*** ***idaṭkāga***	***idil*** ***idanil***	***idin**** * ***idan*** * ***idinadu*** ***idanadu*** ***idinuḍaiya*** ***idanuḍaiya***	***idil*** ***idiniḍattil*** ***idaniḍattil***
These ये	**to these** इन्हें	**w./by these** इनसे	**to these** इन्हें	**from these** इनसे	**Of these** इनका	**in/on/at these** इनमें
ivai ***ivaigaḷ*** ***idugaḷ***	***ivaigaḷai*** ***ivaṭṭai***	***ivaigaḷāl*** ***ivaigaḷoḍu***	***ivaigaḷukku*** ***ivaigaḷukkāga*** ***ivaṭṭiku***	***ivaigaḷil*** ***ivaṭril***	***ivaigaḷ**** ***ivaṭrin*** ***ivaigaḷuḍaiya*** ***ivaṭrinudaiya***	***ivaigaḷil*** ***ivaṭril***

NOTES : (i) * This form of Possessive case is used as Oblique case (inflectional base) to form other cases.

(ii) ** It यह **இது is the (neuter) object that is closer and That** वह **அது is the object that is farther.**

(iii) * The words (pronouns and nouns) begining with letter அ *a* अ that denote fartherness, denote nearness when the initial அ *a* अ is replaced with இ *i* इ.**

This Table is developed for Sanskrit Hindi Research Institute for *"Learn Tamil Through English/Hindi"* by Ratnakar Narale.

THE CASES OF THE PRONOUNS
in Hindi Script
PLEASE FOLLOW THE TAMIL TABLE
Use this table only for reference and varification

TABLE 33-C : CASE SUFFIXES FOR PRONOUNS in Hindi Script

1	2	3	4	5	6	7
Nom.	**Accusative**	**Instrumental**	**Dative**	**Ablative**	**Possessive**	**Locative**
	to = ऐ	**with/by** = आल्	**to/for** = क्कु	**from** = इल्	**of** = इन्	**in/on/at** = इल्
I मैं	**to me** मुझे	**w./by me** मुझसे	**to/for me** मुझे	**from me** मुझसे	**my** मेरा	**in/on/at me** मुझमें
नान्	एन्नै	एन्नाल् एन्नोडु	एनक्कु एनक्काग	एन्निल् एन्निनिन्रु एन्निलिरुन्दु	एन् * एनदु एन्निन् एन्नुडैय	एन्निल् एन्निडत्तिल् एन्निडम् # **(# see Table 27)**
We हम	**to us** हमें	**with/by us** हमसे	**to/for us** हमें	**from us** हमसे	**our** हमारा	**in/on/at us** हममें
नांगळ्	एंगळै	एंगळाल् एंगळोडु	एंगळुक्कु	एंगळिल् एंगळिलिरुन्दु	एंगळ * एंगळदु एंगळिन् एंगळुडैय	एंगळिल् एंगळिडत्तिल्
You तू	**to you** तुझे	**w./by you** तुझसे	**to/for you** तुझे	**from you** तुझसे	**your** तेरा	**in/on/at you** तुझमें
नी	उन्नै	उन्नाल् उन्नोडु	उनक्कु उनक्काग	उन्निल् उन्निनिन्रु उन्निलिरुन्दु	उन् * उनदु उन्निन् उन्नुडैय	उन्निल् उन्निडैय
You आप	**to you** आपको	**w./by you** आपसे	**to you** आपको	**from you** आपसे	**your** आपका	**in/on you** आपमें
नीर्	उम्मै	उम्माल् उम्मोडु	उमक्कु उमक्काग	उम्मिल् उम्मिलिरुन्दु	उम * उमदु उम्मुडैय	उम्मिल् उम्मिडत्तिल्
You all	**to you** आपको	**w./by you** आपसे	**to you** आपको	**from you** आपसे	**your** आपका	**in/on you** आपमें
नींगळ्	उँगळै	उँगळाल् उँगळोडु ऊँगळुडन् **#** **(See Table 27)**	उँगळुक्कु उँगळुक्काग	उँगळिल् उँगळिलिरुन्दु	उँगळ् * उँगळदु उँगळुडैय	उँगळिल् उँगळिडत्तिल्
He वह	**to him** उसे	**w./by him** उससे	**to/for him** उसे	**from him** उससे	**his** उसका	**in/on/at him** उसमें
अवन्	अवनै	अवनाल् अवनोडु	अवनुक्कु अवनुक्काग	अवनिल् अवनिडत्तिलिरुन्दु	अवन् * अवनदु अवनुडैय	अवनिल् अवनिडत्तिल्
She वह	**to her** उसे	**w./by her** उससे	**to/for her** उसे	**from her** उससे	**her** उसका	**in/on/at her** उसमें
अवळ्	अवळै	अवळाल् अवळोडु	अवळुक्कु अवळुक्काग	अवळिल् अवळिडत्तिलिरुन्दु	अवळ् * अवळदु अवळुडैय	अवळिल् अवळिडत्तिल्
They वे	**to them** उन्हें	**w./by them** उनसे	**to them** उन्हें	**from them** उनसे	**Their** उनका	**in/on/at them** उनमें

अवर्	अवरै	अवराल् अवरोडु	अवरुक्कु अवरुक्काग	अवरिल् अवरिडत्तिलिरुन्दु	अवर् * अवरदु अवरुडैय	अवरिल् अवरिडत्तिल्
They वे	**to them** उन्हें	**w./by them** उनसे	**to them** उन्हें	**from them** उनसे	**Their** उनका	**in/on/at them** उनमें
अवर्गळ्	अवर्गळै	अवर्गळाल् अवर्गळोडु	अवर्गळुक्कु अवर्गळुक्काग	अवर्गळिल् अवर्गळिडत्तिलिरुन्दु	अवर्गळ् * अवर्गळदु अवर्गळुडैय	अवर्गळिल् अवर्गळिडत्तिल्
That वह	**to that** उसे	**w./by that** उससे	**to/for that** उसे	**from that** उससे	**Of that** उसका	**in/on/at that** उसमें
अदु ***	अदै अदनै	अदाल् अदनाल् अदिनाल् अदोडु अदनोडू	अदट्कु अदिट्कु अदुक्कु अदट्काग्	अदिल् अदनिल्	अदिन् * अदन् * अदिनदु अदिनुडैय अदनुडैय	अदिल् अदिनिडत्तिल् अदणिडत्तिल्
Those वे	**to those** उन्हें	**w./by those** उनसे	**to those** उन्हें	**from those** उनसे	**Of those** उनका	**in/on those** उनमें
अवै अवैगळ् अदुगळ्	अवैगळै अवट्टै	अवैगळाल् अवैगळोडु	अवैगळुक्कु अवैगळुक्काग अवट्टिकु	अवैगळिल् अवट्रिल्	अवैगळ * अवट्रिन् अवैगळुडैय अवट्रिनुडैय	अवैगळिल् अवट्रिल्
It यह **	**to it** इसे	**w./by it** इससे	**to/for it** इसे	**from it** इससे	**It's** इसका	**in/on/at it** इसमें
इदु ***	इदै इदनै	इदाल् इदनाल् इदिनाल् इदोडु इदनोडू	इदट्कु इदिट्कु इदुक्कु इदट्काग्	इदिल् इदनिल्	इदिन् * इदन् * इदिनदु इदिनुडैय इदनुडैय	इदिल् इदिनिडत्तिल् इदणिडत्तिल्
These ये	**to these** इन्हें	**w./by these** इनसे	**to these** इन्हें	**from these** इनसे	**Of these** इनका	**in/on/at these** इनमें
इवै इवैगळ् इदुगळ्	इवैगळै इवट्टै	इवैगळाल् इवैगळोडु	इवैगळुक्कु इवैगळुक्काग इवट्टिकु	इवैगळिल् इवट्रिल्	इवैगळ * इवट्रिन् इवैगळुडैय इवट्रिनुडैय	इवैगळिल् इवट्रिल्

NOTES : (i) * This form of Possessive case is used as Oblique case (inflectional base) to form other cases.

(ii) ** It यह இது is the (neuter) object that is closer and That वह அது is the object that is farther.

(iii) * The words (pronouns and nouns) begining with letter அ *a* अ that denote fartherness, denote nearness when the initial அ *a* अ is replaced with இ *i* इ.**

EXERCISE : USE OF CASES OF NOUN AND PNOUNS :

Translate into Tamil — Answers are given for your help, if you need

1. Recite (say) a poem (एक कविता को सुनाओ) ஒரு கவிதை சொல்லு *oru kavidai sollu* ओरु कविदै सोल्लु
2. I am going to Mumbai நான் பம்பாயக்குப் ன் *nān bambāykkup pokiren* नान् बंबायक्कुप् पोकिरेन्
3. Banglore's weather (Weather = காலசுபாவம்) பங்களூரின் காலசுபாவம் *bangalurin kālsubāvam* बंगलुरिन् कालसुभावम्
4. In India இந்தியாவில் *indiavil* इन्दियाविल्

5. In the train (Train = ரயில் வண்டி *rayil vaṇḍi* रयिल वण्डि) ரயில் வண்டியில் *rayilvaṇḍyil* रयिल् वण्डियिल्

6. The cities of India (City = நகரம் *nagaram* नगरम्) இந்தியாவின் நகரங்கள் *indiavin nagaraṅgaḷ* इन्दियाविन् नगरंगळ्

7. In Mathura மதுராவில் *Mathurāviḷ* मथुराविल्

8. I am going to Delhi நான் தில்லிக்கும் போகிறேன் *nān dillikkum pogiren* नान् दिल्लिक्कुम् पोगिरेन्

9. In this city (நகரம் *naaram* नगरम् = City) இந்த நகரில் *inda nagariḷ* इन्द नगरिल्

10. A glass of water for you. உனக்கு ஒரு பாத்திரம் தண்ணீர் *unakku oru pāttiram taṇṇīr* उनक्कु ओरु पात्तिरम् तण्णीर्

11. A cup of tea for me. எனக்கு ஒரு கிண்ணம் தேநீர் *enakku oru pāttiram tenīr* एनक्कु ओरु किण्णम् तेनीर्

12. I do not have money (Have = on me). என்னிடம் பணம் இல்லை *enniḍam paṇam illai* एन्निडम् पणम् इल्लै

13. How far is Railway station from here? இங்கிருந்து ரயில்வே ஸ்டேஷன் எவ்வளவு தூரம் *iṅgirundu railway station evvaḷavu dūram* इंगिरुन्दु रयिल्वे स्टोशन एव्वळवु दूरम्

14. I am coming with you (will come with you) to Railway station. நான் உங்களுடன் ரயில்வே ஸ்டேஷனுக்கு வருகிறேன் *nān uṅgaḷuḍan railway stationukku varugiren* नान् उँगळुडन् रयिलवे स्टेशनुक्कु वरुगिरेन्

15. I am going by airplane. நான் விமானத்தில் போகிறேன் *nān vimānattil pogiren* नान् विमानत्तिल् पोगिरेन्

16. She went to England by ship. அவள் கப்பலில் இங்கிலாந்திற்கு போனாள் *avaḷ kappalil engilāndirku ponāḷ* अवळ् कप्पलिल् इंगिलान्दिर्कु पोनाळ् *

NOTE : * In Tamil special particles can be optionally used in place of some case suffixes. One of them is கு or க்கு *ku* or *kku* कु or क्कु = 'to.' A substitute for the Accusative case suffix ை *ai* ऐ e.g. to England = இங்கிலாந்திற்கு *engilāndirku* इंगिलान्दिक For more such particles, please see next lesson.

17. What is the fare for Airport? (கட்டணம் *kaṭṭaṇam* कट्टणम् = Fare, rent) விமான நிலையத்துக்கு என்ன கட்டணம்? *vimān nilayaddukku enna kaṭṭaṇam nagariḷ* विमान निलैयद्दुक्कु एन्न कट्टणम्

18. Whose phone is it (who is calling on phone)? (அழை *aḻai* अऴै = Call, invite) யார் போனில் அழைக்கிறார்கள் *yār phonil araḻikkirārgaḷ* यार् फोनिल् अऴैक्किरार्गळ्

19. Wrong number! (தப்பு *tappu* तप्पु= Wrong; எண் *eṇ* एण् = Number) தப்பு எண் *tappu eṇ* तप्पु एण्

20. You are welcome! (आपका स्वागत है) (நல் *nal* नल् = Well, good) உங்களுக்கு நல் வரவு *uṅgaḷukku nallāvu varavu* ऊँगळुक्कु नल्लावु वरवु

21. This is the key for your room. (சாவி *chāvi* चावि = Key) இது உங்கள் அறையின் சாவி *idu uṅgaḷ araiyin chāvi* इदु उँगळ् अरैयिन् चावि

22. Please give me three rupees. (ரூபாய் *rūpāy* रूपाय् = Rupee, Rupees; தயவு செய்து *dayavu saidu* दयवु सयदु = Please) தயவு செய்து மூன்று ரூபாய் கொடுங்கள் *dayavu saidu mūnru rūpāy koṇḍugaḷ* दयवु सयदु मुन्रु रूपाय् कोडुंगळ्

23. My name is Ratnakar. என் பெயர் ரத்னாகரன் *en peyar ratnākar* एन् पेयर् रत्नाकरन्

24. Mala is my friend. (தோழி *toḻi* तोऴी = Friend f.) மாலா என்னுடைய தோழி *mālā ennuḍaiya toḻi* माला एन्नुडैय तोऴि

25. What will you take with coffee? காபியோடு என்ன சாப்பிடுகிறீர்கள் *kafi enna sāppidu girirgaḷ?* काफी योडु एन्न साप्पिडु-गिरीर्गळ्?

LESSON 11

USING PRE-MADE TAMIL SENTENCES, Part II

PLEASE THINK THIS, BEFORE YOU BEGIN

i. When you learn to make your own sentences, you know what you are doing. You know how each word form is made and why the word is written that way. You will recognize this reality when you try to learn Tamil through the pre-made sentences. If you learn Tamil through only pre-made sentences, as usually done, you will be stabbing in the dark. You should use the pre-made sentences only to improve your learning by studying them in the light of what you have learned.

ii. If you know Sanskrit grammar, you may have figured out from the previous lessons that Tamil grammar is based on similar style like Sanskrit, even though it is not as vast as Sanskrit. If you want to see or learn Sanskrit grammar to any depth, you may like to use my *"Learn Sanskrit through English Medium."*

iii. If you know Hindi, you must have discovered by now that Tamil grammar is much more deep, logical and systematic than the Hindi Grammar you learned in schools. In Hindi grammar, the gender is single most important aspect but it is very arbitrary with no fixed rules, the use of cases is mixed up and the tenses are violated too often. If you want to learn Hindi in a systematic manner, you may like to use my book *"Learn Hindi through English Medium,"* with properly laid out rules, noble truths, grammar dissection and unique tables.

iii. If you studied in English schools, you may have guessed that the English Grammar is too brief, simple, cut and dry, as compared to the Tamil grammar. It is systematic like Tamil.

iv. The present book (Volume I) deals only with the very bsic primary level of the vast Tamil grammar. For the use of Tamil Grammar at next level, and for the use of a fully transliterated English-Tamil Dictionary, please see Volume II of this book.

v. Again, make sure you have studied and understood previous chapters properly, before going ahead with this and the next lessons.

vi. The answers to the questions are provided in this book for your 'help' only. Please first see if you can answer the questions by yourself, theu look at the answers just to verify your answers.

vii. In each exercise, the English transliteration and Hindi is given for your assistance only. Please learn through the Tamil script. Use English and Hindi only wher you are in doubt.

books-india.com

PRE-MADE ENGLISH-TAMIL SENTENCES
Part II

NOTE : You may not understand every part of all these sentences, but as we make more of our own sentences in the following chapters, you will see these sentences more clearly if you revise this over.

1. Excuse me, What time is the train for Mumbai? மன்னிக்கவும் பம்பாய் போகும் வண்டி எப்பொழுது வரும் *mannikkavum! bambāy pohum vaṇḍī eppoḻudu varum* मन्निक्कवुम्! बम्बाय पोहुम् वण्डि एप्पोऴुदु वरुम्?
2. Fifty Dollars ninety cents. ஐம்பது டாலர் தொண்ணூறு செண்ட் *aimbadu dālar toṇṇūru sent* ऐम्बदु डालर् तोण्णूरु सेंट्
3. How far is Washington from here? வாஷிங்க்டண் இங்கிருந்து எவ்வளவு தூரம் *Washingṭon iṅgirundu evvaḷavu dūram* वाशिंगटन इंगिरुन्दु एव्वळवु दूरम्?
4. About five hundred k.m. சுமார் ஐந்நூறு கிலோமீட்டர் *sumār ainnūru kilomīṭṭar* सुमार् एन्नूरु किलोमिट्टर्
5. Where is it? இது எங்கே இருக்கிறது *idu eṅge irukkirdu* इदु एंगे इरुक्किरदु?
6. Please give me ten tickets. எனக்கு பத்துட்டிக்கேட்கள் கொடுங்கள் *enakku pattuṭṭikeṭhaḷ koḍuṅgal* एनक्कु पत्तुट्टिक्केटहळ् कोडुंगळ्
7. What is the news? (क्या खबर है?) என்ன சமாசாரம்? *enna samāchāram?* एन्न समाचारम्?
8. Who is he? அது யார் *adu yār* अदु यार्?
9. Does he know you? அவனுக்கு உன்னைத் தெரியுமா *avanukku unnai teriyumā* अवनुक्कु उन्नै तेरियुमा?
10. When did you (all) come? நீங்கள் எப்போது வந்தீர்கள் *niṅgaḷ eppodu vandīrgaḷ* नींगळ् एप्पोदु वंदीर्गळ्?
11. What does she do? அவள் என்ன செய்கிறாள் *yār avaḷ enna seygirāḷ* अवळ् एन्न सेय्गिराळ्?
12. What happened to you? உனக்கு என்ன ஆயிற்று *unakku enna āyiṭru* उनककु एन्न आयिट्रु
13. Come later! பிறகு வா *piragu vā* पिरगु वा
14. Have a seat. அமருங்கள் *amaruṅgaḷ* अमरुंगळ्
15. Please give me the newspaper. எனக்கு செய்தி ஏடு கொடு *enakku saydi eḍu koḍu* एनक्कु सेय्दि ए‍ॅड्डु कोड्डु
16. Please call the doctor. டாக்டரைக்கூப்பிடு *dākṭaraikkūppiḍu* डॉक्टरैक्कूप्पिड्डु
17. What can I do for you (आपकी मैं क्या सेवा कर सकता हूँ)? உங்களுக்கு நான் என்ன சேவை செய்ய *uṅgaḷukku nān enna sevai seyya* उँगळुक्कु नान् एन्न सेवै सेय्य?
18. I am thankful to you. நான் கடமைப்பட்டிருக்கிறேன் *nān kaḍamaippaṭṭirukkiren* नान् कडमैप्पट्टिरुक्किरेन्
19. Please don't bother me! என்னைத்தொந்திரவு செய்யாதே *ennaittondiravu saeyyaade* एन्नैत्तोन्दिरवु सेय्यादे
20. Let's go. வாருங்கள் போவோம் *vāruṅgaḷ povom* वारुंगळ् पोवोम्
21. May I go now? நான் இவ்வேளை போகலாமா *nān ivveḷai pogalāmā* नान् इव्वेळै पोगलामा?
22. Now you can go. இனி நீங்கள் போகலாம் *ini nīṅgaḷ pogalām* इनि नींगळ् पोगलाम्
23. Don't worry! That's ok! Doesn't matter! பரவாயில்லை *parvā illai* परवा इलै
24. It's none of your fault. உங்கள் மேல் குற்றமில்லை *uṅgaḷ mel kuṭramillai* उँगळ् मेल् कुट्रमिल्लै
25. Don't worry. கவலைப்படாதே *kavalai paḍāde* कवलै पडादे
26. Don't be afraid. பயப்படாதே *bhayappadāde* भयप्पडादे
27. Wonderful. ஆச்சர்யகரமானது *āchcharyakaramānadu* आच्चर्यकरमानदु (आच्चर्यकर–मान्–अदु)
28. Please! தயவுசெய் *dayavusey* दयवुसेय्
29. Please say it again. தயவுசெய்து மறுபடியும் சொல்லுங்கள் *dayavuseydu marubaḍiyum solluṅgaḷ* दयवुसेय्दु मरुबडियुम् सोल्लुंगळ्
30. I understand! என்க்குப் புரிகிறது *enakkup purigiradu* एनक्कु प्पुरिगिरदु
31. Where there is a will there is a way. மனமிருந்தால் மார்கமுண்டு *manamirundāl mārgamuṇḍu* मन–मिरुन्दाल्

मार्ग-मुण्डु.

32. Do you have any books? உங்களிடம் புத்தகங்கள் ஏதேனும் இருக்குமா *ungaḷiḍam puttahangaḷ edenum irukkumā* उँगळिडम् पुत्तहंगळ् एँदेनुम् इरुक्कुमा?

33. Which way is your home? உம்முடைய வீடு எந்தப்பக்கம் இருக்கிறது *ummuḍaiya vīḍu endappakkam irukkiradu* उम्मुडैय वीडु एन्दप्पक्कम् इरुक्किरदु?

34. This way it is. இந்தப்பக்கம் இருக்கிறது *indappakkam irukkiradu* इन्दप्पक्कम् इरुक्किरदु

35. At two-thirty (O Clock) ढाई बजे இரண்டைரை மணிக்கு *iraṇḍarai maṇikku* इरण्डरै मणिक्कु

36. About one week. சுமார் ஒரு வாரம் *sumār oru vāram* सुमार् ओरु वारम्

37. In the trunk of the car. காரின் டிக்கியில் *kārin dikkiyil* कारिन् डिक्कियिल्

38. Today, in the morning. இன்று காலை *inru kālai* इन्रु काल

39. Today the weather is not good. இன்று வானிலை மோசமாக இருக்கிறது *inru vānilai mosamāg irukkirdu* इन्रु वानिलै मोसमाग इरुक्किरदु

40. Where is Mr. Rajan. திரு ராசன் எங்கே *thiru Rājan enge* तिरु राजन् एंगे?

41. Please sign here. தயவு செய்து இங்கு ஒப்பமிடுங்கள் *dayavu seydu ingu oppamiḍungaḷ* दयवु सेयदु इंगु ओप्पमिडुंगळ्

42. Today I am very busy. இன்று எனக்கு வேலைகல் உண்டு *inru enakku velaikal uṇdu* इन्रु वेलैकल् उंडु

43. I am Raman talking. இராமன் பேசுகிறேன் *irāman pesugiren* इरामन् पेसुगिरेन्

44. What is the price of this? இது என்ன விலை *idu enna vilai* इदु एन्न विलै?

45. Are you a dentist? நீங்கள் பல் வைத்தியரா *nīngaḷ pal vaiddiyarā* नींगळ् पल् वैद्दियरा?

46. What (work) do you do? உங்களுக்கு என்ன வேலை *ungalukku enna velai* उँगळुक्कु एन्न वेलै?

47. Anything more, Sir? இன்னும் எதாவது வேண்டுமா அய்யா? *innum edāvadu veṇḍumā, aiya* इन्नुं एदावदु वेण्डुमा, अय्या?

48. Will you come to market with me? என்னுடன் கடைவீதி வரைக்கும் வா *annuḍan kaḍaivīdi varaikkum vā* एन्नुडन् कडैवीदि वरैक्कुम् वा?

49. Do you have my book? உங்களிடம் என் புத்தகம் இருக்கிறதா *ungliḍam en puttaham irukkiradā* उँगळिडम् एन् पुत्तहम् इरुक्किरदा?

50. Yes, I do. ஆம் இருக்கிறது *ām, irukkirdu* आम्, इरुक्किरदु

51. No Sir, thanks. நன்றி, வேண்டாம் *nanri, vaṇḍām* नन्रि, वेण्डाम्

52. Naturally. இயற்கை தான் *iyarkai tān* इयर्कै तान्

53. Yes. ஆம் (ஆமாம்) *ām (āmām)* आम् (आमाम्)

54. How are you, Madam? நீ எப்படி இருக்கிறாய் அம்மணி *enī eppadi irukkīrāy ammaṇi* एप्पडि इरुक्कींराय् अम्मणि?

55. Where is the book? புத்தகம் எங்கிருக்கிறது *puttaham engirukkirdu* पुत्तहम एंगिरुक्किरदु?

56. I will call a doctor (I am calling a doctor). டாக்டரை கூப்பிடுகிறேன் *dakṭarai kūppiḍugiren* डॉक्टरै कूप्पिडुगिरेन्

57. I do not drink (liquor). நான் சாராயம் குடிப்பதில்லை *nān sārāyam kuḍippadillai* नान् सारायम् कुडिप्पदिलै

58. How old are you? உங்களுக்கு வயது என்ன *ungaḷukku vayadu enna* उँगळुक्कु वयदु एन्न?

59. What did the doctor say? டாக்டர் என்ன சொன்னார் *ḍākṭar enna sonnār* डॉक्टर एन्न सोन्नार्?

60. There is no reason to worry. கவலைக்கு காரணமேதுமில்லை *kavalaikku kāraṇamedumillai* कवलैक्कु कारणमेदुमिल्लै

books-india.com

LESSON 12

ADJECTIVES, ADVERBS AND PARTICLES

1. Adjectives and Adverbs

i. An adjective is a word that qualifies or describes a noun.

ii. An adverb is a word that qualifies or describes a verb, an adjective or another adverb.

iii. Tamil adjectives and adverbs are indeclinable. They do not have Gender or Number. e.g.

1. Good boy நல்ல பையன் *nalla paiyan* नल्ल पैयन्
2. Good boys நல்ல பையன்கள் *nalla paiyaṅgaḷ* नल्ल पैयंगळ्
3. Good girl நல்ல பெண் *nalla peṇ* नल्ल पेण्
4. Good girls நல்ல பெண்கள் *nalla peṇgaḷ* नल्ल पेण्गळ्

iv. Tamil adjectives are prefixed to the nouns. e.g. good boy நல்ல பையண் *nalla paiyan* नल्ल पैयन्

v. Some words are by nature adjectives or adverbs. e.g. good நல்ல *nalla* नल्ल, Bad கெட்ட *keṭṭa* केट्ट,

vi. Some adjectives and adverbs are formed from nouns by adding suffixes such as :
ஆன், வான், லான், மான், தான், ளான், பான், உள்ள, இய, ஆத *ān, vān, lān, mān, tān, ḷān, pān, uḷḷ, iya, ād* आन्, वान्, लान्, मान्, तान्, ळान्, पान्, उळ्ळ, इय, आद, etc. Note that some of these suffixes are same as Sanskrit आन्, मान, वान्, ईय adjectival suffixes.

TABLE 34 : NOUNS - ADJECTIVES

NOUN				ADJECTIVE			
Truth	உண்மை	*ummai*	उण्मै	True	உண்மையான	*ummaiyān*	उण्मैयान
Heat	சூடு	*sūḍu*	सूड्ड	Hot	சூடுள்ள	*sūḍuḷḷa*	सूड्डुळ्ळ्
Falsehood	பொய்	*poy*	पोय्	False	பொய்யான	*poyyān*	पोय्यान
Length	நீளம்	*nīḷam*	नीळम्	Long	நீளமான	*nīḷamān*	नीळमान
Shortness	சுறுக்கம்	*surukkam*	सुरुक्कम्	Short	சுறுக்கமான	*surukkamān*	सुरुक्कमान
Use	உபயோக	*upayoga*	उपयोग	Useful	உபயோகமான	*upayogamān*	उपयोगमान
Industry	சுறுசுறுப்பு	*suruuruppu*	सुरुसुरुप्पु	Industrious	சுறுசுறுப்புள்ள	*surusuruppuḷḷa*	सुरुसुरुप्पुळ्ळ
Wisdom	ஞானம்	*jñānam*	ज्ञान	Wise	ஞானமுள்ள	*jñānamuḷḷa*	ज्ञानमुळ्ळ्
Longing	வேண்டி	*veṇḍi*	वेण्डि	Long for	வேண்டிய	*veṇḍiya*	वेण्डिय

This Table is developed for Sanskrit Hindi Research Institute for *"Learn Tamil Through English/Hindi"* by Ratnakar Narale.

books-india.com

vii. From the adjectives, masculine or faminine nouns can be formed by attachinf **வன்** *van* वन् or **வள்** *vaḷ* वळ् suffix. e.g.

1. **நாணயமான** *nāṇyamān* नाणयमान (Trustworthy)
2. **நாணயமானவன்** *nāṇyamānvan* नाणयमानवन् (Trustworthy man) *nāṇyamān*
3. **நாணயமானவள்** *nāṇyamānvaḷ* नाणयमानवळ् (Trustworthy woman)

viii. Adverbs can be formed by attaching **ஆக** *āha* आह or **ஆய்** *āy* आय् suffix to the nouns or adjectives. e.g.

TABLE 35 : NOUNS - ADVERBS

NOUN / ADJECTIVE				ADVERB			
Softness	மெது	*medu*	मेदु	Softly	மெதுவாக	*meduvāh*	मेदुवाह
Speed	வேகம்	*vegam*	वेगम्	Fast	வேகமாக	*vegmāh*	वेगमाह
Beauty	அழகு	*alku*	अळकु	Beautifully	அழகாக	*aḷkāh*	अळगाह
Fine	மென்மை	*menmai*	मेन्मै	Finely	மென்மையாய்	*menmaiyāy*	मेन्मैयाय्
Slow	மெது	*medu*	मेदु	Slowly	மெதுமவாய்	*meduvāy*	मेदुवाय्
Happy	மகிழ்சி	*makiḷsi*	मकिळ्सि	Happily	மாகிழசியாய்	*makiḷsiyāy*	मकिळ्सियाय्
This Table is developed for Sanskrit Hindi Research Institute for *"Learn Tamil Through English/Hindi"* by Ratnakar Narale.							

ix. Adverbs of much emphasis can be made from other regular adverbs by attaching **மிக** *miha* मिह or **நிரம்ப** *niramb* निरंब suffix. e.g.

1. Beautifully **அழகாக** *alǵāh* अळ्गाह
2. <u>Very</u> beautifully **மிக அழகாக** *miha alǵāh* मिह अळ्गाह
1. Fast **வேகமாக** *vegmāh* वेगमाह
2. <u>Much</u> fast **நிரம்ப வேகமாக** *niramb vegmāh* निरंब वेगमाह

EXERXISE :

Translate into Tamil — Answers are given for your help, if you need them

1. I am running fast. — நான் வேகமாக ஒடுகிறேன் *nān vegamāh oḍukiren* नान् वेगमाह ओडुकिरेन्
2. She is running very fast. — அவள் நிரம்ப வேகமாக ஒடுகிறாள் *avaḷ niramb vegamāh oḍukirāḷ* अवळ् निरंब वेगमाह ओडुकिराळ्
3. He is walking slowly — அவன் மெதுவாய் நடக்கிறான் *avaṇ medumāy naḍkkirān* अवन् मेदुवाय् नडक्किरान्
4. She says it very beautifully — அவள் மிக அழகாக சொல்கிறாள் *avaḷ miha aḷgāh solkirāḷ* अवळ् मिह अळ्गाह सोल्किराळ्
5. They are playing happily. — அவர்கள் மகிழ்சியாய் விளையாடுகிறார்கள் *avargaḷ anukūlayāy viḷaiyarukirārgaḷ* अवर्गळ् मकिळ्सियाय् विळैयारुकिरार्गळ्

books-india.com

2. Particles of Emphasis

1. உம் *um* उम् (and, also, even हिंदी : और, भी)

1. Suffix உம் *um* उम् acts like English conjunction 'and.' Like Sanskrit, it is attached to each word or at the end of the linked words. e.g.
   i. Book and pencil. புத்தகமும் பென்சில் *puttakamum pencil* पुत्तहमुम् पेंसिल.
   ii. Ram and Sita. இராமனும் சீதையும் *irāmanum sīthaiyum* इरामनुम् सीदैयुम्.

2. When உம் *um* उम् is attached to a single noun, it means 'also' or 'too' (भी) e.g.
   i. Me too, I also (मैं भी). நானும் *nānaum* नानुम्

2. ஓ *o* ओ (or हिंदी : या)

3. Suffix ஓ *o* ओ acts like English conjunction 'or.' Like Sanskrit, it is attached to each word or at the end of the linked words. e.g.
   i. Book or pencil. புத்தகமோ பென்சில் *puttakamo pencil* पुत्तहमो पेंसिल.
   ii. Ram or Sita. இராமனோ சீதாவோ *irāmano sīthāvo* इरामनो सीदावो.

3. ஆவது *āvadu* आवदु (or, at least हिंदी : कम से कम)

4. Suffix ஆவது *āvadu* आवदु also acts like English conjunction 'or.' Like Sanskrit, it is attached to each linked word. e.g.
   i. Book or pencil. புத்தகமாவது பென்சிலாவது *puttakamāvadu pencilavadu* पुत्तकमावदु पेंसिलावदु.
   ii. Ram or Sita. இராமனாவது சீதையாவது *irāmanāvadu sīthaiyāvadu* इरामनावदु सीदैयावदु
   iii. I or she. நானாவது அவளாவது *nānavadu avaḷāvadu* नानावदु अवळावदु.

4. ஆனால் *ānāl* आनाल् (yet, still हिंदी : फिर भी)

5. Suffix ஆனால் *ānāl* आनाल् acts like English conjunction 'still or yet' e.g.
   i. This book is small yet it is good. இந்த புத்தகம் சிறியது ஆனால் அழகானது *inda puttaham siriyadu ānāl alágānadu* इन्द पुत्तहम् सिरियदु आनाल् अऴगानदु

5. முற்றிலும் *muṭrilum* मुट्रिलुम् (all, whole हिंदी : सब)

6. The adverbial suffix முற்றிலும் *muṭrilum* मुट्रिलुम् is used for saying entire or whole of

something. e.g.

i. The whole countrry. (Country = நாடு *nāḍu* नाडु) நாடு முற்றிலும் *nāḍu muṭrilum* नाडु मुट्रिलुम्

7. Optionally suffix முழுதும் *muludum* मुळुदुम् or அனைத்தும் *anaiddum* अनैद्दुम् can be used in place of முற்றிலும் *muṭrilum* मुट्रिलुम्.

i. The whole countrry. நாடு முழுதும் *nāḍu muludum* नाडु मुळुदुम्

ii. The whole countrry. நாடு அனைத்தும் *nāḍu anaiddum* नाडु अनैद्दुम्

6. பற்றி *paṭri* पट्रि (about, regarding हिंदी : के बारे में)

8. When suffix பற்றி *paṭri* पट्रि is attached to the Accusative form of noun, it means 'about' or 'regarding' that noun. But before attaching this suffix, first Accusative vowel ை○ *ai* ऐ has to be added to the noun before attaching the suffix.

i. About the book. புத்தக்கைப்பற்றி *puttakkai-ppaṭri* पुत्तकैप्पट्रि

ii. About me. என்னைப்பற்றி *ennai-ppaṭri* एन्नैप्पट्रि

7. குறித்து *kuriddu* कुरिद्दु (about हिंदी : के बारे में)

9. In place of suffix பற்றி *paṭri* पट्रि, optionally suffix குறித்து *kuriddu* कुरिद्दु can be attached to the Accusative form of noun, to say 'about' that noun. Again, before attaching this suffix, first vowel ை○ *ai* ऐ has to be added to the noun to make it Accusative.

i. About the book. புத்தகத்தக்குறித்து *puttakathai-kkuriddu* पुत्तकतै–क्कुरिद्दु

8. என்று *enru* एन्रु (that हिंदी : कि)

10. Suffix என்று *enru* एन्रु means the English <u>conjunction</u> 'that' (not the pronoun 'that') e.g.

i. He said that ... அவன் வரவில்லை என்று ... *pavan varavillai enru* ... अवन् वरविलै एन्रु ...

ii. About me. என்னைப் பற்றி *ennaip-paṭri* एन्नैप्पट्रि

9. ஆம் *ām* आम् (is called as हिंदी : ऐसा कहते हैं)

11. When suffix ஆம் *ām* आम् is attached to the end verb in a sentence, it has a meaning of 'they say that, 'is called as, is known as, it is said that, I heard that (ऐसा कहते हैं, सुना है)' etc.

i. He came. அவன் வந்தான் *avan vandān* अवन् वन्दान् → They say that he came அவன் வந்தானாம் *avan vandānām* अवन् वन्दानाम्

ii. He will come tomorrow. அவன் நாளை வாருவான் *avan nāḷai vāruvān* अवन् नाळै वारुवान् → (They say that, I heard that, it is said that) he will came tomorrow. அவன் நாளை வருவானாம் *avan nāḷai varuvānām* अवन् नाळै वरुवानाम्

10. படி *paḍi* पडि (according to, as हिंदी : जैसा)

10. Suffix படி *paḍi* पडि is attached to the verb 'according to' which something else takes place. e.g.

i. Do as I say. (Do accordingly as I tell you) என் சொற்படி செய் *ēn sorpaḍi sey* एन् सोर्पडि सेय्

ii. I did as he said. அவன் சொன்னபடி செய்தேன் *avan seyapaḍi seyden* अवन् सेयपडि सेय्देन्

iii. I do as he says. அவன் சொற்படி செய்கிறேன் *avan solpaḍi seykiren* अवन् सोल्पडि सेय्किरेन्

11. தான் *tān* तान् (only हिंदी : ही)

13. Suffix தான் *tān* तान् is attached to a word to say 'only' that itself. e.g.

i. Only me. (मैने ही) நான்தான் *nāntān* नान्तान्

ii. Only he. (उसीने) அவன்தான் *avantān* अवन्तान्

iii. Yesterday only (कल ही). நேற்றுத்தான் *neṭruttān* नेट्रुत्तान्

12. ஏ *ă* ऍ (only हिंदी : ही)

14. Similar to suffix தான் *tān* तान्, suffix ஏ *ă* ऍ is may optionally be attached to a word to say 'only' that itself. e.g.

i. Only me. (मै ही) நானே *nāne* नाने

ii. Only he. (वही) அவனே *avane* अवने

iii. Only she. (वही). அவளே *avaḷe* अवळे

iv. Only she. (यही). இவளே *ivaḷe* इवळे

v. Only that. (वही). அதுவே *aduve* अदुवे

vi. Only this. (यही). இவனே *ivane* इवने

13. மட்டும் *maṭṭum* मट्टुम् (only; as far as हिंदी : ही, सिर्फ़; तक)

15. Suffix மட்டும் *maṭṭum* मट्टुम् is attached to a word to say 'only' that thing. e.g.

i. Only Rama. (सिर्फ राम, केवल राम) இராமன் மட்டும் *irāman maṭṭum* इरामन् मट्टुम्

ii. Only Sita. சீதா மட்டும் *sītā maṭṭum* सीदा मट्टुम्

16. Suffix மட்டும் *maḍḍum* मड्डुम् can be added to the name of a place to say 'as far as' that place (वहाँ तक).e.g.

i. Up to New York. நியுயார்க் மட்டும் *new york maḍḍum* न्यूयार्क् मड्डुम्

14. தவிர *tavir* तविर (other than, except हिंदी : के सिवा)

17. Suffix தவிர *tavir* तविर is attached to the Accusative form of a Noun to impart a meaning of other than or besides that noun. e.g.

i. Everyone else except Rama. (राम को छोड़ कर बाकी सब लोग) (Everyone = எவனும் *evannum*

books-india.com

एवन्नुम्) இராமனைத்தவிர எவனும் *irāmanai-ttavit evanum* इरामनैत्तविर एवनुम्

ii. Cities other than Chennai. சென்னையைத்தவிர இடங்கள் *sannaiyaittavir iḍaṅgaḷ* सेन्नैयैत्तविर इडंगळ्

15. முன்னை *munnai* मुन्नै (before हिंदी : से पहिले)

18. Suffix முன்னை *munnai* मुन्नै is attached to the Dative form of a Pronoun to say 'before' it. e.g.

i. Before this. (इससे पहिले) இதற்கு முன்னை *idarku munnai* इदर्कु मुन्नै

16. பின்னை *pinnai* पिन्नै (after हिंदी : के बाद)

19. Suffix பின்னை *pinnai* पिन्नै is attached to the Dative form of a Pronoun to say 'after' it. e.g.

i. After this. (इसके बाद) இதற்கு ப்பின்னை *idarkup pinnai* इदर्कु प्पिन्नै

17. போல *pol* पोल (like, similar to हिंदी : के जैसा, समान)

20. The Suffix போல *pol* पोल is attached to a noun as a sign of comparison or simile with another noun. This suffix is also attached to the Accusative form of **the noun to be compared with**. e.g.

i. Fast like a deer. மானைப்போல வேகமாக *mānaippola vegamāh* मानैप्पोल वेगमाह

ii. Slowly like a turtle. ஆமைபோல் மெதுமாய் *āmaippol medumāy* आमैपोल मेदुमाय्

18. வில் *vil* विल् (than हिंदी : से, की अपेक्षा)

21. The comparative suffix வில் *vil* विल is used for comparing one noun with another noun. This suffix is attached to the Ablative form of **the another noun with which first noun is compared with**.

i. Rama is taller than Sita. இராமன் சீதாவில் நெடியவன் *irāman sītāvil neḍiyavan* इरामन् सीदाविल नेडियवन्

19. ஏனென்றால் *enenrāl* ऍनेन्राल् (because हिंदी : क्योंकि)

22. Suffix ஏனென்றால் *enenrāl* ऍनेन्राल् is used as the English conjunction 'because,' to connect two clauses of a sentence.

i. I walk to school because my school is very near. (near = அருகே *aruke* अरुके) நான் கல்லூரிக்கு நடக்கிறேன் ஏனென்றால் என் கல்லூரி ரொம்ப அருகே *nān kallurikku naḍkkiren enenrāl en kalluri rāmb aruke.* नान् कल्लुरिक्कु नडक्किरेन् एनेन्राल् एन् कल्लुरि रांब अरुके.

20. கார் *kār* कार् (doer हिंदी : वाला)

23. The கார *kār* कार is an adjective forming suffix and, therefore, it is gender and number sensetive.

Is used commonly used for making a 'doer' of that noun. e.g. from work to **worker** कामवाला; from vegetable to vegetable maker or **vegetable seller** सब्जीवाला / सब्जीवाली.

i. Vegetable **காய்கறி** *kāyakari* कायकरि + masculine suffix **காரன்** *kāran* कारन् = **காய்கறிக்காரன்** *kāyakarikārana* कायकरिकारन् Vegetable seller सब्ज़ीवाला

ii. Milk **பால்** *pāl* पाल् + masculine suffix **காரன்** *kāran* कारन् = **பால்காரன்** *pālkāran* पाल्कारन् Milkman दूधवाला

iii. Work **வேலை** *velai* वेलै + feminine suffix **காரி** *kāri* कारि = **வேலை** + **க்** + **காரி** **வேலைக்காரி** *velaikkāri* वेलैक्कारि a Female worker.

21. ஆர் *ār* आर् (respect हिंदी : जी)

24. Honorific Suffix **ஆர்** *ār* आर् is attached to the human nouns to denote respect. e.g.

i. Father (पिता) **அப்பன்** *appan* अप्पन् + honorific suffix **ஆர்** *ār* आर् = **அப்பனார்** *appanār* अप्पनार् Father पिताजी

ii. Mother (माता) **அம்மை** *ammai* अम्मै + suffix **ஆர்** *ār* आर् = **அம்மை** + **ய** + **ஆர்** = **அம்மையார்** *ammaiyār* अम्मैयार् Mother माताजी

iii. In order to make plural honorific nouns, first <u>optionally</u> attach the plural suffix **கள்** *kaḷ* कळ् to the noun and then add the honorific suffix **ஆர்** *mār* मार् to it.

(a). Singular : Teacher (गुरु) **குரு** *guru* गुरु + honorific suffix **ஆர்** *ār* आर् = **குரு** + **வ** + **ஆர்** = **குருவார்** *guruvār* गुरुवार् Teacher गुरुजी

(b). Plural : Teachers **குரு** *guru* गुरु + optional plural suffix **கள்** *kaḷ* कळ् + honorific suffix **மஆர்** *mār* मार् = **அம்மை** + (optional) **கள்** + **மஆர்** = **குருக்கள்மார்** *gurukkaḷmār* गुरुक्कळ्मार् Teachers गुरुजन or simply **குருமார்** *gurumār* गुरुमार्

books-india.com

LESSON 13

COMPOUNDING OF LETTERS AND WORDS
संधि और समास

1. Compounding of Characters
संधि

PLEASE READ THIS BEFORE YOU BEGIN THE LESSON

i. This lesson is a brief Tamil version of a the rules outlined in a couple chapters from my book *"learn Sanskrit through English medium,"* for the topics formulated in this lesson are parallel in these two languages.

ii. Sanskrit *sandhi* is a mathematical addition of two characters, vowels or consonants. Sanskrit *samasa* is the linking of two words with a logical definition. The sandhi (கூட்டு *kūṭṭu* कूट्टु) and samasa (பற்று *paṭṭu* पट्टु) are both present in Tamil. Of course, from Sanskrit they have come into Hindi as well, directly and sometimes indirectly.

In Sanskrit, the *samasa* is a huge and one of the most beautiful linguistic aspects. However, in Tamil, only the तत्पुषसमासः aspect is used.

iii. This lesson is presented here in the form of sandhi and samasa rules. You will remember that most of the sandhi rules are appropriately exemplified elsewhere in the earlier lessons of this book and are summarized in Tables 5, 6 and 16.

iv. The sandhi rules can be further subdivided in to three categories of vowel-vowel sandhi, consonant-vowel sandhi and consonant-consonant sandhi.

v. Although the visarga (ஆய்தம் *āytham* आयतम्) is part of Tamil language, the interesting technique of the Sanskrit visarga sandhi has not come into in Tamil. It remains the most unique aspect of the Sanskrit language.

vi. The following collection of rules also serves as a reference checklist of all the rules you need to know for the basic study of the Tamil language.

TAMIL SANDHI RULES

1. (a) Like Sanskrit, the அ, இ, உ अ, इ, उ are Basic or Simple Vowels.

   (b) The rest nine vowels ஆ, ஈ, ஊ, எ, ஏ, ஐ, ஒ, ஓ, ஔ आ, ई, ऊ, ए, ऍ, ऐ, ओ, ऑ, औ are Compound Vowels, composed of the three Simple vowels. e.g.

   ஆ = அ + அ; ஈ = இ + இ; ஊ = உ + உ; எ = அ + இ; ஏ = அ + ஈ; ஐ = அ + அ + இ; ஒ = அ + உ; ஓ = அ + ஊ; ஔ = அ + அ + உ

   आ = अ + अ; ई = इ + इ; ऊ = उ + उ; ए = अ + इ; ऍ = अ + ई; ऐ = अ + अ + इ; ओ = अ + उ; ऑ = अ + ऊ; औ = अ + अ + उ

   a + a = ā; ī = i + i; ū = u + u; e = a + e; ĕ = a + ī; ai = a + a + i; o = a + u; ă = a + ū; au = a + a + u

2. The sound of letter இ *i* इ is normally prefixed to the words that begin with ர or ல र, ल *r, l*, e.g. ராஜன் = இராஜன் राजन् = इराजन् *rājan* = *irājan* (King).

3. When letter இ *i* इ is followed by a retroflex consonant (ट, ठ. ड, ढ *ṭ, ṭh, ḍ, ḍh*), the இ *i* इ is pronounced longer like ई *ī.*

4. When a word (made up of simple consonants and simple vowels) ending in உ *u* उ is followed by a word beginning with any vowel அ *a* अ, the final உ *u* उ is dropped.

5. When a word ending in a mute (half) consonant is followed by a word beginning with a vowel, these two words are joined (just like Sanskrit). e.g. மீன் + இல் = மீனில் *mīn + il = mīnil* मीन् + इल् = मीनिल्.

6. When a word, (other than அது, இது, எது *adu, idu, edu* अदु, इदु, एदु) made up of simple consonants and vowels and beginning with उ, is followed a word beginning with any vowel other than अ, the end उ is changed to व. e.g. சங்கு + இல் = சங்கில் *saṅku + il = saṅgil* संकु + इल् = संगिल्.

7. When a word ending in இ, ஈ or ஐ *i, ī* or *ai* इ, ई or ऐ is connected to a word beginning with any vowel, letter ய் *y* य् is inserted between these two connecting vowels. e.g. பல்லி + இல் = பல்லியில் *palli + il = palliyil* पल्लि + इल् = पल्लियिल्.

8. When a word ending in ஆ, ஊ, எ, ஏ, ஒ, ஓ or ஔ *ā, ū, e, ĕ, o, ŏ* or *au* आ, ऊ, ए, ऍ, ओ, ऑ or औ is followed by a word beginning with a vowel, letter வ் *v* व् is inserted between the two vowels, கானடா + இல் = கானடாவில் *kanadā + il = kanadāvil* कानड़ा + विल् = कानड़ाविल्.

9. When a word ending in **எ** *e* ए or **ஏ** *ai* ऐ is followed by a word beginning with a vowel, consonant **ய்** *y* य् or **வ்** *v* व् is optionally inserted and the two words are joined together (Sanskrit style).

10. When a monosyllabic word with a short vowel ending in a mute (half) consonant is followed by a word beginning with a vowel, the mute consonant is doubled. e.g. **கல்** + **இல்** = **கல்லில்** *kal + il = kallil* कल् + इल् = कल्लिल्.

11. When a word ending in vowel उ is followed by आ, the उ is dropped. e.g. **காரு** + **ஆ** = **காரா** *kāru + ā = kārā* कारु + आ = कारा. (kāru = Washerman)

12. A noun beginning with **க், ச், த், ப்** *k, ch, t, p* क्, च्, त्, प्, when preceded by its adjective, doubles the initial letter. e.g. **பாட புத்தகம்** = **பாடப்புத்தகம்** *pād puttaham = pāḍpputtaham* पाड पुस्तहम् = पाडप्पुस्तहम्.

13. Vowel **ஏ** *ĕ* ऍ is pronounced like English *eye* when it comes as initial letter of a word, or when it comes in a word of mono-syllable. e.g. **ஏகம்** ऍकम् *ekam* (unique); Sanskrit ऍकम् *ekam* (unique); **தேர்** थेर् *ther* (a Chariot, a divine Chariot, a Chariot or vehicle for God, a Chariot driven by Gods).

14. The sound of **க** is like English letter *k* (as in *Kit*) or Hindi क (as in कमल), when : (a) a Tamil word starts with letter **க**, (b) when the **க** is in the word is mute (i.e. half **க்** क् *k*), (c) when it is doubled (**க்க** क्क *kk*), (d) **க** is at the end of a syllable, (e) or when **க்** comes after letter **ட்** *ṭ* ट, (f) or when **க்** comes after **ன** (n न), (g) when **க்** comes after letter **ற்** *ṛ* ऱ्, and (h) when **க்** is between two vowels. e.g. **கடல்** *kaḍal* कडल = Ocean; **சக்கரம்** *chakkaram* चक्करम् = Wheal (Sanskrit चक्रम् *chakram;* Hindi चक्र *chakra);* **வைகாசி** *vaikasi* वैकासि = April-May (Sanskrit वैशाख, Hindi बैसाख); **கட்கம்** *kaḍkam* कट्गम् = Sword (Sanskrit खड्गम् *khaḍgam;* Hindi खड्ग *khaḍga);* **பற்கள்** पऱ्कळ, पर्कळ् *parkal* (teeth); **வணக்கம்** वणक्कम् *vaṇakkam* = Hi (Sanskrit/Hindi नमस्ते).

15. The sound of **க** is like English letter *g* (as in *gut*) or Hindi letter ग (as in गरम), when **க** comes after the nasal consonants **ங்** (ng ङ) , **ண்** (ṇ ण) or **ர்** (r ऱ्) , e.g. **சங்கம்** सङ्गम् *saṅgam* = Group (Sanskrit सङ्ग: Hindi संग, संघ); **அவர்கள்** अवर्गळ् *avargaḷ* (they).

16. When letter **க** क *ka* comes in the middle of a word between two consonants, that letter **க** *ka* क has a sound like letter ह *h* or घ *gh.* e.g. **நகம்** नहम्, नघम् *naham, nagham* (Nail), **மகன்** मगन्, महन्,

मघन् *magan, maghan, maghan* (Son). Also, The **க** *ka* क at the end of a word, if follows vowel आ *ā,* it sounds like ह *h.* e.g. **உனக்காக** (For you) उनक्काक् = उनक्काह् *unakkāk = unakkāh.* Similarly, In a word of several syllables, the **க** क *ka* of the last syllable sounds like ह *h.* e.g. **அவர்கள்** अवर्गळ् *avargaḷ* (They).

17. When a word ending in letter **ம்** *m* म् is followed by a word beginning with letter **க** k क, the letter **ம்** *m* म् is changed to letter **ங்** *ng* ङ् (like the *parasvarna sandhi* of Sanskrit grammar). e.g. **பழம்** *paĺam* पळ्म् Fruit + **கள்** *kal* कळ् a suffix of pluralization = **பழங்கள்** *paĺangaḷ* पळ्ंगळ् Fruits. However, in some cases the **ம்** m म् changes to **க்** *k* क् e.g. **நகம்** *Inaham* नहम् Nail +**கண்** *kan* कण् Eye = **நகக்கண்** *nahakkan* नहक्कण् Nail and Eye.

18. When a word ending in letter **ம்** *m* म् is followed by the honorary suffix **ங்க** *ngg* ङ्ग, the **ம்** m म् is dropped, like the Sanskrit *parasvarna sandhi*..e.g. **வணக்கம்** *vanakkam* वणक्कम् (Hi नमस्ते) + **ங்க** (Sir जी*)* = **வணக்கங்க** *vaṇakkang* वणक्कङ्ग (Hello Sir, नमस्ते जी).

19. When an adjective ending in letter **ம்** m म् is followed by its noun, the end letter **ம்** m म् of the adjective is dropped.

20. When a Tamil word starts with letter **ச**, or when the **ச** in the word is mute (i.e. half **ச்** च् *ch*) or when it is doubled (**ச்ச** च्च *chcha*), the sound of **ச** is like the Hindi letter च (as in चम्मच), and Sanskrit letter च *ch,* as in the Sanskrit verb चर्च् *√charch* (to violate, to rebuke). English language does not have letter *ch*, but only the sound of *ch* is there as in English word *Church*.

21. Like the Sanskrit rule of Third Consonant, when letter **ச** *cha* च comes after letter **ஞ்** (ञ् *ny*), the letter **ச** takes sound of Hindi letter ज English j. e.g. **பஞ்சு** पञ्जु *pañju* (Cotton).

22. When **ச** *cha* च is mute or doubled, it sounds like छ *chh*. e.g. **இச்சை** इच्छै *icchai* (Desire), Sanskrit and Hindi इच्छा *ichhā*..

23. When **ச** *cha* च comes after letter **ட்** ट् t or **ற்** र् r, it maintains its च *ch* sound. e.g. **திராட்சை** दिराट्चै *diratchai* (Grapes); Sanskrit, Hindi द्राक्ष *drāksha.*

24. When **ச** *cha* च comes after letter **ட்** प *p*, it sounds like स *s*. e.g. **பசு** पसु *pasu* (Cow), Sanskrit पशु *pashu* (Animal).

25. When letter ச *cha* च comes after letter ஞ், the letter ச *cha* च is pronounced as ज *j* and letter ஞ் is pronounced somewhat like न् *n*. e.g. பஞ்சாபி (written पञ्चापि) spoken पंजाबी *pañjābī*..

26. When ச comes as initial letter, or if it comes in the word as a full simple consonant, it sounds like स *s*. e.g. சரம் सरम् *saram* (Movement) Sanskrit सर *sar* (move); ரசம் रसम् *rasam* (Juice) Sanskrit रसम् *rasam* (juice).

27. When a word ending in ம் म् *m* is followed by a word starting with letter ச च *ch*, the ம் म् *m* is usually changed to ஞ் ञ् *ny*; in some cases it is changed to ச் च् *ch*. e.g. (i) பழம் (fruit) + சோறு (food) = பழஞ்சோறு पळञ्चोरु *palañchoru* (fruit diet); (ii) மரம் + சட்டம் = மரச்சட்டம் मरच्चट्टम् *marachchaṭṭam* (a Wood-frame).

28. Letter ஞ *ny* ञ forms sandhi with only vowels அ, ஆ, எ, ஏ, ஒ अ, आ, ए, एँ, ओ (*a, ā, e, ĕ o*).

29. When a word ending in ண *ṇ* ण् is followed by a word beginning with க், ச், or ப் क्, च् or प् *k, ch* or *p* , the final ண *ṇ* ण becomes ட் ट् *ṭ*. e.g. மண் + குடம் = மட்குடம் मण् + कुडम् = मट्मूर्त्तम् *maṇ* (Earthen) + *kudam* (pot) = *maṭ-kudam* (Clay-pot मटकी).

30. The letter த is stand alone, initial letter, mute or doubled, it has a sound of त, थ *t, th*; but when it is in the middle or at the end of a word, it sounds like द, ध *d, dh*. In Sanskrit originated words, it is pronounced accordingly. e.g. தானம் दानम् *dānam* (Charity); தேவி देवि *devī* (Goddess).

31. The Tamil ட *t* ट (ट, ड, ढ) gives the preceding vowel a wider sound than it's normal sound. e.g. ஈடு ईडु *eedu* (Suffer); ஏடு एँडु *ĕdu* (a Leaf); ஓடு ऑडु *odu* (Run, hasten).

32. When letter த *t* त comes letter ந் *n* न्, it sounds like द d. e.g. இந்த इन्द *ind* (this), வந்தனம் वन्दनम् *vandanam* (Salute).

33. When letter ப comes as stand-alone, initial, mute or doubled, it sounds like प *p* as in பணம் पणम् *paṇam* (Coin); Sanskrit पण् *paṇ* (to buy), English word *pan* (Pot). When letter ப is doubled, it also sounds like प *p* as in கப்பல் कप्पल् *kappal* (Ship).

34. When letter ப comes as after letter ட ट *t* or ற र *r*, it also sounds like प *p* as in பாடம் पाठम् *pāṭham* (Lesson); Sanskrit, Hindi पाठ *pāṭh* (Lesson).

35. Other than above three situations, when letter ப comes in the middle or at the end of a word, it

sounds kike ब or भ *b* or *bh*. e.g. **கம்பர்** कम्बर *kambar* (A Tamil Poet).

36. Between two vowels, the Tamil **ப** *p* प has *ph* फ like sound. e.g. **தபம்** तफम् *tapham* (Austerity) Sanskrit तपम् *tapam* (Austerity).

37. When a word ending in **ம்** म् *m* is followed by a word beginning with letter **க** क *k*, the **ம்** म् *m* changes to **ங** ङ् *ng*. e.g. **வணக்கம்** *vaṇakkam* वणक्कम् (Hi नमस्ते) + **குமார்** (Kumar कुमार*)* = **வணக்கங்குமார்** *vaṇakkaṅgkumār* वणक्कङ्कुमार (Hello Mr. Kumar नमस्ते कुमार जी).

38.. When a word ending in **ம்** म् *m* is followed by a word beginning with letter **ச** च *ch*, the **ம்** म् *m* changes to **ஞ்** ञ् *ny*. e.g. **வணக்கம்** *vanakkam* वणक्कम् (Hi नमस्ते) + **சந்த்ரா** (Chandra चन्द्रा*)* = **வணக்கஞ்சந்த்ரா** *vaṇakkañchandrā* वणक्कञ्चन्द्रा (Hello Miss. Chandra नमस्ते चंद्रा जी).

39. When a word ending in **ம்** म् *m* is followed by a word beginning with letter **த** त *t*, the **ம்** म् *m* changes to **ந்** न् *n*. e.g. **வணக்கம்** *vanakkam* वणक्कम् (Hi नमस्ते) + **தாகுர்** (Tagore ठाकुर*)* = **வணக்கந்தாகுர்** *vaṇakkaṇthākur* वणक्कन्ठाकुर (Hello Mr. Tagore नमस्ते ठाकुर जी).

40. When a word ending in **ம்** म् *m* is followed by a word beginning with letter **ம** म *m*, the **ம்** म् *m* is dropped. e.g. **வணக்கம்** *vanakkam* वणक्कम् (Hi नमस्ते) + **முருகன்** (Murugan मुरुगन्*)* = **வணக்கமுருகன்** *vanakkamurugan* वणक्कमुरुगन् (Hello Mr. Murugan नमस्ते मुरुगन् जी).

41. In a word where **ய** *y* य comes after **ஆ எ ஏ ஒ** आ, ए, ऍ, ऑ *ā, e, ĕ ŏ,* the **ய** sounds like इ *i*. e.g. **ஓய்வுக்காலம்** ऑयवुक्कालम् *Oyvukkālam* (Life at retirement); Double **ய்ய** has pure य *y* sound. e.g. **அய்யா, அய்யர்** अय्या, अय्यर *iyyā, iyyar* (Sir); Final **ய்** has ई *ī* sound. e.g. **தாய்** दाई *dāī* (Mother).

42. The initial **ர** *r* र, is compounded with vowel **உ, ஐ, ஒ** or **ஓ** उ, ऐ, ओ or ऑ (u, ai, o or ŏ), or vowel **இ** इ *i* is prefixed to it. e.g. **இரண்டு** इरण्डु or रण्डु *iraṇḍu* or *raṇḍu* (Two).

43. When a word ending in **ல்** ल् *l* is followed by a word beginning with **க், ச்,** or **ப்** क्, च् or प् *k, ch* or *p* , the final **ல்** ल् *l* becomes **ற்** र् *r*. e.g. **பால் + பசு** = **பாற்பசு** पाल् + पसु = पार्पसु *pal* (Milk) + *pasu* (Cow) = *pārpasu* (Milch cow).

44. When a word ending in **ள்** ळ् *ḷ* is followed by a word beginning with **க், ச்,** or **ப்** क्, च् or प् *k, ch* or *p* , the final **ள்** ळ् *ḷ* becomes **ற்** र् *r*. e.g. **பொருள் + கள்** = **பொருட்கள்** पोरुळ् + कळ् = पोरुर्कळ् *poruḷ* (Matter) + *kaḷ* (Suffix of pliral) = *porurkaḷ* (Many बहुत).

books-india.com

45. When **ற** *l* र् is doubled, they sound like *ṭr* ट्र. e.g. **காற்று** *kaṭru* काट्रु (Wind).

46. When this **ன்** *n* न् comes before **ற்** र *r* , it's sound changes to ण *ṇ* and then the **ன்ற்** न्र् *nr* is pronounced as ण्ड्र *ṇḍṛ.* e.g. **கன்று** कण्ड्रु *kaṇḍṛu* (Calf).

47. When a word ending with letter **ல்** *l* ल् is joined with or followed by a word beginning with letter **க, ச** or **ப** क, च or प *k, ch* or *p,* the **ல்** ल् *l* is changed to **ற** *l* र्. e.g. **கடல் கப்பல்** = **கடற்கப்பல்** कडल् कप्पल = कडर्कप्पल कडर्कप्पल *kadal kappal - kadarkappal* (Ocean liner).

48. When letter **ல்** ल् *l* is followed by letter **த** त *t*, both these letters are changed in to **ற்ற** र्‍ *rr*. e.g. **கூந்தல் தலை** = **கூந்தற்தலை** कून्दल् तलै *kūndal talai* = कून्दर्तलै *kūndartalai* (Hairy head).

49. **ற** *r* र् never comes before letters **க் க ச் ச த் த ப் ப** क्, क, च्, च, त् त, प् प *k, ka, ch, cha, t, ta, p, pa.*

50. When this **ன்** *n* न् comes before **ற்** र *r* , it's sound changes to ण *ṇ* and then the **ன்ற்** न्र् *nr* is pronounced as ण्ड्र *ṇḍṛ.* e.g. **கன்று** कण्ड्रु *kaṇḍṛu* (Calf).

51. When a word ending in a vowel is followed by a word beginning with consonant क्, च्, त्, or प्, *k, ck, t,* or *p* that consonant is doubled.

52. The Tamil letter used in place of **ஜ** is **ச** and pronounced as ज j or स s. e.g. **சனம்** जनम् *janama* (People) Sanskrit जन *jana* (People); **பசு** पसु *pasu* (Cow), Sanskrit पशु *pashu* (Animal, Cow).

53. Tamil **ஸ** *sa* स is always used as a mute character and joins another consonant or a vowel. e.g. **புத்தகம் (புஸ்தகம்)** पुत्तहम् *puttaham* (Book), Sanskrit पुस्तकम् *pustakam*, Hindi पुस्तक *pustak* (Book).

54. The **த** त *t* that joins with स *s* has a sound of थ *th*. e.g. **ஸ்தரீ** स्त्री स्थ्री *stree* (Woman).

55. Tamil letter used in place of **ஷ** is **ட** and pronounced as ट t. e.g. **கஷ்டம்** कष्टम् *kashṭam* = **கட்டம்** कट्टम् *kaṭṭam* (Trouble).

56. Tamil **ஹ** *ha* ह is used only for the words that came from Sanskrit. For Tamil words letter **க** is used for ह *h*. e.g. **நகம்** नहम् *naham* (Nail),

2. Compounding of Words

समास

i. In Tamil (तत्पुरुष) Samasa, compound words are formed by (sandhi) linking two nouns with a third noun, observing the above given sandhi rules.

ii. Like Sanskrit samasa, the words to be joined must be first put in their Nominative Singular forms before joining them. And like the Sanskrit *tatpurusha* samasa, the first word qualifies the second word, but the last word stands for the compound word. e.g. Heartache **உள்ளம்நோவு**

உள்ளம்-நோவு *uḷḷam-novu* उळ्ळम्-नोवु Heartache = **உள்ளம்** heart + **நோவு** ache. **உள்ளம்** Heart is the qualifier of the ache. Heart is the secondary word. Heart is the adjective of the word ache. **நோவு** Ache is the primary word. Ache stands for the word heartache. i.e. Ache represents the compound word and takes the gender and number suffixes. Secondary word can easily be replaced with any other suitable noun or adjective, like **தலை-நோவு** headache, **இரைக்குடல்-நோவு** stomachache, etc.

LANGUAGE LEARNING BOOKS by RATNAKAR NARALE
www.ratnakar-books.com

CPSIA information can be obtained
at www.ICGtesting.com
Printed in the USA
LVOW09s1602020118
561519LV00012B/372/P

9 781897 416587